# EXHIBITING RELIGION

STUDIES IN RELIGION AND CULTURE

Frank Burch Brown, Gary L. Ebersole,
and Edith Wyschogrod, *Editors*

# EXHIBITING RELIGION

## COLONIALISM AND SPECTACLE AT INTERNATIONAL EXPOSITIONS 1851–1893

### John P. Burris

UNIVERSITY PRESS OF VIRGINIA
CHARLOTTESVILLE AND LONDON

THE UNIVERSITY PRESS OF VIRGINIA
© 2001 by the Rector and Visitors
of the University of Virginia
All rights reserved
Printed in the United States of America on acid-free paper

*First Published in 2001*

Library of Congress Cataloging-in-Publication Data
Burris, John P.
  Exhibiting religion : colonialism and spectacle at international expositions, 1851–1893 / John P. Burris.
    p. cm — (Studies in religion and culture)
  Includes bibliographical references and index.
  ISBN 0-8139-2083-3 (cloth : alk. paper)
  1. Religion—Study and teaching—Great Britain—History—19th century. 2. Exhibitions—Great Britain—History—19th century. 3. Religion—Study and teaching—United States—History—19th century. 4. Exhibitions—United States—History—19th century. I. Title. II. Studies in religion and culture (Charlottesville, Va.)
BL41 .B87 2001
200'.74—dc21                                           2001005107

*For Kathy*
*Without you there is no us*

# CONTENTS

|   |   |   |
|---|---|---|
|   | List of Illustrations | ix |
|   | Acknowledgments | xi |
|   | Introduction | xiii |
| 1 | International Expositions in Historical Context | 1 |
| 2 | Britain's Great Exhibition: Ideology Materialized | 23 |
| 3 | Social Evolutionism and International Expositions: A Cultural History | 63 |
| 4 | Exhibitionism, American Style | 86 |
| 5 | Exhibiting Religion at Chicago's Columbian Exposition | 123 |
|   | Conclusion: A Parliament for the World's Religions? | 167 |
|   | Notes | 179 |
|   | Bibliography | 195 |
|   | Index | 207 |

# ILLUSTRATIONS

1. Joseph Paxton's initial proposal for the design of the Crystal Palace — 30
2. Interior of the reconstructed Crystal Palace — 34
3. The East Indian Palace inside White City — 105
4. Japan's Ho-o-den Palace — 106
5. Booth displaying "Hindoo" magic — 115
6. The Islamic-based "Street in Cairo" — 116
7. Victorian ladies admiring Samoan gentlemen — 118

# ACKNOWLEDGMENTS

THE LIST of people who need to be thanked for making possible the production of this book is indeed long. A brief list of the most directly relevant contributors is what follows. I would first like to thank my teacher, mentor, and good friend Charles H. Long for teaching me *how* to think rather than *what* to think. I had the privilege of being one of Professor Long's students in a seminar that introduced me to graduate study in the field of religion after I had taken some time away from the discipline. This was one of those pieces of luck that one can only look back upon with deepest gratitude. This book has grown out of a long and deeply engaged relationship with him in which the "other" has shown profound generosity. Long's unpublished paper about the Columbian Exposition entitled "Fair: No Fair" helped establish the blueprint for this book.

My other dissertation committee members were both instrumental in shaping the direction of this book as well. Richard Hecht taught me a great deal about method in the study of religion. Catherine Albanese did a tremendous amount of work on the manuscript, both theoretically and editorially—a debt that can never be repaid.

William Pietz read the manuscript at a critical point and made indispensable contributions to it, one of which involved pointing out that the book did not have an adequate thesis and that the one it had was not in fact what the book was about. David Chidester rendered an exhaustive and invaluable report on the manuscript at a very late stage, nearly all of which has been incorporated into the final version of the book. Chidester's study entitled *Savage Systems* and the present one were in fact written coterminously, and both have acknowledged the significant influence of Charles Long in their formation. Thanks in a different category goes to David L. Miller, whose influence on me has found its way into these pages in so many different ways that the sum cannot be totaled.

In the absence of a laundry list of funding agencies that made the production of this book possible, I would like to thank my parents, John Sr. and Selby, for their generous support of this lengthy project, both emotionally and financially. I would also like to thank the graduate program at Syracuse University for funding in the early stages of my studies and for providing an outstanding program for its students—specifically, the chairman at the time, James B. Wiggins, and the graduate director, Charles E. Winquist, each of whom taught me a great deal intellectually as well.

The help I received from the professional librarians on both sides of the Atlantic at the following libraries was invaluable: the National Arts Library, the Guidhall Library, and the British Museum Library in London; and the DePaul Library's Department of Special Collections, the Chicago Historical Society, the Chicago Public Library, and the University of Chicago Library in Chicago.

My editorial team at the University Press of Virginia has been instrumental in developing and shaping this study from the beginning. Cathie Brettschneider has done an outstanding job in reconceiving the book as what it is: a study in religion and culture. David Sewell has provided a number of valuable suggestions about how to improve the mechanics of the book. And last, but hardly least, my copyeditor, Jill R. Hughes, has transformed the original manuscript with quite brilliant literary insight.

My gratitude to my wife, Kathy, a professional librarian herself, who has contributed immensely to this project both directly as an editorial advisor and indirectly as a divine companion, can never be placed into words, though I have tried my best in the dedication.

# INTRODUCTION

AT A MEETING attended by a few key members of Britain's Royal Society on June 30, 1849, Prince Albert was asked if he had considered whether the national industrial exhibition planned for 1851 should be expanded to include participation by foreign nations. Queen Victoria's "German Consort" had most certainly reflected on the matter carefully. The apprehension and uncertainty with which this fateful decision was attended within the British intelligentsia was enormous. Free trade had only recently dawned in Europe, and the principal nations involved in that development were fearful that allowing foreign products into their countries without severe regulations might prove ruinous for the national economy. Nonetheless, by 1849 Britain felt it had established itself as the modernizing world's industrial giant and decided to take the fateful step toward the promotion of international trade by hosting the first world's fair, or "international exposition." The "Great Exhibition" of 1851—often referred to as the "Crystal Palace," which was the nickname given to the novel glass building in which it was housed—inaugurated a tradition of international expositions in Western society. These unprecedented events, as gatherings that sought to represent materially the whole of the known world within single settings, were to have a decided effect on the formation of the human sciences in general and on the emergence of a field of religion in particular.

At the time they occurred, the international expositions of the nineteenth century were the most comprehensively global intercultural events that had ever been staged. As unprecedented gatherings of disparate peoples who had long heard of but never actually laid eyes on one another, the events lent support to universalizing theories about relations among the world's many cultures. The international expositions were simultaneously a reflection of and a forum for emerging concepts of "culture" and "religion" as subjects for objective analysis. They proved to be important in the development of a field of religion in particular, because for the vast majority of those writing about the expositions at the time of their occurrence, religion was perceived as both the essence of cultural structures and the most plausible point of departure for intercultural comparisons. The events thus provided ideal settings in which religion, as a unique new field of intellectual inquiry, and religions, as the most basic source matter for that field, could come into clearer focus than ever before.

The international exposition tradition was a microcosm of many of the key developments in the surrounding culture that contributed to the birth of the new field of religion, and certainly, the events themselves did promote the objectification of religion. Of the two primary expositions surveyed in this study, it is estimated that as much as 20 percent of the English populace visited the first international exposition—London's Great Exhibition of 1851. Comparably, Chicago's "World's Columbian Exposition" admitted twenty-seven million visitors, while the country's population stood at around sixty-six million. Even accounting for foreigners and multiple visits, the figures are significant. The international expositions were focal points through which many of the elements of modernization and secularization were introduced to the public. Their message did not require literacy but instead demonstrated the extent to which Western society was being transformed from a localized medieval mentality to a sprawling urban monster that stood in a deeply ambiguous relationship to traditional religion.

This study is concerned with utilizing international expositions as a means of identifying some of the key elements that allowed a field of religion to become a distinct, differentiated, and permanent feature of the Western intellectual landscape. It is not concerned with identifying when the concept "religion" originated within the history of Western thought. The question of whether or to what extent "religion" was separable from its sociohistorical settings in the premodern period is a subject for a different study. Both Gavin Flood and Richard King have recently recounted the subtle changes in how the Latin roots of the term "religion" were employed in antiquity when Christianity came into existence. The ultimate fruitfulness of this etymological approach to understanding fundamental terms that are so largely shaped by the historical settings in which they are used is certainly debatable. At the very least, however, it demonstrates that the argument can be made that "religion" could be separated from its historical contexts to some degree in the premodern period, however nominal.[1]

# INTRODUCTION

Regardless of how this broader question about the origins of "religion" might be approached, my primary concern here is to use the international exposition tradition as a guide to explore how a field of religion became possible. The question of to what extent a "field" of religion may have existed before the time of the Great Exhibition is an open one, as David Chidester has pointed out. Nonetheless, I maintain that before the time of London's Great Exhibition of 1851, and even before circa 1870 and the cultural revolution marked by the success of evolutionary theory, there were no distinct outlines for a field of religion comparable to those that emerged after these periods. A study such as that made by F. D. Maurice in 1846 demonstrates that while "religions" had come into existence by this time, their relationship to a distinct theoretical model that could be called "religion" and clearly differentiated from Christian theology was negligible. The international exposition tradition made critical contributions to demonstrating where definitive parameters for a distinct field of religion might be drawn by locating all religions in an evolution-based hierarchy and displaying them according to that model.[2]

Because I am using the international exposition tradition as a barometer for assessing some of the key developments in the formation of a field of religion, I have no intention of making any summary statements about how the present discipline of religious studies came into being or even how it originally developed. I have spoken of "a" rather than "the" field of religion here because the approach I am taking to the subject is expansive rather than contractive. A history of the academic study of religion specifically, for instance, might feel more confident in speaking of the history of "the" field of religion. This is a more limited view of the topic than I wish to present, however, and I readily acknowledge that a broader methodological approach to the subject such as this cannot possibly be exhaustive. The reference to "a" rather than "the" field of religion signifies an attempt to expose some of the conditions that led to the possibility of such a field rather than to determine where precise boundaries might be drawn around it. Similarly, it is difficult to forge the connection between how a field of religion emerged and how the field of religion is presently constituted. I have made a limited number of observations about possible connections between the two in the conclusion of this study.

Understandings of the concept of "religion" in the nineteenth century largely revolved around the various usages of the term "culture." As Terry Eagleton has recently observed, the term "culture" went through various incarnations in the nineteenth century. Usage of the word changed according to both historical epoch and national tradition. While "culture" could be distinguished from the term "civilization" only through more sophisticated analysis early on, the latter increasingly came to carry colonial implications toward the end of the nineteenth century. Robert J. C. Young has noted that the anthropological, comparative meaning of "culture" was not decisively introduced into English until E. B. Tylor defined it as "the specific variable culture of different nations and periods" in *Primitive Culture* in 1871. Before this time, "culture" had no distinctly comparative connotation as a way of defining social differences.[3]

The term "civilization," borrowed from the French, gradually grew in use in the English context after the time in which Tylor was writing. According to Young, "Civilization was fundamentally a comparative concept that took on its meaning as the end-point in an historical view of the advancement of humanity." As a counterpoint to the potentially imperialistic new meaning of "civilization," the Germans employed the term "culture"—also borrowed from the French, which became "*Kultur*" in German. *Kultur* promoted the idea that the highest social ideals did not have to emerge on a comparative basis and lead to imperialism. *Kultur* was marked by an indigenous-based, more ethnically defined sense of "cultivatedness" that was not dependent on comparison with other peoples to gain legitimation.

As these designations affect understandings of the term "religion," then, the interpretation of the term *Religionswissenschaft* in English, for instance (ostensibly the "science of religions"), would need to take into account differences between the German conception of *Kultur* and the British notion of "civilization." The guiding notion of *Kultur* developed within and contributed to the German historiographical tradition beginning with Leopold von Ranke, where historical data must ultimately be grasped through a self-reflective intuition to be fully understood; in the end, it must grant that all knowledge is to some extent subjective and self-referential. Peter Novick has effectively made this point in his analysis of how German historiography was reconceived in an excessively literal manner in the pragmatic context of the United States. By contrast, the British designation "comparative religion" increasingly reflected the colonial political world in which it was developing, and involved the more logistical construction of a mass of data from cultures across the world. Within the colonial context, the term "culture," with its new sense of rootedness in ethnic makeup and geographical identity, was eventually made to apply to foreign societies who were perceived as "savage" and later as "primitive"—peoples who were perceived as not yet having developed "civilizations" on par with the West.[4]

INTRODUCTION                                                                    xvii

The Anglo-based international exposition tradition in Britain and the United States, which is the primary subject of this study, well reflected these trends in modern thought. "Civilizations" became clearly demarcated from "cultures" in the exposition setting. Civilizations became identified with "world religions" and were the basic fodder for a field of religion. Cultures largely became the subjects (and objects) of anthropology, which was the science of "culture" as distinguishable from "religion." I have not undertaken to forge the distinction between culture and civilization at every point in this study, because it was not a precise one in international exposition literature and it only became clearly identifiable toward the end of the period I am examining. Nonetheless, the exposition tradition did model the cultural usages of these terms through the way in which it exhibited cultures and religions.

I have conducted an analysis of the international expositions as a means of creating a different approach to the early history of a field of religion than that which has traditionally been adopted. To explore the emergence of a field of religion on the basis of Enlightenment categories or how it finally came about as an academic discipline does not cast the net wide enough in attempting to account for all that contributed to its manifestation. In the place of these more common approaches, I am interested in developing what could be described as a cultural history of a field of religion in its formative stages. With this approach, I intend to use the example of the international exposition tradition to show that the emergence of a field of religion, particularly among the humanistic disciplines, was dependent on cultural and political factors that stretched across all levels of Western society as well as most of the rest of the world beyond it. A number of recent studies have been fundamentally concerned with the context out of which theories of religion emerge, but generally these have been confined to the more elite intellectual spheres of Western society in the manner in which the "context" of the field of religion is conceived. In this study, I have tried to examine a wider range of influences on an early field of religion that moves beyond elite culture into popular culture and also beyond the West in general and into the global mentality of colonialism.

A work of cultural history such as this cannot be reduced to a singular thesis or formalized argument, because to arrange such a broad mass of historical data around too limited a theoretical theme would be dogmatic and tendentious. There were an indeterminable number of elements that contributed significantly to the possibility of a field of religion. Instead of advancing a single thesis, I have aimed to demonstrate that four distinct elements were foundational in allowing a field of religion to come into existence.

First, and as the guiding premise of this book, I will demonstrate the extent to which the early field of religion, as a fundamentally comparative-based mode of inquiry, was formed on the basis of colonial interactions. At the international expositions, the manner in which cultures were "exhibited" materially had a determined influence on the way in which the concept of "religion" developed and also on the way in which "religions" came to be defined. The insight that theoretical approaches to interculturalism within the humanistic disciplines and the field of religion formed to a significant degree around the material, economic, and political relationship between the peoples involved may not be novel. However, I maintain that within the field of religion in particular there does not exist an extended study of the material context that contributed to the formation of the discipline during the period surveyed by this book. I certainly cannot claim to have exhausted the possibilities for such a study here, but this book nonetheless appears to me to be a necessary step in that direction.

Second, for such a field to have any chance of success early on, it needed to be made viable at the level of popular culture, a project expositions helped to further. It was not until the churches were forced, due to flagging attendance and the general tenor of popular sentiment, to adapt traditional religious dogma to accommodate notions about religion emerging from within the human sciences that they actually did so. Without a significant degree of popular support, the human sciences and a field of religion would have had a difficult time gaining the degree of visibility they did. The demise of the absolute authority of what I have called "traditional biblical religion"—meaning religion prior to the impact of evolutionism—was a necessary prerequisite for their success. It was only after the popular embrace of evolutionism that new approaches to religious questions emerging from within the humanistic disciplines and by a field of religion became enduring features on the horizon of Western religious thought.[6]

Third, the international expositions were instrumental in popularizing social evolutionism in particular as a tool for comparing religions. Social evolutionism was the idea that if there was a teleological progression in nature, the principles by which it operated could also be used to define the extent of progress made by different human societies. The international expositions were able to demonstrate, even to persons who were illiterate, that presumptions about "exotic" and "savage" or "primitive" peoples being culturally backward were for all appearances true. When "exotic" or "primitive" peoples were lined up along exposition midways, as they were at Chicago's Columbian Exposition, a subliminal message was delivered that such peoples belonged only in the carnival, that they were comparable to domestic freaks, and that they did not need to be taken in full seriousness. The facade of the expositions, with their melodramatic demarcations between "primitive" and "civilized," *distorted* any serious attempts to conduct interreligious comparison in such an environment. This practice sent a message to all levels of society that the social evolutionary model for intercultural relations was one that was clearly advantageous to all Western peoples. Social evolutionism contained its own moral vision about chosenness and cultural superiority that religion had long implied. The difference was that the new basis for claims of uniqueness was a scientific analysis of natural processes rather than claims of revealed truth.

Finally, what occurred within the international exposition tradition was that the encroaching global division between "primitive" and "civilized" peoples resulted in peoples deemed primitive becoming defined predominantly by cultural affiliation, or "race," as opposed to "religion." The result of this was that they became usurped under the aegis of anthropological studies—as cultural rather than religious "specimens." On the other hand, peoples identified with major civilizational centers became defined by religious affiliation. This dichotomy was finally reflected definitively at the first "World's Parliament of Religions," which was held in conjunction with the Chicago international exposition of 1893. There, the peoples who had been defined ethnically and predominantly in relation to "cultural" orientation were excluded from the event, while the remainder of the world that was identified with major civilizational centers gathered in a meeting of the "ten great world religions." In this, the concept "religion" can be seen as reinforcing colonial categories rather than acting as a point of critique of them.

While I have used the international expositions as a means of locating certain themes that were important to the emergence of a field of religion, I am just as concerned to show some of the effects the expositions had in specific historical contexts. This is what I understand the history of religions to be: the concerted attempt to contextualize both theories and events within as complete an understanding as possible. One reason why definitions of religion have not been as satisfactory as they might have been in the field of religious studies is that they have not paid enough attention to national differences in the way the concept "religion" has been conceived. In acknowledgment of the significant problem of national differences in the interpretation of "religion," as noted above, the present study is largely limited to the international exposition tradition as it unfolded in Britain and the United States. As such, its limitations in developing any summary statement about the field of religion in general are clear. The early history of a field of religion in Germany or France would certainly be a formidable undertaking—to the point where the attempt to account for the appearance of the concept of "religion" within each of the principal national European traditions in a single volume might well be impossible.

In this study, I have confined myself to the less ambitious task of exploring how the international expositions may provide important clues about the way in which the concept of "religion" manifested in the latter half of the nineteenth century in the British-American context. I have forged a connection between British and American international expositions largely because of the cultural continuity between the two countries. In addition, these were the cultural settings in which the first international exposition took place and also where the first interreligious intellectual congress occurred within the exposition tradition. While much contemporary work in the history of religions has come to focus on one geographical setting at a time, in the case of Britain and the United States in the nineteenth century we find an instance of one dominant cultural tradition becoming observable in two quite distinct historical contexts. The cultural contexts of both Britain and the United States help to explain the appearance of a field of religion in complementary ways; they are distinct yet connected historical manifestations of a field of religion.

Britain's Great Exhibition initiated the international exposition tradition and stands as a classical point of departure for the formalization of theories seeking to classify the emerging "global village." At Chicago's Columbian Exposition of 1893, the global classification of cultures developed into a more definitive taxonomy of "religions" than had appeared before. The creation of taxonomies of religion took place largely on the same basis and with the same biases as did cultural classification. The World's Parliament of Religions that was held in conjunction with the Chicago exposition appeared as an appropriate symbol of this phenomenon. The United States was the forum in which the presumptions of Anglo-based colonialism were played out within a sociological rather than a colonial setting, and the culturally complex event of the World's Parliament of Religions brought together peoples from across the globe in a face-to-face encounter that was unprecedented in its scope. By observing some of the ways

# INTRODUCTION xxi

in which the international expositions act as guides to the rise of a field of religion in both Britain and America, it will become more possible to show how objective approaches to "religion" transformed traditional biblical religion in more than one social context.

I have concluded this study with an analysis of the centenary of the first World's Parliament of Religions. The latter Parliament was revealing in showing that although the historical context had changed radically in the intervening century since the first Parliament, there were still important structural similarities between the two events. These similarities call into question the degree to which the colonial mentality that defined the first Parliament has changed, especially at the level of popular culture. I have ended with some brief reflections about how this study might be relevant to the field of religion of today.

# EXHIBITING
# RELIGION

# 1

# INTERNATIONAL EXPOSITIONS IN HISTORICAL CONTEXT

THE INTERNATIONAL exposition tradition was motivated by commercial interests, but it helped produce a discourse about intercultural relations that was unique within the history of Western thought. The events that were part of this tradition produced an atmosphere of increasingly intense competition between the many disparate peoples involved in them. As the tradition developed, this led to a greater interest in new conceptual models through which the integrating world might be envisioned as an interconnected whole. French historian Fernand Braudel has pointed to the importance in historical analysis of what he calls "conjuncture"—the creative but explosive effervescence that appears when long-developing cultural traditions come into close and extended contact with one another. This phenomenon occurred in an extreme and largely unprecedented way at the international expositions and is pivotal in attempting to understand the structure of international expositions and the power with which the events were invested. The international expositions were sites for mass conjunctures between several modern nations, colonies, and little-industrialized societies from across the world. They promoted the development of elaborate and highly differentiated "human" sciences—such as religion—that sought to organize conceptually this new historical information. The international expositions were instrumental both in acting as a reflection of humanistic theories already emerging at the time and in providing a forum in which they could be applied to actual peoples as a kind of case study.[1]

Religion appeared most definitively within the international exposition tradition at the first "World's Parliament of Religions," which was held in conjunction with Chicago's Columbian Exposition of 1893, sometimes referred to as the "Columbiad." The Parliament is revealing on many fronts in attempting to reimagine the appearance of a field of religion beyond the confines of the university. It was the first extensive gathering of religious representatives from across the world, but it was also the first intellectual gathering of any kind in the modern West to include extensive representation of cultures outside the Western bloc of nations. Equally important for this study, the Parliament also stands as an example of legions of peoples from across the globe being excluded from an event that was defined by specifically religious categories. Both the explicit and implicit agendas of the Parliament—who was in attendance, who was not, and why— merit our attention in assessing the event as an important symbol for the formation of a field of religion.[2]

To understand how an event like the World's Parliament of Religions became possible—and desirable—it is necessary to consider in historical context the principal ways in which the international exposition tradition influenced how the Parliament was structured. For that central purpose, the expositions need to be located historically in four contexts: (1) the rise of truly global commerce, (2) exhibitionism and museum display, (3) interculturalism in general, and (4) cross-cultural discourse in particular.

First and foremost, international expositions were commercial enterprises. They were aimed at enhancing domestic production by boosting national morale, stimulating consumption through the aesthetic display of commodities, and promoting international trade via costly exhibitions of industrial might. Through these basic strategies, the stage was set for increasingly complex material interactions between the countries and exhibitors attending the events. The classical cultural form underlying international expositions was the trade fair. While international expositions differed from trade fairs in that they did not revolve around the actual exchange of commodities, the two were fundamentally similar in that they always involved commercial negotiations across unfamiliar cultural borders, with all the discursive complexity that went along with it.

Second, what was so unique about the nineteenth-century international expositions was that the displays of industry and available commodities were accompanied by choice samples of a country's most prized and representative possessions—both their own and those of any colonies they may have had. Such possessions were displayed as symbols of cultural prestige designed to subtly enhance a country's image in the eyes of its international trade competition. When this element of "cultural display" is isolated from the initial focus on "industrial display," international expositions look more like exhibitions, or even museums, than fairs or expositions. The success of an international exposition was dependent largely on its ability to transform itself into a spectacle that to some degree transcended the more mundane commercialism on which the events were founded. As such, the expositions were greatly influenced by the exhibition and museum traditions that for centuries had been developing in Europe. These developing systems of display—the element of spectacle at the expositions—would have a strong influence on how international expositions promoted hierarchies of global culture and global religion that were decidedly to the host's advantage.

Third, the expositions were historically significant because they were of an *international* character and were unprecedented as such. The specific character of the modern "nation"—never easy to define—came into sharp focus at the expositions as many emerging nations found themselves in close proximity to one another. Further, beyond being international, the expositions were also *intercultural* at a time when concepts of "culture" had scarcely begun to make inroads. The idea of interculturalism—as an addition to, and in tandem with, internationalism—appeared in embryonic form within the international exposition tradition. The application of the term "culture" was never precise at the expositions, but it was regularly used to distinguish "nations" and full-blown "civilizations" from social entities that were seen as being somehow less than that. With all the world's peoples represented within the single setting of, as the initial example, the Great Exhibition, these long-developing and previously vague categorizations of the world's many peoples began to emerge in crisp detail as politically charged global hierarchies.

Finally, and of central importance to this study, the nineteenth-century international expositions produced the first international and intercultural intellectual congresses. These gradually became important features of the events. The international intellectual congresses of later expositions developed into complex exchanges of ideas about global issues and cultural ideologies involving a wide range of subjects, which eventually included religion. This developing discourse was the theoretical aspect of what Karl Marx identified around the time of the Great Exhibition as "dialectical materialism." This dialectic—the interplay of material exchange and the politicized discourse surrounding it—was central to the exposition phenomenon. International expositions appeared as classical case studies of Marx's theoretical structure. They began as adventures in international commerce but eventually produced an encompassing global discourse that had a decided effect on commercial interactions.[3]

In this first chapter, I will briefly discuss the historical contexts of the four principal themes of the international expositions of the nineteenth century identified above: international commerce; the exposition as spectacle; interculturalism; and expositions as forums for cross-cultural discourse. Each of these contributed significantly to the central focus of this book: the rise of a global discourse about religion that was shaped by the material exchanges between the cultures involved.

## The History of Fairs before the Great Exhibition

The historical precursor of international expositions was the ubiquitous phenomenon of the trade fair. Hebrews, Greeks, Romans, and Asians have all been identified as having discovered their own unique forms of this universal human institution. The word "fair" derives from the Latin word "*feria*" meaning holy day; in German the word "*Messe*" signifies both fair and mass. From time immemorial, trade fairs facilitated the exchange of common goods while simultaneously providing a context in which the most exotic aspects of material culture—both commodities and cultural novelties—could periodically be put on display. That is to say, the trade fair was always part market and part carnival; it was set apart from the ordinariness of daily life. To lure visitors and accomplish their desired ends, trade fairs, like the later international expositions that would grow out of them, were always partly dependent on their ability to offer something beyond the predictability of daily life.

The search for historical precursors to the nineteenth-century international expositions is best confined to the history of trade fairs extending back into the late medieval period in Europe. The economic structure of those early fairs was similar to the later international expositions in that the cost of staging a fair was always difficult to justify directly. Societies hosting both trade fairs and international expositions sought to gain some form of leverage, different in each particular situation, in exchange for all that was required in hosting one of the events. Nearly all international expositions lost money; the expense was considered an investment in a country's future on the burgeoning international market. Historically, earlier trade fairs had to be justified on the basis of the same kind of speculation. Like the international expositions, the trade fairs were capable of distorting standard values of goods in favor of the hosting society because of the prestige factor attached to hosting an extravagant fair. The international expositions would expand the prestige factor of hosting fairs—its immediate benefit to the image of a nation internationally—by creating the most elaborate material displays in history. In ways that would distinctly favor the hosts, these opulent displays of cultural potency had the ability to shape the discourse about foreign cultures that was emerging out of them.[4]

The Champagne fairs of France, which reached their height around 1260, are the most plausible precursors to the international expositions of the nineteenth century due to the simple fact that they included the exchange of both immediate and deferred value, the latter in the form of money. Direct barter was never an exact science, but more and more the exchange of money led to these fairs becoming centers for negotiations about an emerging international economy that could never be defined concretely.

When the Champagne fairs began to decline around 1320, the system reformed around Geneva in the fifteenth century, later at Lyons, and at the start of the seventeenth century in Italy at the Piacenza fairs around Genoa. Braudel observes that these relatively modern fairs can be pictured as a three-level pyramid. At the base were numerous transactions in cheap and mostly perishable local goods. Moving up, there was an exchange of luxury goods that were expensive primarily because they had been transported a significant distance to arrive at a fair. At the top of the pyramid was the exchange of monies, without which not nearly as much business of any kind could be transacted. As the fairs developed, there was a definite movement toward monetary exchange and the creation of new forms of credit, and away from the exchange of commodities per se.[5]

Braudel cites the Piacenza fair in Italy around the start of the seventeenth century as an example of a fair that had moved away from commodities altogether:

> Four times a year it was the scene of decisive but discreet meetings. No merchandise came to the fairs, and very little cash, but literally masses of bills of exchange, which in fact represented the entire wealth of Europe, with payments by the Spanish Empire as the mainstream. About sixty business men attended, Genoese for the most part. They were members of a club to which one could not be admitted without paying a very heavy caution [fee]. These privileged men fixed the *conto*, that is the exchange rate for liquidation at the end of each

fair. This was the big moment of these meetings, which were secretly frequented by foreign exchange dealers, and representatives of large merchant firms. There was a total of perhaps 200 initiates, behaving with great discretion and handling vast amounts of business.⁶

While exchanges at the Champagne fairs of the thirteenth century were primarily centered on commodities, by the start of the seventeenth century the ratio had changed entirely: it was now monetary exchange and credit that dominated the exchange of commodities. The international expositions would represent the culmination of this age-old tradition by moving beyond direct exchange altogether and exclusively into the sphere of speculation about commercial potentials.

The internal mechanics of European politics were only a part of the total development of the trade fairs, however. Another significant contribution came from the great international voyages—marked initially by those of Columbus. The effects of those voyages began to be felt in a variety of ways throughout the sixteenth century. Such expeditions stimulated the growing money market in Europe by introducing gold and silver in great quantities, a process tied intimately to the encounter with the Americas. As important, they began to bring diverse peoples into contact with one another en masse, greatly facilitating interest in, and utilization of, intersocietal interactions of all kinds. The trade fairs provided an existing cultural structure that was instrumental in integrating the early fruits of the new practice of mercantilism into European societies. This made the fairs much more global and exotic than they had been and set the stage for their maturation into international expositions.

After the middle of the seventeenth century, fairs began to decline as the driving force of the European economic structure. The exchange of money and credit came to be controlled largely through the Amsterdam Exchange, which replaced the old center of Antwerp. After 1695, the Royal Exchange in London came to predominate over Amsterdam. More business came to be transacted within the growing European cities, which were now home to more sophisticated shops that could handle uncommon commodities in the form of foods, spices, and other material goods. Fairs continued as a subsidiary component of the European economy, however, still providing a medium through which the exchange of the most unusual commodities could take place on an intermittent basis.

The early history of trade fairs is informative in trying to grasp the underlying structure of the international expositions. What began as more localized attempts to influence the setting of exchange rates by the hosting of fairs is directly analogous to the displaying of industry and its commodities by modern nations at international expositions for the purpose of defining and gaining a controlling interest in potential markets across the world. What was always at stake at fairs was the determination of value across unfamiliar borders. Fairs represented attempts to negotiate value in its most abstract of forms. Early on, it may have been exotic consumables like pepper that were the focus of a trade fair. Later, differing interpretations of the value of metals, coinage, and creative forms of credit predominated. The process was taken a step further at international expositions: aesthetically minded displays promoting "imagined communities" called "nations" were the means by which international commercial speculation was advanced. The value of various currencies at earlier fairs was dependent on a host of mitigating political and economic factors, as was the potential commercial value of particular industrial displays at international expositions.[7]

Fairs did not just define values, however; they *distorted* them because of the attractive light in which they cast their hosts. This fact more than any explains the desire to hold fairs, both in ancient times and modern, even with the great expense involved in doing so. The assessment of value is never neutral or objective. At the early fairs, as at later international expositions, value was determined by the structure of political power, which inevitably was in the hands of the hosts of a fair. Early fairs privileged some commodities over others in the same way they privileged some currencies and metals over others. At the international expositions, national ideologies would vie with one another for abstract forms of international prestige, a process involving unprecedented displays of material culture and, eventually, direct discussion and debate. Fairs were always the conduits for negotiations between peoples who did not regularly interact with one another. It is not surprising that later fairs in the form of international expositions would be forums for the rise of a unique tradition of international intellectual congresses and the first global congress of religions.

## *Collections, Exhibitions, and Museums:*
## *The Carnivalesque at International Expositions*

While the long history of international expositions can be traced back to the early trade fairs, the more immediate precursors to international expositions were national industrial exhibitions. These events differed from trade fairs in that they generally did not involve a trade in goods, but instead functioned to enhance the image of the nation in the eyes of its people. They did this through displays of productive capacity and attractive exhibits of the finest artifacts a culture had to offer. As the national industrial exhibitions grew into international events, they evolved from selling a more hopeful national future to a country's own working classes, to selling either international trade or colonialism (depending on the region) to the whole of the world. This marked a movement from *intra*nationalism to *inter*nationalism, from promoting nations as effective governors of their own people to promoting nations as beneficent empires with amorphous boundaries throughout the world.

Strictly national exhibitions were focused almost exclusively on the display of industry and domestic products. At the international expositions, however, displaying colonial territories of Europe and subordinated domestic peoples (Native Americans and African Americans) within the United States made the events into ideologically complex intercultural exhibitions involving much more than just industry. Little-industrialized human cultures, both their artifacts and their peoples, provided points of contrast against which the industrial progress of modern Western civilization could be gauged.

The displaying of exhibits that were not directly connected to commercial aspirations grew out of a centuries-old tradition of exhibitions and museums in Europe. Especially with regard to the representation of colonized societies and cultures deemed "primitive," these exhibits bear careful scrutiny as a part of international expositions that contributed significantly to the complete picture of how religious categories developed from within the exposition tradition. The collective "Other" outside the West was not only more industrially simplistic but also became caught up in the potentially denigrating carnivalesque atmosphere at international expositions. While "civilized" modern nations were invited to occupy the austere section of an exposition's main fairgrounds, various peoples judged "savage," and later "primitive," took up places in the circuslike atmosphere of the carnival area. This served to reinforce implicit stereotypes about the backwardness of such peoples based simply on a lack of industrialization.

While the most dramatic manifestations of the dichotomy between "savages" and "primitives" versus the "civilized" would be reserved for later international expositions, such manifestations did appear in embryonic form at London's Great Exhibition. On the surface, the Great Exhibition was designed to display the greatest advances to date in the realm of industry, but with the whole world invited to the event, it proved exceedingly difficult to separate something that could be specifically identified as "industry" from the wider world of material culture. Myriad handcrafted objects and geological artifacts from places such as Melanesia, Africa, and the Native Americas, for instance, were placed on display a few aisles away from immense British steam engines and other au courant displays of industrial potency. In the exhibition setting, these trinkets from small-scale cultures appeared more as cultural curios belonging in museums than as bonafide examples of international industry. In addition to these potential museum pieces from abroad, the Western countries themselves sent countless nonindustrial displays of cultural exotica of their own, which were also sources of great fascination. The combined features of serious commercial aspiration and aesthetic display made the expositions complex in terms of how they promoted the collective image of the attending countries.

The official motivation behind the noncommercial, nonindustrial exhibits at international expositions was altruistic: to provide cheap education for the masses that might counterbalance the potentially shameless commercialism of these events. This was a multifaceted endeavor participated in by governments, trading companies, and individuals alike. The unofficial reason for such displays was to engage in a subtle competition of aesthetic sensibilities and technological innovation with other modern nations and foreign commercial competition. It was not enough to demonstrate production capability. Nations also had to demonstrate that their potential wealth could be put to good use.

Non-Western cultures were predominantly represented by interested Western parties at the international expositions. The art of displaying the collective "Other" from across the world went through a process of continual refinement at the events. It became an indispensable part of the proceedings—a growing science in and of itself. Eventually, in what would amount to the ultimate example of turning foreign peoples into spectacles, actual peoples were put on display in distinct villages at the expositions. Displaying actual peoples as cultural artifacts significantly affected the extent to which peoples deemed "savage" or "primitive" were marked off from those held to be part of "civilizations." The religious categories of the World's Parliament of Religions would dramatically reflect this dichotomous global division by calling for a meeting of the "ten great world religions," all of which were identified with major centers of civilization.

The long history of the exhibition trade can be traced back to the medieval churches, which qualified as the common man's first museum. This fact is surprising only when considered within the Protestant-dominated context of the international expositions. Patrick Geary has shown that there was an enduring trade in relics housed in the churches throughout the medieval period. The churches were repositories for a revolving stock of holy relics that acted to spark the public's religious imagination and proved quite profitable as well. These objects were seen as bestowing certain spiritual benefits, and the less frequently they were shown, the greater those benefits might be imagined as being. By custom, a small monetary offering was left as an act of homage toward the religious commodities.⁸

In the pre-Reformation period, religious objects were often displayed side by side with natural curiosities in the churches. The survey of English religious houses supervised by Thomas Cromwell from 1535 to 1540 found that "hardly a house was without its prized relics, most of them enclosed in reliquaries of precious metals and stones." With the Reformation dawning in England, part of Cromwell's duty was to eradicate all traces of this "abomination of idolatry." It was the fact that the church *specifically* housed these collections, rather than the nature of the collections themselves, that led to their being confiscated and sent up to the place of national collection at the Tower of London.⁹

Once the Reformation hit England full force, an irremediable fissure occurred in the relationship between religion and its material symbols. During Cromwell's crusade, a magical cross made of old sticks and wire that had been an object of great veneration for the people of the Cistercian abbey in Boxley, Kent, was collected and brought to London. Outside St. Paul's Cathedral, a Bishop Hilsey of Rochester exposed this lowly abuse of the symbol of the cross by taking the overtly mundane and unholy object and breaking it into pieces as he preached. Hilsey ended by slinging the pieces of the dreadful cross out into the crowd, who then "broke the pieces into further pieces." Soon after Elizabeth I's reign had begun, in fact, "The last objects that had been used for the 'increase of lucre' [in the churches] had been disposed of, and along with them had gone not only the superb reliquaries which were themselves works of art but also most of the wall paintings, tapestries, statuary, and liturgical accessories that had made the pre-Reformation church a gallery of art as well as a museum. Such art as escaped mutilation or outright destruction then was merely reprieved, to become the victim of Puritans' hammers, whitewash brushes, and torches in a later epoch."¹⁰

Once collections of relics were eliminated as objects of veneration and relocated safely into the domain of the secular after the middle of the sixteenth century in England, the exhibition business began to expand. English ships began to return from remote regions of the world with the most unearthly natural and cultural phenomena. Honest expository about the nature and origin of such obscure objects was expected within the church setting, but the purveyors of commercial collections were free to exploit the desire to observe cultural exotica that was emerging everywhere in Europe by 1600.

By the beginning of the eighteenth century, when such novelties as the encyclopedia were coming into being, knowledge about the more arcane curiosities of human culture had become a marketable commodity. English "virtuosos"—amateur scholars and collectors—began to market collections in increasingly profitable public displays. In the middle of the eighteenth century, the famous collection of Sir Hans Sloane was sold to the government and formed the basis for the British Museum, which opened in 1759. As the first European museum designed specifically for the public, it was hoped that the British Museum's displays would surpass the often embarrassing collections of the past proffered by gentlemen amateurs. The museum's purpose was "to promote Science and the Arts," rather than to satiate the "curiosity of . . . multitudes . . . in quest of amusement." Thus, the more altruistic themes of London's Great Exhibition—the promotion of science, art, and industry (affiliated with technological innovation)—emerged early on from within Britain's museum tradition.[11]

The exhibition trade began to make an important transition beginning in the middle of the eighteenth century. At a growing rate, what was once a business built primarily on exhibiting technological innovations, relics and natural oddities from foreign lands, and domestic human freaks gave way to the simple displaying of exotic—but normal—foreign peoples for purposes of education and entertainment. The image of the "savage" satiated the English curiosity with its authentic otherworldliness, and it had the dual advantage of not requiring the pity that was often bestowed upon domestic freaks. It went beyond that, though. Unlike that of domestic freaks, the image of the "savage" proved fully capable of being exalted. The term "noble savage" actually has a rarely discussed, implicit meaning. Representatives from foreign lands such as Africa or Polynesia who claimed the status of nobility were a much greater drawing card at English exhibitions than were more common "specimens." In fact, instead of repulsing European audiences, the more dignified "savages" often mesmerized them. The "ethnic villages" that emerged at later international expositions—

small troupes of peoples from cultures considered "exotic" who were set up in displays of their native lands—thus grew out of a lengthy tradition of turning foreign peoples into spectacles.¹²

In any case, the displaying of foreign peoples was not just a simple byproduct of European explorations. The rise of an exhibition trade was partly dependent on the early profits of the industrial revolution, which by the beginning of the nineteenth century had put a small amount of spare change in commoners' pockets. This as much as anything made it possible for exhibitions to be reconceived as potentially serious business in the form of larger-scale exhibitions and, eventually, international expositions. The willingness of the working class to spend hard-earned money to see foreign subjects placed in potentially condescending displays for entertainment purposes was an important piece of the puzzle that formed the full picture of the displaying of foreign peoples. This phenomenon was an example of a sophisticated form of colonialism based on aesthetic rather than exclusively economic or military principles being bought into at virtually every cultural level within the colonizing countries, with conscious choices made by all.

Another contributing factor to the success of the exhibition trade in the West was that the process of usurping heretofore unknown peoples into Western modes of representation was in large part a result of the Christian worldview that guided such expansion in its early phases. As Bernard McGrane has pointed out, newly discovered cultures had to be represented within the Christian worldview if they were going to be acknowledged as human at all. It was not until the Enlightenment (or later, depending on whether one is speaking about elite or popular culture) that Christianity became *a* religion in Europe, among other religions, rather than the single worldview by which all others were defined. Before the Enlightenment, the Christian encounter with peoples it had never before witnessed dictated that those other peoples be "nominated," as in being "Christened," so that they could become intelligible within the monolithic Christian worldview: "The implicit sovereignty of giving names, of nomination, has a historically specific character. In the sixteenth century, names did not name in a neutral sense, nor did they function as naming in a geographical sense, rather, fundamentally, *names Christened*. To name was to Christianize and to Baptize." Interaction within the early colonial context, then, dictated that for any discursive interaction to take place at all meant that those being interacted with by Christian nations would be "converted" as well, at least in the eyes of the explorers.¹³

The long history of exhibiting foreign cultures in the West thus took place within a religious context that dictated that those cultures be pulled into Western modes of representation in a powerful way. The international expositions of the nineteenth century would extend the act of "nominating" foreign cultures in an increasingly abstract and symbolic manner, with everything from aesthetics to religion becoming involved in the way other peoples were displayed. The events would succeed in reinforcing the Western sense of dominance by exhibiting foreign peoples in a manner indicating that their rightful place in the emerging globally defined world was as at some level of subordination. Drawing from a deep and rich tradition, the carnivalesque aspect of the international expositions was instrumental in delivering this message from an area somewhere beneath the level of discourse.

## *Defining Human Culture Globally before International Expositions*

What made the nineteenth-century international expositions most significant was, quite simply, that they were genuinely global events to a greater degree than any that had come before them. They began as eminently cautious forays into limited international trade within Europe and rapidly expanded beyond Western internationalism to become encompassing global events. This set the stage for the appearance of various taxonomies of the world's cultures and also of its religions. Industrial potency was the barometer for how both cultures and religions were placed into hierarchies within these taxonomies. As the international exposition tradition developed, a dichotomous global division emerged in which some peoples were relegated to the expositions' carnivalesque "midways," while others were represented only within the utopian cities that marked the main fairgrounds. This global dichotomy was never entirely distinct and changed in emphasis depending on where any given exposition was being held, but its existence is testified to by the simple development of this dualistic structure within the expositions' grounds.

Within the West itself, the burgeoning world of commerce was being quickly redefined within an international arena after the middle of the nineteenth century. The international expositions proved ingenious in refining this emerging art of international commerce. Their strategies went well beyond simple economics. Patriotism was promoted heavily in the new international context and welled up at the events like some supernatural force—or perhaps like a newly discovered cultural instinct, the preservation of which was imperative for maintaining the tenuous collective identity of newly constituted nations. The expositions combined several elements—ideas for stimulating domestic production and commerce, the promotion of international trade, and a renewed focus on national pride—to redefine what it meant to seek a better way of life and what exactly would be involved in attaining it. All were necessary components of the attempt to promote nations in the eyes of the world at the expositions.

Anthropologist Burton Benedict has made an intriguing analogy between international expositions and the potlatch ceremonies of "archaic" societies, first given significant attention by Marcel Mauss. In the potlatch, ever greater gifts are exchanged to place rivals in debt and advance one's own social position. To fail to return a larger gift than one has been given is to endure humiliation and loss of social status. For Benedict, international expositions are like potlatches in that they involve "a collective representation that symbolizes an entire community in a massive display of prestige vis-à-vis other communities. All kinds of institutions find simultaneous expression: religious, legal, moral, and economic. Potlatches and world's fairs are not simply concerned with the exchange of goods in a purely economic sense, but with the exchange of entertainments, courtesies and rituals."[14]

Benedict's analogy is effective in describing the dynamics behind the interaction between the Western countries at international expositions. Because the events were so speculative in their relation to future commerce, there was a great fear on the part of competing nations that to fail to match another country's "gift" in the form of an exposition spectacle was to run a great risk indeed. This dynamic was played out primarily between France and Britain early on, but it was also evident between Britain and the United States when Americans constructed their own version of the Great Exhibition at the "New York Crystal Palace" in 1853. By the turn of the century, it was France and the United States who engaged in the most earnest competition, and the exposition phenomenon touched most parts of Europe through the twentieth century.

The interaction between "civilized" political units called "nations" invites two questions that have remained surprisingly open debates since the middle of the nineteenth century, when awareness of these designations was first becoming solidified: what did it mean to be "civilized," and what precisely was a "nation" or "nationalism"? The possible answers to these questions bring into view all aspects of the structure of international expositions.

Benedict Anderson has observed that nations are amorphous entities and thus difficult to define. He writes, "Like Gertrude Stein in the face of Oakland, one can rather quickly conclude that there is 'no there there.'" Anderson argues that nations combine the essential cultural structures of the ancient world—what he calls "dynastic realms" and "religious communities." In the dynastic realm, people were "subjects" in a divinely sanctioned political structure headed by a king. The older political structures were defined more by the gravitational pull of a center than by distinct geographical borders. They were able to govern multilingual and heterogeneous populations without having to account for, answer to, and in some manner unite each separate population under their aegis in a concise manner. Similarly, the ancient religious community was defined by a sacred script more symbolic than the precise languages of modernity and more easily transferred across dynastic borders. This contributed to the formation of less clearly defined, mass groupings of peoples in the ancient world.[15]

In the modern period, however, the continual and significant increase of populations within different cultures, the "weight of numbers" in Braudel's terminology, caused borders to overlap one another at a growing rate. Modern peoples gradually became "citizens" rather than subjects and were members of sovereignties adjudicated by a "state." Thus, a more concise drawing of boundaries around each respective cultural center became inevitable. Anderson follows Eric Hobsbawm in noting that modern nations are defined primarily by linguistic affinity, with a host of other contributing factors. While numerous linguistic groups used to be capable of being united under one dynastic realm, nations in the modern world have come to be separated by linguistic affinity. Thus, nations have increased in number in the modern period, while their separate characters as distinct political units have become more clearly defined.[16]

According to Anderson, by appealing to new continuities in the form of the modern nation, modernity has replaced the deep sense of continuity provided by the religious communities of antiquity. Individuals are transformed into the imagined community of the nation by various means. The most important of these early on was the capacity of the print medium—especially newspapers—to unite, within the common cause of the nation, disparate peoples who had never met one another. Once this transformation was accomplished, the nation could invite cohesion, impose coercion, and gain a power over individuals comparable to that which only the religious community used to be capable. This transition to a series of satellite nations from what used to be more massive dynastic realms was crucial in allowing something like the Great Exhibition—as a congress of many nations that promoted trade between them—to come into existence.

Indeed, keen competition between civilized nations was the central focus of the first international expositions, and those nations attending would come to define themselves much more concisely as a result of it. As the events progressed, however, international trade became more accepted and standardized. As this occurred, cultures regarded as "savage" or "primitive" began to be represented much more elaborately at the events as key players in the blossoming international market for exotic consumables and commodities made from raw materials gleaned from their lands. The juxtaposition of these less-industrial cultures with the imagined communities of civilized nations at international expositions, given the latter's material dominance, legitimated national identities in a way that comparison exclusively with other similar nations could not. By the time the Chicago exposition was staging the first World's Parliament of Religions in 1893, the religions affiliated with the cultural areas deemed "savage" or "primitive" by the international exposition tradition would be excluded from the first global discussion of religion altogether. This would only serve to reinforce the cultural hierarchies that had grown up initially on the basis of industrial capacity.

## *International and Intercultural Discourse before International Expositions*

While London's Great Exhibition was significant for the material displays of world culture it boasted, it also brought together unprecedented international juries to judge which of those displays were the best in their respective categories. The gathering of international awards juries was a necessity at the Great Exhibition, because juries had been a regular feature of national exhibitions. However, until the juries were formed, it did not seem to dawn on anyone that they posed a potential threat to one of the stated purposes of the event: to promote a congress of, rather than a competition between, civilized nations. The historical significance of the international juries was readily apparent to all of those involved as the Great Exhibition progressed and the juries completed their work. Just how unique were these first international gatherings of prominent persons from the arts, sciences, and world of commerce at the Great Exhibition?

The Great Exhibition juries opened the door to the possibility of a large number of persons from different national, and later different cultural, traditions congressing about various aspects of human culture that were not bound by any particular societal context. That is to say, they lent great impetus to the development of human scientific categories that did not see themselves as being confined to a single intellectual tradition. When all of the possibilities of such discussions are considered in sum, what appeared much more clearly than it had before was the possibility of developing an objective approach to *all cultural* phenomena, or a science of human culture. With all of the world's material productions and raw materials ostensibly set before them, the Great Exhibition's award juries had more tangible data from which to conceive such a vision than had previously been available. This was, at the very least, largely how the persons involved in the jury process themselves understood their work.

In the Enlightenment and before, numerous purportedly comprehensive taxonomic schemas were advanced that attempted to fill in the many blanks of the complete picture of human culture. The categories proposed by the Swedish scientist Linnaeus in his *Systema Naturae* in 1735, which divided the species *Homo sapiens* into types *americanus, asiaticus, afer,* and *europaeus,* are a prime example of the generality of the earliest taxonomies. However, these earlier schemas were unduly limited by existing geographical conceptions of the exterior world. One can go all the way back to Aristotle to identify the first attempts to create sciences of various branches of human knowledge that conceived themselves as complete explanations of their respective areas of study, but those attempts were much more successful in some fields than others. The specific field of geography, for instance, made tremendous strides between the time of Linnaeus and that of the Great Exhibition. The attempt to create a more or less complete picture of human culture was not feasible, of course, even at the time of the Great Exhibition, but for the first time, it had become possible to sketch an outline of that picture. Eric Hobsbawm writes of the 1780s, for instance: "Even the best-informed men then living—let us say a man like the scientist and traveller Alexander von Humboldt—knew only patches of the inhabited globe. The main outlines of the continents and most islands were known, though by modern standards not too accurately. Outside of a few areas—in several continents they did not reach more than a few miles inland—

the map of the world consisted of white spaces crossed by the marked trails of traders or explorers."[17]

Advances made in cartography by the middle of the nineteenth century allowed for a complete reassessment of the total human context. The world had been an interminably shifting shape before the nineteenth century; its potential for radically diverse cultural forms remained endless. The journeys of Captain James Cook, for instance, continued to uncover new terrain until the end of the eighteenth century. When the exterior world could be mapped in outline with confidence, it became much more feasible for a "science" of human culture to emerge as a unified sphere of study. If that science was incomplete, it was incomplete in a very different way than prior, more geographically limited attempts to define a science of culture. When a science of human culture emerged as a real possibility, it became feasible to create definitive global hierarchies that could begin to be carved in stone, as it were. The Great Exhibition, with its implicit colonial ambitions, did much to promote the idea that a comprehensive science of human culture was not only plausible but desirable as well.

Earlier discussions about intersocietal and intercultural themes took place in vastly different contexts than did the international awards juries at the Great Exhibition. The most powerful institutions responsible for holding significant discussions on far-reaching social issues prior to the Great Exhibition would have been the following: governments, trading companies, churches, universities, and learned societies. In terms of more genuinely objective approaches to intercultural conceptions, however, each of these bodies was severely limited for what should be obvious reasons: they were comprised of members of either single countries or single ideological persuasions—generally both.

The most potentially objective of these institutions, the universities, were dominated by their national orientations to a far greater degree than today and were still in a fledgling stage of their development. The learned societies were involved in very specific intercultural topics—like cartography, for instance—which did not lend themselves immediately to the more universal and meaningful observations about topics like the whole of human culture that would develop out of the Great Exhibition. Governments and trading companies were not in the business of education and theory making but rather of commerce and national defense. The ideological hindrances to ecclesiastical attempts to conceive of human culture generically scarcely require comment. The universal proclamations issuing forth out of Protestant and Catholic church councils, for instance, varied markedly depending in which, or about which, country the meetings took place.

It has always proven exceedingly difficult to establish anything approaching the objective basis for knowledge across cultural borders that the human sciences would later seek. This problem was paramount for those sciences in their early development. In fact, apart from natural philosophy (what is now called physical science), the distinct fields of study we now take for granted were surprisingly vague before the Great Exhibition. Knowledge was eminently local to a much greater extent than it is today, even if it was self-fashioned as "enlightened" and universal. The first academic chairs in a modern discipline as seemingly fundamental as history, for instance, were not even appointed until 1810, at the University of Berlin, and in 1812, at Napoleon's Sorbonne.[18]

The specific focus of interculturalism as an area of study was even later in arriving. It was not until after the advent of evolutionary theory in the second half of the nineteenth century that the birth of anthropology as an academic discipline took place. Anthropological conceptions prior to that time were based on interactions with a relatively small range of individual cultures, and they were focused primarily on one or a small grouping of cultures. They also lacked the more scientific basis they would eventually have after the rise of archaeology and the advent of evolutionary theory as a means through which human culture as a whole could be comprehended as an extension of nature and conceived, at least as a series of working hypotheses, as consisting of some hard data. Without this definitive material basis, the link between the "human" science of anthropology and the hard sciences would have been difficult to forge.

While plausible precursors to the objectifying intercultural conceptions emerging out of the international exposition tradition are difficult to locate, what contributed more directly to the possibility of objective-minded, international debates was a change in the language used for creating important works of scholarship toward the end of the eighteenth century. Johann Gottfried Herder was among those who led the march in promoting the use of common languages in the treatment of serious subjects to replace more elite languages, primarily Latin. Herder also drew attention to the need for a study of the differences between the cultural contexts in which the various languages were in use as a way of grasping with greater precision the differing modes of interpretation that had developed in the increasingly distinct European countries. The earliest comparative projects in Europe were analyses of literature that called attention to national differences in aesthetic judgments. Great Britain, perhaps stimulated into an awareness of the importance of cultural comparison through its early colonial activity, was ahead of nations on the Continent in the comparative literary movements of the eighteenth century.[19]

These changes in the linguistic context of Western thought marked a crucial change in Western scholarship. The use of common languages began to generate the necessary amount of divergent yet sophisticated scholarship to allow for the exacting and distinctly contrasting points of view necessary for the emergence of definitive human sciences. Without the increased use of the more common languages in the world of scholarship, it would have been difficult for so many people in the arts and sciences from different countries to represent divergent points of view about, say, the relative value of commodities at the Great Exhibition, or later, to discuss the subtleties of cultural values or the process of comparative religion at the expositions' intellectual congresses.

## National Exhibitions prior to the Great Exhibition

The popular commercial exhibitions of the eighteenth century were conceived by early capitalists as attractive containers that would catch whatever loose change their prospering industrial societies might dump into them. Government-sanctioned national exhibitions utilized the popularity of the exhibition business as a means of attracting large numbers of people to events ostensibly designed to promote the welfare of society (or perhaps to maintain its existing structure, depending on one's political perspective).

The French were the first to turn the display of industry, art, and manufactures into an art form that more closely resembled the later international expositions. Post-Revolutionary France was in desperate need of an industrial jumpstart, with stockpiled goods and a low level of production. The first French national exhibition took place in Paris in 1797. English blockades had cut off French ports, making the export of goods all but impossible. It was hoped that the display of goods in the forecourt of the Louvre would not only sell the tapestries, carpets, and ceramics presented, but also that it would be a symbol for the French people that the country's industry was alive and well. In the four days it ran, this initial French exhibition did sell many of the goods it set out, but just as important, the event proved capable of attracting crowds. Visitors appeared willing to amble through endless stalls of commodities even if purchase was not a definite reason for attending the event.[20]

The next year, another event took place at a more prestigious site with elaborately prepared buildings and a greater emphasis on creating appealing displays of goods. Whereas there were only three exhibitors in the 1797 exposition, the event of 1798 was host to 110 firms and private entrepreneurs. Again many goods were sold, but what drew the most attention was the pageantry surrounding the event. Military parades, fireworks, and dozens of sideshows created a festive scene of "carnival and ceremony, of circus and museum, of popularism and elitism" that was to mark all ensuing events. A catalogue printed for the event was mainly a compilation of the addresses of the exhibitors, and it quickly became apparent to the world of free enterprise that exhibitions could be effective advertising showcases. The French government took a keen interest in the careful staging of these events. The carnivalesque and educational aspects of these early national exhibitions were carefully planned for the purpose of  attracting the largest possible crowds and making them feel good about their country and its productions. By 1849, the French were staging their tenth national exposition, which attracted 4,352 exclusively French exhibitors and a considerable amount of international interest as well.[21]

The British exhibitions also increased in scope after the start of the nineteenth century. The British events tended to include a wider variety of material goods and industrial displays, even if they were no match for the pageantry of the French events. After 1837, the Mechanics Institute began to stage regular events that had a more philanthropic focus than did the earlier, more economically minded events. The intention was to cast industrially driven modernizing society in a better light by advancing all aspects of the industrial process, including calling attention to the plight of the working classes.[22]

Throughout the first half of the nineteenth century, there were also comparable national exhibitions in other countries. Some of the most significant were at Munich (1918), Stockholm (1823), New York (1828), Moscow (1829), and Brussels (1830). The Brussels exhibition included principalities from the Netherlands and thus had an international element to it. The most international event prior to the Great Exhibition was the Berlin "All German Exhibition" of 1844, which united the separate German states within a single enterprise. This event clearly showed that exhibitions could exert influence in the political arena as well as in the economic one. The German event "had an eye on the foreign visitor and was intended as a showcase for German national identity."[23]

It was virtually certain, though, that the first international exhibition would be in France or Britain. Their respective levels of industrial production were the only ones that would stand a reasonable chance of benefiting from exposure in the international market. Britain's Great Exhibition would become the first exhibition to acknowledge the growing symbiosis between internal and external economics, between domestic production and international trade. At the same time, it would become the first event in history seeking to incorporate the whole of the known world into its vision of a modern world system. The appearance of a field of religion at the Great Exhibition was truly embryonic in terms of its stage of development, but realizing that the seeds for its birth were being sewn by that time helps to explain its rapid development in the coming decades.

The historical radicality of the Great Exhibition, as an international gathering of nations and cultures that included formal discussion between them, can be put into perspective only by observing the difficulty of locating a number of its key elements within plausible historical contexts. This problem shows the real significance of both the event itself and its juries. As international gatherings founded on the principles of egalitarianism and objectivity—difficult to establish in actuality as these principles may have been—the juries were important precursors to what would become passionate, face-to-face debates at later international expositions about such sensitive topics as religion. London's Great Exhibition and the international exposition tradition it gave birth to need to be viewed as a complex interplay between economic, political, aesthetic, and discursive cultural forces. When all of these elements are understood as being fundamentally interrelated to one another and inseparable, it will become more feasible to understand the extent to which they combined at international expositions to have a decided effect on the formation of a field of religion.

# 2

## BRITAIN'S GREAT EXHIBITION
### IDEOLOGY MATERIALIZED

The Great Exhibition of 1851 has remained a national historical treasure in Britain for the nearly 150 years since it took place. The event has been made a part of the British school curriculum so that children might be indoctrinated into the enduring vision of a progressive Britain that led the world forward in its Victorian heyday. Most commoners recall the exhibition with great fondness and it remains a kind of a guiding national fable, but only a few photographs remain of the Great Exhibition. The event predominantly has been set away safely in the stores of the literary imagination, where there is a decided movement away from scientific reduction and toward historical amplification.[1]

So encompassing was the spectacle of the Great Exhibition that it represented virtually anything its patrons desired it to. In 1851 it was the very definition of the word "evocative." Some of the visions it evoked were valid; others were illusions. The danger in treating the event historically today is that it can present itself as a tabula rasa. The contemporary writer can project the pressing issues of the early twenty-first century onto the mass of data that was generated by an event like the Great Exhibition and forget that tacit assumptions about cultural hegemony, commodification, and power/knowledge dynamics were but vague apparitions in 1851 compared to what they have become today.

My purpose here is not to explore how the Royal Commission that organized the Great Exhibition masterminded the event from the beginning as a means through which to advance the interests of

British colonialism abroad and "sell" an unjust class structure at home. Few would deny that hegemonic inclinations did exist to some extent in 1851 Britain, but it is only by placing such proclivities clearly within their *own* historical context that the Great Exhibition is genuinely informative as a pivotal point in Western history. What is still so fascinating about the nineteenth-century international expositions today is that they provide such effective summations of the cultural events unfolding around them. The Great Exhibition stands as a definitive symbol for the beginning of mass global integration. The unfolding exposition tradition that followed provides a glimpse of the diverse means by which Western society as a whole succeeded in acquiring the inordinate degree of power it did within the emerging modern world system.[2]

In this chapter, I confine my analysis of the Great Exhibition to a search for the specific historical developments that prompted the formation of a field of religion. This same historical data is equally informative about how a field of "culture"—what would eventually be called anthropology—emerged parallel to a field of religion.[3] These two fields of study appeared as alternate approaches to conceptualizing a new mass of data that appeared most clearly within the international exposition tradition. In the earliest periods of colonial expansion, cultural and religious comparisons were difficult if not impossible to distinguish from one another. Religious understanding was always central rather than peripheral to the developing art of cultural comparison as a whole.[4]

The connection between religion and culture was driven home most forcefully at the Great Exhibition when it became clear that determinations of value in the act of religious comparison were based almost exclusively on the economic status of the society each religion represented rather than on more definitively religious criteria. This was true of both the subtle religious comparisons exclusively among Western nations and the more sweeping religious comparisons between "civilized nations" as a whole, with cultures categorized as "savage." Because of this, cultural and religious comparisons greatly informed one another and, as we will see, were often difficult to distinguish.

The most general outlines of the intercultural hierarchy that began to emerge at the Great Exhibition revolved around a basic dichotomy between "savage" and "civilized" societies—a conceptual tool that was sharpened considerably during the course of the event. The term "savage" was originally used to demarcate a geographically based division between "civilized" modern society and the unmapped "wild-erness" beyond it. Between the Great Exhibition and Chicago's Columbian Exposition, the term "primitive," as referring to the "first," or the "original," largely supplanted the term "savage" and denoted an opposition between an originary form of "primitive" humanity and "evolved" modern society. This occurred predominantly through the work of E. B. Tylor. Tylor's work, along with too many others to name, expedited the eventual triumph of the doctrine of social evolution, which maintained that certain social groups had "evolved" further out of an original state of animal nature than had others (discussed fully in chapter 3). While intimations of the concept of social evolutionism had begun to appear at the Great Exhibition, it was primarily after that event that the concept emerged as the most prevalent schematic through which the intercultural world was conceptualized. The concept of "culture," as a purportedly neutral descriptive term for human societies, did not emerge triumphant in anthropological circles until the twentieth century, though the term was certainly in use before then.[5]

The emergence of a global division between "savage" and "civilized" at the Great Exhibition was a natural outcome of an exhibition based on "industrial" display. The "civilized" countries were those that produced the many commodities that were beginning to drive the international economy; the "savages" were vaguely affiliated with the regions that supplied the bulk of the raw materials from which those commodities were produced. Within this formulation, the United States represented a kind of wild card in the new international game, since it was dominated politically by the civilized but included many persons who would have been considered "savage," and it also was in the business of supplying raw materials. This untamed foal with wobbly legs and questionable judgment was clearly imbued with a frightening amount of potential and remained difficult to place within global cultural hierarchies because of that.

The remainder of the global hierarchy was more covert. It was based on a magnificently biased analysis of the material displays presented by the various countries attending the Great Exhibition. The quality of those displays—especially the technological prowess of the most sophisticated exhibits—carried definitive implications for the general religious prestige accorded to one or another country. With China and Japan absent, the displays of Islamic countries and the displaying of the prize colony of India by the British East India Company formed a liminal cultural world between "savage" and civilized. The religions of these regions—or those equated with them through a truly imprecise science—were correspondingly viewed as semibarbaric.

In the case of the Western countries—all of which were dominated by traditional biblical religion, either Protestant or Catholic—the identification of religious differences came out at least as much in the form of subtle judgments about nations and their economic potency as in assessments of separate and identifiable religious positions. Southern Europe meant Catholicism and all that went with it, just as northern European culture implied Protestantism. The newly emerging forum of international expositions led quite naturally to these nationally based religious interpretations and even promoted them. It was on this basis—judgments of the world's cultures based on industrial capacity—that a "science" of comparative religion began to emerge from within the international exposition tradition.

## Laying Plans for an Unprecedented International Exhibition of Industry

The Great Exhibition of 1851 got off to a very slow start. Early in 1848, Prince Albert was against the idea of hosting an exhibition of any kind in Britain. Exhibitions were costly to stage, and their beneficiary value for industry had come into question. Henry Cole, a member of the Royal Society of Arts, which would eventually organize the Great Exhibition, was convinced of the economic efficacy of exhibitions and sought to change the prince's mind. The Royal Society thus elected to send its secretary to Paris for the French national exposition of 1849 to study the event and to make a recommendation about whether Britain should hold a national exhibition of its own and, if so, what form the event should take. The question of hosting an international exhibition had not yet been broached.

It was actually the French who were the first to consider seriously making their exhibitions international. The president of the Societé Royale d'Emulation, Monsieur Boucher de Perthes, recommended that French exhibitions become international at the early date of 1834. The French would indeed have been well advised to host the first international exhibition: hosting countries were inevitably cast in a most favorable light at international exhibitions. French manufacturers were skeptical, however. Ever wary of the possibility of Britain flooding their markets with cheap products, they did not buy the idea of inviting the British and the rest of the world to display their products on French soil. The same process occurred a second time during preparations for the French exhibition of 1849, and again the notion was aggressively rejected by the interested French parties.

The principle of free trade, which sought to incorporate rather than avoid international trade relations in stimulating domestic production, was still a new concept. French manufacturers thought it best to leave well enough alone regarding such an uncertain enterprise.

By 1850, however, British production had reached a level that allowed the prospect of an international market to appear for the first time and, despite many grave reservations, as a door to potentially limitless economic possibilities. The repeal of the Corn Laws in 1846, which removed the long-standing tariff on imported corn and sounded the gong for the advance of free trade in Britain, removed bureaucratic obstacles to international trade. When Royal Society secretary Matthew Digby Wyatt made his report on the 1849 French exposition, he spoke directly to the prospect and promise of an international exhibition: "Smarting under the protracted misery of actual and threatening civil war, and the effects of sudden commercial stagnation, the manufacturers of that generally enlightened nation may perhaps for once be pardoned for the short-sighted policy which induced them to forego the splendid opportunity thus offered them of acquiring . . . a knowledge of those slight points and qualities which might convert many of her strictly local manufactures into articles of foreign demand and export trade, thus relieving the wretchedness of her laity."[6]

It goes without saying that neither Britain nor France wanted to be shown up by the other, but the prospect of being shown up on one's own turf could be disastrous. What had been negotiated for centuries by quick-starting, full-scale wars between the two countries was becoming in the nineteenth century a subtler chess game of economics in which exhibitions were beginning to be valued as considerably more than pawns. Wyatt's report blamed the failure of the French to promote their commercial relations internationally on the unfounded fears of French manufacturers and challenged his own country to avoid a similar pitfall.

After a meeting of notable Englishmen at the Paris exposition of 1849 where the idea of an international exhibition was discussed, the process leading to such an event proceeded swiftly. A day before plans for a British exhibition were to be announced, Henry Cole recalled a conversation with Prince Albert: "I asked the Prince whether he had considered if the exhibition should be a national or an international exhibition. The Prince reflected for a minute, and then said, 'It must embrace foreign productions,' to use his words, and added emphatically, 'International, certainly.'"[7]

The tide had turned. The powers that were in mid-Victorian Britain had decided that it could only be an advantage to place Britain in fair competition with the productions of the rest of the world. It is difficult to grasp how significant a leap this was for an old-world, mid-Victorian society. No one knew for sure what would really result from staging a joint exhibition of domestic and foreign productions, but the increasing scope of national exhibitions made it likely that they would eventually become international. The final step to hosting an international exhibition deserves its own special place in history, and the British have most certainly preserved it carefully for themselves. At the meeting held on June 30, 1849, Prince Albert publicly announced plans to host an unprecedented international exhibition.

Once the Great Exhibition was officially proposed, it became fodder for some classic Parliamentary debates. The cantankerous Colonel Sibthorpe, an irreverent iconoclast, led the conservative vanguard that sought to veto all creative movements aimed at making a British international exhibition a reality. Prince Albert quickly announced that the event would be funded exclusively through the private sector, thus relieving the government of any financial burdens related to the event. His statement was again indicative of the exhibition's aims and ideals: "The experiment is of a national character . . . it ought to rest for its support upon national sympathies, and upon such liberal contributions as those sympathies may dictate." Queen Victoria opened the bid for public support by donating one thousand pounds to the cause. Prince Albert then contributed another five hundred pounds. The success or failure of the Great Exhibition was to rest on a gamble: would the strength of the national sympathies of the populace save the day for Britain or bring her down in international shame? This was a gamble, but how much of a risk was it to attempt to garner *national* sympathies for an *international* event to be hosted on the nation's own turf? The question points to the symbiotic relationship between the encroaching reality of international relations and attempts to invoke nationalist sentiment.[8]

There were plenty of other problems besides financial ones, and at many moments through the first half of 1850 it looked as if the Great Exhibition would not happen. The primary fears and concerns of the naysayers were not entirely unfounded and would finally be assuaged and resolved only with the greatest difficulty. First, there was always the threat of plague when all manner of peoples were to be gathered in one place. In addition, subversive and revolutionary activity was a recurring concern at any major gathering in the mid-nineteenth century in Europe. In this regard, Britain was in a significantly different position from France, since the events of 1848 had caused only a murmur in the London underground. Nevertheless, the disenchanted

Chartists were still a force to be reckoned with, and working-class conditions at mid-century were by all accounts appalling. Another concern was how to police an event whose eventual dimensions were an unknown quantity.

The central pragmatics that remained to be solved in staging the Great Exhibition were more immediate: where to have it, and in what type of facility. Event organizers were in favor of a central London location to insure easy access, promote attendance, and insure that the event would be solvent. There was really only one good choice—Hyde Park. It was centrally located, accessible, and had plenty of space to accommodate crowds. But Hyde Park was also an oasis in the middle of an industrializing and suffocating city that was generally covered with a layer of smoke emitting from inefficient factories. As the "lungs of London," Hyde Park was not a disposable commodity; it stood between old-world England and a pathological level of urbanity.

The question of the venue was just as critical. The principal buildings at France's three previous expositions were temporary but impressive constructions that added considerably to the favorable light in which the events were perceived internationally. An appropriate setting for the first international exhibition was critical. Exhibition commissioners solicited proposals from the public, but the two hundred received were all inadequate. Threatened again with dissolution by the impasse, the Great Exhibition instantly turned into an unfolding fairy tale when a greenhouse architect named Joseph Paxton submitted a proposal for an unprecedented three-tiered building made of reusable glass plating. The public fell in love with the sketches of Paxton's colossal glass palace, and the Great Exhibition was all but assured of becoming a reality.

Once construction got under way, the *Illustrated London News* ran otherworldly artistic renditions of the emerging structure. Paxton proceeded creatively. A row of large elm trees ran through Hyde Park on the proposed building site. Many thought it an outrage to even consider cutting them down. Paxton's solution was to build a rounded transept along the middle of the building to create extra space so that the trees could be contained inside the building. The final effect would prove exquisite: three towering elms reached up to the top of the glass building, creating the feeling of an enclosed garden rather than an exhibition hall. The building was technically 1,848 feet long, but measured from the outside it was 1,851 feet long—a symbolic touch that was perhaps a bit over the top. Fears about the building's inadequacies and dangers proved to be almost uniformly unfounded: it was, architecturally speaking, a true stroke of genius for which Paxton

Figure 1. The advertisement run by the Crystal Palace architect Joseph Paxton in the *Illustrated London News*. Paxton's novel proposal to construct a transparent exhibition hall out of glass plating won over the public and transformed the Great Exhibition into the spectacle it became.

would be knighted at exhibition's end. In November of 1850, a friend of Paxton's who wrote for the irreverent British periodical *Punch* nicknamed the creation the "Crystal Palace." The name proved so catchy and appropriate that the Great Exhibition is still affectionately referred to in Britain, and in many other quarters, almost exclusively by this nickname.⁹

With the inevitability of the event becoming apparent, other preparations had to be accelerated. Commodities and raw materials had to be arranged into an ambitious classification scheme that ended up being a statement of the progress of nineteenth-century science, arts, and industry. Displays were divided into four primary categories, the order of which was not arbitrary: raw materials, machinery, manufactures, and fine arts. As the "workshop of the world," responsible for transforming raw materials into usable commodities, Britain sought to emphasize their importance at an industrial exhibition designed in part to validate the colonial process. The four basic exhibition categories were further divided into thirty classes, each of which had endless subdivisions.

A critical decision about how the Crystal Palace displays would be arranged also required special attention. Prince Albert's initial plan was to arrange all Great Exhibition displays by category rather than by country in order to emphasize the commonality of the productions of the world. However, this plan would prove unfeasible due to the impossibility of trying to place every item entering the Crystal Palace into the appropriate category. This was unfortunate, because the theme of the oneness of nations was intended to unite rather than divide the participating countries at the Great Exhibition. The ensuing arrangement by country was therefore accomplished in a carefully arbitrated manner. Britain and its colonies would occupy one half of the Crystal Palace. The foreign half was to be arranged such that equatorial countries were located nearest to the center of the building, while more northerly countries were placed farther out. In this way, it was hoped that national jealousies about placement might be averted.

The most sensitive area of concern for the commissioners, and the one about which the greatest precautions were taken, was the matter of how to award prizes to the finest displays in the thirty exhibition categories. Many would have liked to avoid the issue of awards altogether—both organizers and exhibitors alike—but the commissioners were adamant about refusing to admit articles that were marked "not for competition." Awards had always been a standard feature of continental exhibitions and were seen as a means of luring foreign exhibitors. They had to be included.[10]

The inevitability of international competition among nations remained a major concern that affected the planning of all aspects of the Great Exhibition. The problem of giving awards took on an especially deeper significance than would have been the case at a strictly national exhibition. The *Morning Chronicle* (London) expressed a sentiment (and fear) for many nations by noting that the exhibition is for "nothing less than to select out of the widespread legions of combatants who have been struggling on the great battle-field of commerce of the world . . . the valiant warriors to battle against each other—the victory to decide on the supremacy of this or that nation." With such challenges having been posed, it was determined that the awards juries would reflect the structure of the Crystal Palace itself. Half of the jurors would hail from Great Britain and half would be from foreign nations. The gathering of jurors would be extensive. There were 318 appointed jurors in all, and each of them was allowed to call in assistants for special cases.[11]

The makeup of the Great Exhibition's awards juries was unprecedented. The international assemblages would be comprised of preeminent persons in the arts, sciences, industry, and commerce gathered for the purpose of assessing the relative value of more than a million articles displayed by seventeen thousand exhibitors. The most sophisticated industry to date, the most unexpected of commodities, and the most obscure, newly found raw materials were all assigned a team of international experts who would judge their relative value based on the theme of progress, both industrial and social.

The nature of the awards was also delicate. An initial plan called for significant cash awards to be given out to insure that exhibitors would be motivated to attend. It was quickly determined, however, that at an international event a monetary incentive had to be eliminated as potentially too inflammatory. Thus, in place of money there would be three medals distinguishing different forms of quality (as opposed to degrees of quality) among the displays in the thirty subdivided categories.

The commissioners of the Great Exhibition went to significant lengths to minimize competition at the event, both in its organization and especially in its adjudication of awards. This careful planning calls attention to the fact that all participants at the event were very much aware of the lurking tensions with which this first international gathering of nations would be imbued. It was an acknowledged possibility that at the first international exhibition, where the most prized productions of rival nations were on display, there was a definite potential for hostilities to emerge triumphant. This potential for conflict had to be treated with the utmost seriousness.

## *Imagining Global Culture inside the Crystal Palace*

The Great Exhibition opened on May 1, 1851, with observers unable to reach for enough arcane adjectives to do justice to their feelings about the occasion. With anticipation heightening for a year, many of the grand statements describing the actual opening exceeded themselves and toppled over into melodrama. A writer for *Punch* summed up the problem best by noting: "The scene I witnessed was the grandest . . . and most splendid show that eyes had ever looked on since the creation of the world—but as everybody remarked the same thing, this remark is not of much value." William Makepeace Thackeray published an especially presumptuous ode in the *London Times*. As a whole, the press felt compelled to extol the virtues of its beloved nation in a way it never would have at a strictly national event, where more attention would have been paid to domestic problems. A small minority of critics was not so sanguine. One writer called the exhibition "an undertaking that united . . . the rivalry of nations with the sentiment of peace." British press reports of the opening ceremony also amounted to a collective "three cheers for us," though there was indeed a great deal of which to be proud. It would have been a national sacrilege to diminish the gravity of this moment in any inappropriate way: "The pens of all the ready writers of Great Britain, continental Europe and America are engaged upon this one theme," the *Illustrated London News* reported. "There is no other topic of interest or importance."[12]

The Crystal Palace itself received the greatest portion of the accolades, and deservedly so. When one considers the appearance of any modern city and then recalls that glass buildings had been almost nonexistent before 1851, the architectural breakthrough marked by the Crystal Palace is readily apparent. In constructing an encompassing historical chronology leading up to the Great Exhibition, one observer made the rather prophetic observation that the Crystal Palace marked the emergence of a "glass age." Mainly, though, the Crystal Palace was staggeringly beautiful in the eyes of the Great Exhibition's patrons, and in the context of its old-world setting of 1851, it was awe-inspiring in its immensity. The unique structure proved to be the quintessential symbol of British industrial and technological progress. The sky shone straight through the towering roof and lent a spirit of lightness and gaiety to the experience inside. Paxton's Crystal Palace would eventually win the Great Medal, a special award given to only two Great Exhibition displays.[13]

Much of the reflection about the world-historical significance of the Great Exhibition became caught up in the subjectivity of the moment. The appearance of such a palace at this particularly auspicious time in history could only portend the greatest of blessings. The congress of nations at the Great Exhibition has "made us all understand one another better than we did before," wrote one contemporary observer. "[It has] broken down the ancient barriers of jealousy and exclusiveness. Who shall say, that if we had a railroad system pervading Europe in 1780 . . . whether Napoleon Bonaparte might not have become a great sculptor or a great cotton-spinner in 1810."[14]

In psychological terminology, the Crystal Palace was the perfect "projection hook": it presented a too-perfect opportunity to make summary statements about far-reaching social and philosophical issues hovering in the backs of writers' minds where they should have stayed. Few could resist the glittering image of British prowess marked by the exterior of the Crystal Palace. The Great Exhibition made plain for British analysts what heretofore had been less definite intuitions about the structure of the emerging, globally defined world. Inside there were just as many achievements to boost the collective ego and to make reassuring comparisons with the rest of the world's countries. Foreign nations were greatly disadvantaged in having to transport less impressive displays various distances to the event. By contrast, domestic British exhibits arrived early, were all in place by the exhibition's opening, and had been carefully organized to place them in the best possible light. It proved a tremendous advantage for a country to host an international exhibition, and at the first international exhibition, Britain stood triumphant over her international compatriots. At an event that had carefully orchestrated the theme of "peace between nations" with that of "fair competition," it was possible for Britain to appear as the world leader of industrial progress as well as the diplomacies of peace keeping.

Figure 2. The interior of the Crystal Palace as Londoners would have seen it. This is the reconstructed version of the building in Sydenham. (Courtesy Cooper-Hewitt National Design Museum, © 2001 Smithsonian Institution; photographer unknown)

Concerning the actual spectacle of the Great Exhibition, there was no better forerunner than the Crystal Palace to those hallmark features of modern society—the department store and the shopping mall. The combined British and foreign naves of the building provided a look at enough previously unknown commodities and raw materials as to leave its unaccustomed visitors exhausted at the end of the day. It is impossible to do justice to the spectacle of the Crystal Palace by choosing a few choice examples of displays, because there were so very many such articles that might qualify. The display of the famous Kohinoor diamond, lent by Victoria herself, was a first stop for countless spectators who found it disappointing because it was uncut and whole and hence very dull in appearance. Follet Osler's cut-crystal fountain, which was carved from four tons of pure crystal glass, stood at the apex of the Crystal Palace and was an object of great admiration. The Indian court, constructed by the East India Company, also provided a self-contained spectacle of cultural exotica that was not to be missed.

Yet it was the whole of the effect of so many sights coexisting with one another that left the most lasting impression on the old-world minds enjoying this unique cultural experience. Charles Dickens, who was given the last word in the *Official Catalogue* of the Great Exhibition, was unable to stay inside the building for more than a short period at a time and was fairly repulsed by seeing so many things in one place at once. Most were completely fascinated by the sights of the Crystal Palace, though. And "sights" were all the Great Exhibition consisted of, since nothing was allowed to be sold inside the building save for a few nonalcoholic refreshments. This cultural experience was about gazing, a pastime that would grow to improbable proportions in the century to come. It was a lesson in the possibility of possessing rather than actual acquisition. It was a hidden promise to a beleaguered working class—which would be admitted for just a shilling after the third week—pointing to the shape of better things to come. At the exhibition's close, Prince Albert's own "model dwellings," representing a proposal for how to build en masse affordable and more comfortable housing for the working classes, was awarded the other Great Medal besides Joseph Paxton's.[15]

In an exhibition of articles representing so many facets of culture, there were bound to be uncomfortable discrepancies in bringing the twin themes of peace and industry into concert with one another. Such problems were apparent, for instance, when visitors attempted to properly appreciate the aesthetics and material progress of the displays of instruments of war: "Turning to the more civilized instruments of destruction at the Crystal Palace . . . we have improved rifles . . . splendid specimens of gunbarrels . . . a beautiful steel cannon [and] elegant blades suggesting the remembrances of ancient chivalry." Such disparities were perhaps predictable at an event that attempted to represent all the productions of culture attractively.¹⁶

There was an undercurrent of complaint about the event, but it remained just that—a minority voice viewing the Great Exhibition as a grand irony within British social life. The unearthly level of opulence inside the Great Exhibition was an uncomfortable spectacle for some, existing as it did within a city marked by squalid poverty: "Shall we ostentatiously show off all manner of articles of comfort and luxury," questioned one writer, "and be ashamed to disclose the condition of those we have to thank for them?" Still, it generally proved difficult to disparage an event that promised everything to everybody. More than anything, the Great Exhibition promised that a strong and united Great Britain would be indispensable in allowing the many promises of the future to be kept. It was Britain itself that was for sale inside the Crystal Palace. The country was being sold to its own working classes, which, ironically, provided it with something to sell; to its colonies, which provided it with raw materials to produce; and to its intercontinental partners in trade, which held the keys to the most promising future markets of all.¹⁷

With so much at stake for Britain, then, it was imperative that the rest of the world on which she depended to maintain her position as world leader understood their respective places in the emerging global scheme of things. The global picture had been coming into focus for some time, but to this point it had consisted of a collection of cultural bits and pieces garnered together in a haphazard manner over the course of centuries. There was really no substitute for having the whole of the world's culture (or a fair piece of it) gathered under one roof for the purpose of taking inventory. The Great Exhibition provided the perfect opportunity for fine-tuning a vision of the world that had been sensed more than experienced and imagined more than actually gazed upon.

Once the world was together under one magnificent British roof well suited for the occasion, the cultural pieces were surprisingly easy to assemble. The single most remarkable aspect of the press coverage of the Great Exhibition was the uniformity of its judgment about the comparative level of "civilization" exhibited by nations and cultures represented at the event. There was remarkably little disagreement as to which pieces should fit where:

Let us commence at home and see what appearance this island of ours puts on at this peaceful *reunion* of nations. Her genius is mechanism, her tendencies to relieve labour from its drudgery. Look at the great department of machinery. Watch that vast collection of interesting objects . . . lighten immeasurably the burden of life and relieve hundreds of hands from the most irksome forms of industry. You will there see how mechanism is extending her dominion over the whole empire of labour. [Ours is a] vast and remarkable collection of objects. And now let us cross the transept and endeavor [to discuss] foreign countries and their respective social developments. Let us mark their order. We pass to Spain. How are the mighty fallen! This country, which once ruled as wide a dominion as ours . . . and sent its Armada, called Invincible, in vain to conquer England, occupies but a third-rate place in the Crystal Palace. No new springs of healthy enterprise appear, nothing that gives promise for the future. Pass on to Italy and there see the fine arts still clinging to their ancient home, emasculated by their long separation from liberty and commerce, degenerating from their lofty and vigorous conceptions into curious Dilettantism, and [yet recalling] the traces of a happier era. From Italy we enter France—and what do we find there? Not the mechanical genius of England, not its utilitarian tendencies. They show that kings and queens are their customers. The state looks down as a patron upon . . . industry and takes [it] under special protection. Austria [has] little . . . to sustain her industrial character. Germany shows the desire to enter into competition with us. Yet the German collection as a whole is greatly wanting in that variety and expansiveness which mark the industrial development of the great powers.[18]

While comparable taxonomies had been emerging in intellectual circles since the Enlightenment, the fact that the press coverage exhibited such uniformity of judgment in placing the world into a desirable order demonstrates the extent to which such assumptions about the global hierarchy had begun to permeate popular culture as well. Through the exquisite example provided by the Great Exhibition, literate laypersons were being allowed to see the potential value of intercultural taxonomies in justifying the British position as world leader.

The only country that could not be dismissed easily was France. As Whitney Walton has argued, French artistic sensibility was far superior to that of Britain in 1851. Britain had made some headway in creating more attractively designed, mass-produced products for daily use—Henry Cole's inexpensive tea set being a prime exhibition example. Generally, though, while Britain's products were attractive because of their affordability and superior construction, they were accepted only grudgingly due to their aesthetic clumsiness. The French were particularly unforgiving on this account. On the other hand, French artisans who created fewer but more attractive products were on the whole much more likely to be granted subsidies by the French government. It was argued with some validity that this practice benefited the rich, who could afford the expensive subsidized products, more than it did the working classes. Then again, government subsidization also provided the opportunity for more and better public displays of artistry that could be enjoyed equally by all, thus improving a culture's collective image of itself.[19]

British observers sought to resolve the argument by claiming that excessive government involvement came replete with inevitable psychological ramifications. They argued that British industry produced a much greater quantity of utilitarian products because it was all a product of private enterprise. Hence, its working classes were afforded better lives, with a larger number of useful products made available to them for daily use. The inadequacy of French manufacturing was offered as the reason why French products could not match the general efficiency and affordability of British products. The British went too far, however, in arguing that their aesthetic sensibilities, while admittedly lagging in the past, were now moving ahead by leaps and bounds. There was only nominal evidence of improvement in that arena.

This ideological debate between Britain and France about cultural style became materialized through the mass exhibition of commodities, which provided concrete examples of what was at stake. The dispute also provided the parameters for Britain's claim to superiority over the rest of the world as well. Britain had decided definitively on the general value of utilitarianism and based its sense of social superiority on it. That sense of superiority increased exponentially as one moved away from the aloof little island to the north, past the only viable threat (in the form of France), and out into the rest of a confused and backward world.

The surprises in the above passage from the *Times* among the "civilized" world powers of 1851 were Austria and Germany. Austria was a formidable central European empire at mid-century and was to some extent acknowledged as such at the Great Exhibition. The states of the Zollverein, on the other hand, which would not become Germany until 1873, were still struggling to define themselves as a unified nation to the same extent as the other European powers. The southern European powers of "bygone eras," Italy and

Spain, were acknowledged by the British press only as nations in decline, whose sun had long since set.

Representatives of Islamic countries near the southern or eastern Mediterranean and beyond were treated as perennially dangerous "shifty-eyed Arabs" who had made wandering a way of life: "Take Tunis, first," with its "gaudy brocaded costumes" and its "stilettoes, quick to avenge a hasty word." "This Tunisian tent marks the nomade man [whose] voluntary habit it is to wander. [This is] the principle cause of unsubdued barbarism." These mostly Islamic countries represented a kind of netherworld between the normative civilization of Europe, the vagaries of the Orient, and the abomination of savagery. Japan did not send exhibits, nor did China, though British merchants put together some Chinese displays, as they did with nearly all the "uncivilized" countries. The argument used to dismiss the second tier of "semicivilized" countries was the same as the one used to dismiss highly cultured France: "The general impression produced by the productions of such countries as Egypt, Tunis, Turkey and native India is the same; the more civilized nations excel most in common comforts—comforts which all classes may enjoy."[20]

It was this philosophical predilection that was used to justify Britain's colonial ambitions. The colonial enterprise was warranted because of Britain's capacity to produce commodities that, at least potentially, could be enjoyed by all the peoples of the world and not just the ruling classes.  The basic idea may have been simple enough, but its implementation required that the rest of the world be subordinated to the British administrative genius. This necessitated the development of political strategies that went well beyond the show of industrial potency to include subtler claims of supremacy in areas such as aesthetic sensitivity, diplomacy, and social philosophy. There was little question that economic success and the social philosophy attending it were the primary basis for assertions about a general British triumph in all spheres of culture, but the subsidiary claims of cultural dominance reinforced these more overt apologetics seeking to justify the colonial enterprise. Brute force would never work in the face of the whole world. British culture had to demonstrate its desirability at many levels to maintain the colonial structure, and the Great Exhibition provided the perfect forum in which to do so. Religion was but a minority voice as one of the claims to cultural superiority—mainly because the idea that a country's religion could be compared and hence had to be justified in some manner was so bizarre in 1851 Britain, at least everywhere but within a very elite intellectual circle. Still, the affiliation of industrial success with religious orientation was unmistakably present and was voiced intermittently, as we will see.

## The United States at the Great Exhibition

The United States was in a unique position at the Great Exhibition in that it fell between so many of the world-defining categories set up by the British. The reason for this was that in 1851 the renegade colonies were still not so far removed from the homeland itself. On the whole, the American sensibility was decidedly British, which made it difficult to simply dismiss the young nation as an extensive exercise in cultural folly. Similarly, while the American presence at the Great Exhibition would leave much to be desired in the eyes of British analysts, there was no denying that the country would soon be a force to be reckoned with and that its potential was in no small part attributable to its implementation of British cultural values and the British social philosophy.

Despite the emotional connections that bonded them together—or perhaps *because* of those connections—the two countries had been involved for some time in ongoing negotiations regarding various disputed regions of North America, primarily along the Canadian border. The War of 1812 had not been fought to a definitive end, instead being "concluded by a treaty formally recognizing that nothing had been changed in the basic relationship between the two belligerents." More recently, the ill-defined boundary extending over the areas of Washington State and Oregon had been in dispute throughout the 1840s, a process that rekindled hostilities on both sides. It is against the immediate history of this ongoing competitive relationship between the two countries that the participation of the United States in the Great Exhibition and Britain's reaction to it needs to be understood.[21]

The inability of the United States to extract itself altogether from negotiations with the British was only a part of the story of American international uncertainty during the period. Although beginning to significantly increase its production by 1850, the United States was never unified to the same extent as the European nations, especially England—a fact that would become blatantly obvious with the Civil War. Equally, the continental United States was a shifting shape geographically until the middle of the nineteenth century, when a boundary was finally set between Texas and the Pacific Ocean just above Baja. The changing geographical boundaries only added to the confusion of defining what it meant to be an American in the mid-nineteenth century. Railroads, which were a key to the boom in

American industry at mid-century, would not come into full swing until the 1850s. Finally, the vast internal territory of the country, which clearly set the United States apart from European nations in providing ample room for domestic expansion and growth through immigration, reduced motivation for international commercial expansion. All of these elements contributed to the relatively late start made by the United States in developing international relations. They help explain the anxieties and difficulties by which its participation in Britain's Great Exhibition would be marked.[22]

It is not surprising, then, that from the beginning, the United States was unable to bring into concert its grand ambitions for participation in the Great Exhibition and what was required to turn them into reality. That there were strong ambitions is undeniable. President Millard Fillmore sent his regrets about being unable to attend the Great Exhibition a full six months before the opening but nevertheless saw fit to fire a few volleys for his country in doing so: "I should be most happy to be able to make a personal comparison between the leading men of the country [England] and my own and to see how far we have improved on the political institutions of the mother country." The Great Exhibition called for a *united* American response in presenting an image of the country at an international event, and it is safe to say that in 1851 this called for a specific kind of effort Americans were not capable of making. Various excuses were trotted out for the inadequate preparations made by the United States for the Great Exhibition. The most common were claims of miscommunications regarding the extent of the Great Exhibition and the appropriate level of American participation. A more plausible explanation is that the country could not collectively decide how important an event this strange European exhibition phenomenon was for its present interests.[23]

Exhibition representatives for the United States got as far as requesting the second largest foreign space next to that of France—forty thousand square feet next to France's fifty thousand and the thirty thousand of the Zollverein. The months leading up to the event were then spent scrambling about for exhibitors, but ultimately an embarrassing amount of the space was left empty. France occupied 90 percent of its space, and most countries were close to that figure. But the United States could fill only thirteen thousand of its confidently requested and graciously allotted forty thousand square feet. British exhibits eventually took over some of the spare area. For months the newspapers had run articles declaring that the United States "promises largely" and followed American progress, and the lack thereof, toward that end. The interest in American displays was genuine, especially in raw materials from the intriguing lands of the Wild West. Once the event got under way, reports noted that "those newly settled Western states" such as California "disappoint us dreadfully" in failing to send "what we had been so curious about."[24]

The American performance did provide just cause for criticism, but the British were already poised to pounce on their erstwhile brethren. They did so with the kind of half-hearted British attempt at diplomacy that only exacerbates a situation. The *Times* noted that of all departments, that of the United States was the most empty:

> Our Transatlantic descendants, following out their New World instincts, have no idea of being jostled by other nations or being pinched for space, even in the Crystal Palace.[25] England is not given to boasting and swaggering; she generally understands her strength, and studies moderation of language about herself though she has some excuse for being proud. Her Republican progeny are not so modest. The American department is the prairie ground of the exhibition, and our cousins, smart as they are, have failed to fill it. They cannot keep pace with the great strides of European industries. Let them, therefore, await the future with patience and humility.[26]

Exhibition commentators sought to appropriate foreign countries through a language that at once made them subordinate but nonetheless integral and valued participants within the British vision of world civilization. America was just a child with much to learn; but she was also accorded a measure of respect for what she might become if she could muster the humility to follow Britain's lead. At times, however, the commentary did get a bit nasty in its attempt to keep the United States in its place. In a spin-off from one of the more admired American displays—a piece of marble sculpture called *The Greek Slave* by a little-known American sculptor named Hiram Powers—*Punch* ran some nasty comics that lamented the emptiness of the American department and chided the Americans about their continued practice of slavery. Below one comic was written, "Why not have sent some specimens of slaves. We have the Greek Captive in dead stone—why not the Virginian slave in living ivory. Let America hire a black or two to stand in manacles, as American manufacture."[27]

The strength of the United States lay in its vast store of natural resources, many of which were uncommon, and in its technological ability to develop those resources into usable raw materials. Early on, however, much of the American department consisted of several simple mounds of the raw materials exhibited unattractively in gaudy displays, "giving to them more the look of a display of goods for purchase than of articles of taste and art for exhibition." Piles of soap; Henry County tobacco; ginned cotton; malted Indian corn; and lard oil, for instance, looked rather out of place next to the 170 mostly hand-carved pianos, billiard tables, and elaborate Gothic furniture that were chosen for display by other countries.[28]

As much as anything, however, the exhibits of the United States were like those of so many other countries in that they were merely late in arriving rather than failing to appear at all. By the close of the Great Exhibition, a handful of articles demonstrating a dose of Yankee ingenuity would salvage what otherwise might have been an exhibition disaster for Americans. Henry Goodyear's rubber could be put to enough practical uses to demand some admiration for American pragmatism. Cyrus McCormick's reaper stunned its British counterparts in a public competition—an incident so unexpected that it caused endless controversy and calls for repeat competitions. Both inventions would win Council Medals, which were practically, if not officially, first-place awards. The locks of Day and Newell, exhibited by a Louisiana man named Thomas Hobbes, who became a sensation when he picked a London company's famous Brahma locks, were roundly applauded. And Samuel Colt's revolvers were also acknowledged as superior. But like so many other deserving exhibits from across the globe, the latter two, unaccountably, would not be awarded prizes. Finally, a win by the New York yacht *America* over the English Royal Yacht Squadron in a contest on British waters secured the greatest measure of respect for the upstart Americans from a maritime-proud nation.

The Americans had displayed just enough capability in areas the British prized most to be accorded a token of respect. A significant part of the criticism aimed at the United States was based on an acknowledgment of her inevitable emergence as an international superpower. Most were afraid to think where and how far that potential might lead. For now it was thought best to put the adolescent nation in its place when possible. By exhibition's end, a dinner held by a wealthy American merchant named George Peabody for a distinguished group from both sides of the Atlantic produced some reconciliations and a mending of fences. Several American spokespersons stood and made conciliatory remarks, though none were equal to a British diplomat's summary of the meaning of the yacht race won by the Americans: "They had taught us how to win the race and we had taught them how to bear the loss of one."[29]

Regardless of the grace-saving triumphs, the report of the American commissioner at the Great Exhibition had to finesse a situation that was something quite other than the definitive American victory that had been expected. The report gave the impression that the reason for the young American nation's questionable performance in the face of the formidable international competition was simply that it had extended the utilitarian political philosophy of Britain to even greater effectiveness:

> The history of our portion of the exhibition—of the lack of all pecuniary aid from the government—of its early discontentments, vicissitudes, and trials—of its gradually emerging from the darkness—of its stoutly fought battles, its victories, its successes, and of its hardly, but fairly won honors at the close—is all too well known to the whole world to need recapitulation here. It is sufficient to say we were not misunderstood. We alone of all people exhibited the products of unfettered, untaxed, unpatronized labour. We showed the results of pure democracy upon the industry of men. We demonstrated the progressiveness of the human mind when in the enjoyment of liberty. And we alone, from among the assemblage of the two score nations, bore away the palm for intelligent labour.[30]

The report by the commissioner, a Mr. Riddle, concluded by noting that he hoped the United States would never have the concentration of wealth that produces spectacular articles of art. This was a way of apologizing for why American exhibits were on the whole so pragmatic in character. To this ideal England had to bow, because it was precisely the same rationale it had used to pronounce its own social superiority over the rest of the world. The United States had taken the ideal of laissez-faire utilitarianism one step further, even if many of the moral and aesthetic results, similar to those of Britain, were unsatisfactory.

The American press was generally able to claim American credibility at the Great Exhibition, even if an outright victory was out of the question. Horace Greeley, who was probably the most visible interpreter of the American performance in London, cautioned about becoming overly optimistic based on America's late successes. The truth of the American performance, he concluded, lay "midway between the extremes." The legacy left by American participation at the first international exhibition, however, was that the United States was left with some work to do to become credible as an international political power and a great deal more work to do to become a cultural power. The uncertain performance by the fledgling, insecure, yet eminently boastful American nation at the Great Exhibition proved woefully inadequate in establishing the country's international identity. A hastily planned and unfortunate international exhibition would take place in New York in 1853, indicating a desire for immediate redemption from the Great Exhibition experience; later, Philadelphia's Centennial Celebration of 1876 and especially Chicago's Columbian Exposition of 1893 would go to outrageous lengths to stake American claims in the international world. The Chicago exposition would become the most magnanimous ever staged, and in so doing would lend itself, to some extent unwittingly, to the grandest visions of Western, Christian, and especially Protestant supremacy to date.[31]

The historical contrast between Britain and the United States at mid-century is revealing for understanding the different themes that ran through their respective international expositions. British and American events produced quite different conjunctures of cultures and divergent understandings of the relationships between those cultures and how they might be adjudicated. With its vast internal territory and negligible international connections—which was due in part to the country's remote location—American expositions would reflect the need to organize the intercultural world internally and societally. In contrast, at the colonially based British events, intercultural organization was external and intersocietal. Further, the process of comparative culture at American expositions would eventually come to also include the first direct discussion of comparative religion—a development that was plausible only in the context of the United States during this period, as will be explored in the final chapter. While religion remained an implicit and tacit assumption within cultural analysis at the Great Exhibition, at the Columbian Exposition its relationship to culture would be made explicit.

## *Colonies and Primitives Invade the Palace*

As noted in the first chapter, Bernard McGrane has observed that exotic cultures (by Western standards) were initially "nominated" into the worldview of Christianity by being given Christian names. At the Great Exhibition, these more peripheral "savage" cultures were almost exclusively displayed by British merchants who "nominated" them materially into the structure of this Western event. Private collections of cultural exotica gleaned from centuries of global explorations and colonial activity accounted for all but one exhibit from colonized and "savage" cultures.

The fact that the more peripheral societies of the world did not actually represent themselves at the Great Exhibition certainly contributed to the dubious status accorded them. No country was more negatively affected by this inevitable circumstance, and hence more unfairly represented at the Great Exhibition, than India. It was not until 1857, six years after the Great Exhibition, that India became a proper interest of the British government. Before that time she had been the colonial property of the East India Company. Indeed, it was to the East India Company that exhibition organizers first turned to inquire whether the company would be willing to organize a full display of its many articles representative of India's rich cultural heritage. If Britain's prize colonial possession could not be represented in all its glory, the exhibition could not possibly be a success. The East India Company responded in a manner appropriate to the grandiosity of the occasion by setting up a separate "Indian Court" comprising some thirty thousand square feet, which was devoted strictly to the display of articles native to its prize possession. The Indian Court was a popular stop inside the Crystal Palace, and many Indian designs were acknowledged as far superior aesthetically to anything the West, including France, had to offer. As one of Britain's most treasured colonial possessions, India was clearly demarcated from the primitive world, although this proved a hollow concession. Indian articles were almost entirely overlooked in the awarding of prizes, much to the consternation of Owen Jones, who was in charge of the interior design of the Crystal Palace. To make matters worse, all medals were given to the East India Company as the official exhibitor of the wares.[32]

While the Crystal Palace was divided by country, each of which then set up their displays according to the exhibition's thirty categories, Britain was in a unique position in that it had domestic displays as well as colonial displays. Hence, the colonies became a category unto themselves—as if they were commodities falling into a specific exhibition category, which in a sense they were. The exhibition catalogue shows only a single display sent by a country that would have qualified as "primitive." The reason for this was that exhibitors had to pay for all of their own items to be sent. Queen Pomare of the Society Islands (Tahiti) commissioned eight pandanus mats made from *fara* leaves, five headdresses, a vase, and some handmade cloth to be shipped to the Great Exhibition. The queen remained the lone full-fledged exhibitor from a society falling outside the civilized or semicivilized designation. Some countries donated items to British exhibitors, the chief's throne from the king of Dahomey being a notable example.

# BRITAIN'S GREAT EXHIBITION 47

The worlds of colonies and "savages" as displayed inside the Crystal Palace were not about those worlds themselves. They were about Western representations of those worlds. The appellation of "industry" to most colonial displays and to the displays of nearly all noncolonized, "uncivilized" peoples was ludicrous. The Crystal Palace was a museum every bit as much as it was an "exhibition of the industry of all nations." That fact was made apparent by the extent to which the least industrialized societies functioned as peripheral entertainments to the principal theme of advances in technological industry in analyses of the event. It was this glaring discrepancy at the level of "industry" that made dogmatic the attempt to define an intercultural hierarchy at the event.

The manner in which the world's many "savages" were incorporated into the schema of British civilization was based almost exclusively on what might be termed the moral imperative of industrial development:

> The first and perhaps most powerful and lasting impression [of] the exhibition is that all men *labour*. The most careless glance, however, at the material results of men's industry establishes some striking differences in quality among them. The productions of those who are commonly called Aborigines, or the less civilized races—are substantially the inferior fruits of human industry. Yet the most polished nations may trace in them their own perfection backwards to its source. The highly civilized man, rendered by science familiar with the works of uncivilized people will subdue his own prejudices in regard to their incapacity, and soon come . . . to aid them.[33]

This passage went on to make an eminently arguable conclusion that rather vaguely linked a lack of industry with an inclination toward violence: aboriginal civilization "has not yet discovered a better way to manage than by almost incessant wars."[34]

Such analysis may seem excessively defensive in retrospect, but the Britain of 1851 was still a relatively insecure social entity that had been watching multitudes of its Irish brethren a mere stone's throw away starving from the potato famine. Arguably the world's most civilized country in 1851, Great Britain still had a significant rate of starvation, was continuously threatened by pestilence, and had a social condition that made revolution an irremediable hazard. These mitigating factors notwithstanding, the rhetoric that was applied to the world's least industrial societies was as irrational as the dreaded savagery it sought to keep at bay.

What complicated the problem of encountering "savages" immeasurably, however, was the constant reappearance of the theme of the "noble savage," which was continually interspersed within all the vitriolic assessments of "savagery." It was not the actual noble savage who made an appearance at the Great Exhibition but rather his wares. Commentators simply could not prevent themselves from admiring what they simultaneously deplored, often within single sentences of description: "Malta's contributions" though "not very important" have nevertheless "attracted considerable attention, and have elicited much praise by [their] beauty and tastefulness." A little colony of copper figures from the Gold Coast is "very grotesque and interesting" in appearance. Guiana is distinguished by "an abundance of rude furniture [that] nevertheless have a sort of littery picturesqueness. They carry us back to Waterton's delightful 'wanderings.' In one of these huts he must have rode upon the caymen's back—in such a hammock he must have lain awake . . . with his leg hanging over . . . to tempt the great winged vampire bat, the surgeon of the forest, who lets sleeping men's blood for nothing."[35]

The enamoring and the despicable continually presented themselves as the obverse of one another in these passages. The savage and the grotesque *were* genuinely fascinating in the rapidly civilizing London of 1851. They represented worlds becoming quickly lost in modernizing Western society. It was a regular feature of exhibition commentary that once the obligatory moralizing about savagery ceased, admiration quickly followed on its heels. Literary embellishments flowed over the top and beneath the surface of the actual encounter with the material culture of "savages" in an apparent attempt to reinforce negative assessments of those unfamiliar cultures. In the end, however, those morally laden judgments could not always maintain themselves in the face of the diverse intercultural world when it was observed firsthand. The ambiguity of the encounter with "savagery"—its "grotesque appeal"—could never be finally overcome and explained away.

The same dichotomy held true of the description of the social lives of "savages," whose simplicity was seen as appalling, yet also eerily attractive. To those living in a society where it was unclear if the growing monster of urbanity signified progress, as those in power sought to convey, or apocalypse, as revolutionaries attempted to convince the working classes, the collective cultural world of the "savage" had a dual meaning. The year 1851 was the first in which more British persons came to live in urban rather than rural settings. The result of that trend, as has so often been noted in histories of the period, was something other than the certainty that urbanization was synonymous with progress. "Savagery" had to be defined in sharp distinction from the civilized at all times so that the value of civilization might be made clearer and the project of modern society could proceed apace.

Peoples who showed the capacity to adopt civilized ways, such as the New Zealanders, were ranked higher on the emerging cultural hierarchy than "the mere savage [who] is content with what nature has provided. The miserable Australian aborigines are perishing from the face of the earth [while] the New Zealanders are mingling and blending with the white men, learning his skills and practicing his arts." Of course, no mention was made about the extent to which various degrees of *coercion* influenced various "savages" to show an inclination to become "civilized." While "exotic" foreigners who attended the Great Exhibition were of great interest to observers of the event, analysis of domestic "exotics" was virtually nonexistent in the literature on the Great Exhibition, as was analysis of the place of Jews at the event. The official denouncement of slave-holding allowed for new approaches to conceiving a grand vision of human culture in which all cultures were "equal," but this did not seem to extend to the disenfranchised within British society.[36]

The vague history of ideas about foreign cultures became materialized and concretized at the Great Exhibition. The incorporative global hierarchies that emanated from within the Crystal Palace on that basis were efforts to define how all of the world's cultures related to Britain as potential "interests" rather than attempts at objective cultural analysis. Ideology at the Great Exhibition issued forth from a definitively material base. This manner of conceiving the intercultural world would predominate in how international expositions would categorize the world's cultures and their religions in the half-century to come. The Great Exhibition initiated a division that would become ever more pronounced within the international exposition tradition of defining the world's least industrialized peoples strictly on the basis of their limited material culture, while more industrial societies were accorded some connection to one or another religion.

## *The Great Exhibition of Religion:*
## *A Match Made in Heaven?*

Religious organizations were among the first to comprehend the tremendous opportunity presented by an international exhibition on

British soil. An advertisement in the *Times* from April 25, 1850, written by a converted Jew named Ridley H. Herschel, proposed a "conference of Christians of all nations" in connection with the Great Exhibition. Though it was an exciting proposition, such a gathering gave pause for reflection. The precise parameters within which a meeting of the "Christians of all Nations" might take place were complex:

> It may be objected that if the invitation is given to Christians at large, without some specification as to creed, the assemblage will consist of a motley collection of persons holding opposing views. I would simply say to obviate this difficulty that the invitation is sent to those only who believe the Scriptures to be the Word of God, and who hold the cardinal doctrines of the divinity of Christ and justification by faith. These truths include all other truths that are of essential importance. With those who deny the inspiration of the scriptures, and who view Christ simply as a gifted man, sent to be an example to us, we have no Christian sympathy or fellowship.[37]

The "justification by faith" is left unspecified here—no doubt to avoid a blatant attack on Catholicism. Nevertheless, this was clearly a proposal for a congress of *Protestants* of all nations. The idea that Catholics might be invited, or participate if they were invited, was inconceivable. Throughout the period of the Great Exhibition, the *Illustrated London News* ran a regular article titled "Papal Aggression" that observed Catholic activities throughout Great Britain with a watchful eye. Catholicism in Ireland was continually mocked and blamed in part for the difficulties of that country.

In the middle of the nineteenth century, traditional biblical religion was still very much intact. It had a very local and, in a place like London, a very nationally specific meaning. Thus, the mass printing of religious tracts designed specifically for the exhibition represented "some measures adopted by the bishop and clergy to counteract . . . the moral and spiritual evils arising from a large and miscellaneous group of strangers, including many of the worst and most dangerous character, not only of the other countries, but of our own." Even a benign meeting among like-minded Protestant brethren was a prospect that caused considerable trepidation when it became apparent that it would have to involve troubling negotiations of religious differences based on its varying national contexts. After all, what believer could want Christianity itself to be usurped into endless distinctions between nationalities?[38]

Certain technical obstacles also had to be overcome for such international religious meetings to become feasible. It was noted prior to the exhibition, for instance, that "in churches and consecrated chapels the liturgy can only by law be read in English." Hence, seven other temporary chapels had to be set up by the committee to accommodate non–English-speaking Protestants. Deeper anxieties surfaced in an early *Times* article, which could only hope that "the Church of England, as a true witness to the pure faith of the gospel, will be advantageously exhibited to the eyes of Europe and America." An example of the kind of religious diversity that was being faced by religious organizers is the fact that there was even significant Mormon participation at the event.[39]

At the opening ceremony, the Archbishop of Canterbury was in a difficult position: how to put into perspective an event based on rampant materialism that had all the markings of a new age of profound irreligion. He set the tone for later religious analyses of the Great Exhibition by downplaying materialism and emphasizing the hopeful, if tenuous, possibilities of brotherhood. The potentially alarming proliferation of commodities was viewed as evidence of the Deity's omnipotence and beneficence. An alternative choice in interpreting the event, given the blatant images of idolatry with which it was attended, would have been to sentence it to eternal damnation, decry it as the quintessential symbol for humanity's collective degradation, and declare such doings to be the work of the devil. Sentiments like the following, after all, were commonplace in the period: "In all true Protestant houses of prayer no gaudy images or meretricious decorations will meet the view of our visitors. The congregations will be found here adoring the invisible God [and] asking no aid of the senses."[40]

In mid-nineteenth-century Britain, however, the tide had turned regarding the need to accept the seeming inevitability of advancing commodification. Or if the tide had not yet turned, there was no event more instrumental in British or perhaps even Western history than the Great Exhibition for instigating such a change. By 1851, the offices of religion could only hold to traditional wisdom to a certain degree. It was by no means accepted that a social revolution was imminent at the Great Exhibition, but there were some unmistakable hints. The rapid rise of industry, with its gravitational pull toward urbanization, and the encroachment of evolutionary theory were the two most blatant. Thus, the archbishop decided—no doubt wisely—to go with the tide rather than to risk being buried in what would become, in the decade following the Great Exhibition, a tidal wave:

Almighty and everlasting God, governor of all things. We acknowledge, O Lord, that thou hast multiplied the blessings which Thou mightest most justly have withheld. Instead of humbling us for our offenses, Thou hast given us cause to thank Thee for Thine abundant goodness. It is of Thee that peace is within our walls and plenteousness within our palaces. While we survey the works of art and industry which surround us let not our hearts be lifted up that we forget the Lord our God, as if our own power and the might of our hands had gotten in this wealth.[41]

The overwhelming power of the material display of the Great Exhibition had virtually forced the archbishop's hand. It had to be divine inspiration that had "gotten in this wealth," because the wealth itself was becoming undeniable.

Still, exhibition organizers were determined at every point to avoid having the Great Exhibition turn into a preposterous commercial spectacle with no redeeming social value whatsoever. Religious organizations were one of the first places to which they turned for help. Early on, the commissioners declared that while the Great Exhibition was focused on social progress, it was also "no less calculated to influence the mind and better the feelings; that whilst the inspection of the works of industry should tend to elevate taste . . . it should impress enduring lessons of higher moment."[42]

Education was a predominant if obligatory theme, and religious groups led by the British and Foreign Bible Society devoted their full energies toward that end. "Enduring lessons of higher moment" were impressed upon Great Exhibition visitors through the impressive 457,000 religious tracts on various themes that were passed out at the event. No less than 382,971 Bibles were handed out and sold. Extra church services in foreign languages—some fourteen per week—were arranged for visiting Protestants from foreign countries by several religious organizations in the area. Sermons in French, German, Swedish, and Dutch were delivered by visiting foreign Protestant ministers. A fortnight into the event, a dinner for two hundred was held for the most prominent of the Protestant participants at Freemason's Tavern.[43]

While the Christian form of religion found a significant niche in relation to the Great Exhibition, determining how religion might be displayed inside the Crystal Palace was entirely another matter. The *Morning Chronicle* ran a series of articles on religious objects inside the Crystal Palace, but this mostly involved an excessive analysis of stained glass. The more pressing issue regarding the commodification of religion inside the Crystal Palace was predictable enough: surely among one million commodities there must be some small corner for that greatest commodity of all time—the Holy Bible. Then again, with exactly what branch of industry might the Bible be affiliated? It was a difficult question for which the exhibition commissioners could not initially find an answer. Hence, a proposed display of Bibles in 130 languages was rejected because it did not fit neatly into any of the Great Exhibition's thirty prescribed categories.

The decision that the Bible had no place inside the Crystal Palace initiated an inflamed debate that those proposing the display of Bibles did not take lightly. After several scathing editorials in which the exhibition commissioners were lambasted for their handling of the matter, the commissioners saw fit to make the unusual gesture of recounting the regrettable incidents in the official minutes. The commissioners explained that a Mr. Roberts, requesting space for a Bible display on behalf of the British and Foreign Bible Society, had been unable to "explain under which of the commissioner's categories for admittance he considered translations of the Bible to have a title of admittance. He distinctly stated they were not specimens of the art of printing, but as showing the energetic efforts of the Society." Given the special circumstances, and in spite of the rules, the commissioners acquiesced and offered space for the Bibles in the machinery department near the printing machines. The space was gratefully accepted, but it was soon discovered that a stairway had been built over the Bible display, and further, that the display sat adjacent to a malt machine and a distilling apparatus. Not wanting to ruffle any more delicate feathers, the commissioners agreed to move the display again. The new location was "an improvement," complained Mr. Roberts, but had still been chosen "without consulting the Society."[44]

The Bible's nomadic legacy inside the Crystal Palace left it entirely unclear whether its presence was indeed welcome at an event that ran so contrary to the prevailing biblical interpretations of the time. Nevertheless, aside from the problem of categorization and placement, the display of translated Bibles was generally appreciated for what it was: the presentation of a unique and powerful commodity. Comparative philology was in its early stages, and the spectacle provided by Bibles in 130 languages gave pause to many observers. The profusion of knowledge of other languages was a novelty in 1851, the power of which was just beginning to be appreciated: "While England was a Roman Catholic country and this volume was a sealed book, she remained an inferior political power. When the seal was taken off it, however, the great mental faculties of England's children were unchained. When its truths are dimmed by Romish error our country's sun will have begun to set. Connoisseurs in the arts will examine with minuteness the exquisitely finished weapons of destruction. But the Christian will gaze with deeper emotion on the weapons of our warfare which are [from] God. By these the church shall conquer the world for Christ."[45]

Most religious commentators were concerned to explore the general meanings of the Great Exhibition through the most recurrent themes of mid-nineteenth-century theology. The authority of the Bible was still almost wholly unchallenged. Enduring religious assumptions were firmly implanted in the social consciousness. In relation to those assumptions, contemporary events appeared as ephemeral phenomena, the essential function of which was to prove what had already been known with certainty: that even Great Exhibitions are preordained.

Long-suffering ministers consistently fell prey to what might be termed a "prophetic syndrome" in assessing the Great Exhibition. They could finally say, collectively, "I told you so!" This had to be it—the ominous "gathering together of all nations." This was to be a repetition of Belshazzar's Feast, about which one minister claimed to have received countless letters. The eschaton had arrived, or it would most certainly not be long now until it did. In reaching for that extra special sermon for the unprecedented event of the Great Exhibition, almost all ministers had the same ammunition held in reserve for just the right occasion. One writer took more than a hundred pages to gaily describe the fascinating secular spectacle in all its aspects, only to conclude with a religious intimation: "The first assembling together of nations [leads us to that day] when they will meet on a still grander scale, and on a very different occasion." No greater homage can be paid to the culturally transcendent quality of the Great Exhibition than the many testimonies witnessing to it as a signal for the culmination of the world.[46]

A more surprising theme, considering Protestantism's enduring ambivalence toward the spiritualization of matter, was that the majority of clergymen adopted the stance of the Archbishop of Canterbury. They viewed the proliferation of commodities as a symbol for the material omnipotence of the Deity. Scientific progress had opened up endless possibilities for imagining and interpreting the many courses of nature in a religious way. In fact, most saw the religious age as being dominated by the advance of deism. This was a religious period in Britain, defined as much as anything by William Paley's seductive musings about the Deity's phenomenal brilliance. Was it such a big step to deify—in a relative way, of course—the transformation of nature into useful human products? Perhaps it was, but such an interpretation of the spiritual status of exhibition commodities predominated in the religious literature. In the exhibition, "we trace the minute and comprehensive illustrations of the plan according to which He is bringing out the capabilities of mind [and] raising men from barbarism to civilization."[47] The Reverend Thomas Binney would go a step further in a passage that might well have served as an inspiration to Karl Marx, who at the time was just beginning his masterwork *Capital:*

> [The countries] are not summoned together by trumpet blast. They are to bring with them, in their tranquil march . . . the bloodless trophies of their industry and skill. However unable the most of them may be to understand the spoken languages of the rest and interpret what will be written, everywhere on the whole scene [all will recognize] the common voice that shall seem to be issuing from the objects around them. The products . . . will recognize each other as belonging to one and the same world [and] will have among themselves a common dialect—a language of their own—which all the workers alike shall understand.[48]

The gap in the relationship between material productions and the divine was clearly closing at the Great Exhibition, and as it did, it was becoming more feasible to equate industrial and technological progress with some form of religious sanctification. This allowed for a global hierarchy to emerge that did not have to have immediate recourse to a particular form of religion but could use material success, in a kind of distorted Calvinism, as a gauge for attunement with the divine.

As a purportedly global gathering, the Great Exhibition also lent itself to the idea that the event symbolized a new unity among all humankind. Yet the sentiment of world unity and its actual explication inevitably diverged from one another. There was a recurrent incommensurability between British ideological fantasies claiming world unity and the actual encounter with foreign peoples and their cultures. Some of the world's races and religious beliefs clearly presented a greater challenge to the flexibility of the British cosmology than did others. A particularly perceptive analysis by the Reverend Edward Higginson revealed the limits of the extent to which a liberal reading of world religions could go in the Britain of 1851. After calling for open arms in encountering the rest of the religious world, Higginson got down to specific religions and their shortcomings:

"Here are Protestants from Germany . . . Lutherans [who] are less dogmatized than our 'orthodox' Churches. Here are the Roman Catholics from countries where Romanism is established by human law, and not [as among us, by] a mean and despised church. Shall we anathematize their Church, as she with her voice of authority does ours? Jews we have always with us—would that our Churches shewed Christianity to them in a light not less rational as regards its theology, while more spiritual in its worship, than their own ancient faith!"[49] Great Exhibition religious commentary did not get any more liberal than this. Still, the open-minded Reverend Higginson drew careful boundaries right down the line. Lutherans could teach something only to English *orthodox* churches. Catholic authoritarianism, bound as it was by human (read *papal*) law, was to be risen above. Jews needed to be taught, but only an informed pedagogical approach would do; their intelligence could not be dismissed like other religious peoples, because too often it had been witnessed firsthand. Thus, it was their worship that was seen as misguided.

Just as with cultural analyses, however, the farther one moved from British shores, the greater the problems presented by the internalized fantasies regarding the religious unity of the world. Of Muslims, Higginson wrote, "Mahometans, think as we may and must of his conquering sword and self-excusing, self-indulgent Koran—to them Mahomet's claims are true." "Mahometans" simply could not be praised, merely acknowledged as believing differently. The Orient represented another matter altogether: "Men are among us from the Far East," Higginson observed, "from China and from India, from Japan—strange men, bodily and mentally." Their sages have "ascribed to the physical universe itself the attributes of Godhead," and "their populace have bowed to graven images," Higginson noted. "It is under the Providence of the Great Faith of all that they have erred and we have been guided to truth."[50]

In the contemporary period, comparative religion has become so commonplace in Western culture that it has become exceedingly difficult to project oneself back into the world of 1851, which was peopled with what for Victorians seemed the strangest of religious beings. To speculate about foreign religion was to enter a world of "strange men, bodily and mentally" for whom reality might be an exclusively material affair. The interreligious world of 1851, even in a preeminently cosmopolitan locale such as London, was mostly exotic and heathen, with but a few small islands of civilization and religious sanity.

An international meeting between Protestants was tenuous enough in the Britain of 1851; an international meeting between religions—that is, a direct debate about the subtlest aspects of cultural ideology, which was how religion was perceived in the literature of the event—would have been unthinkable. The state of comparative philology was only a technical stumbling block. Fears about the unpredictable nature of religious fervor were more responsible for the fact that the idea of a congress of distinct religions could never have even been broached. Religion still symbolized the unknown in a very direct way; intercultural religion thus symbolized an unknown that was more opaque still—a dark mystery indeed. Some mysteries are just a little too dark, however, and in 1851 London, a discussion of religion among representatives from across the world was most certainly one of them.

Nevertheless, while international juries were considering the relative value of a million attractively displayed commodities, British theologians attempted to make at least some sense of the strangest and most heathenish elements of the world of intercultural religion. But the religious world about which they ruminated was largely one of their own making: "Christian missionaries are the only European residents" in some countries and "possess peculiar facilities for obtaining the productions of both barbarous and civilized nations on behalf of the benevolent and noble object of 1851." Indeed, it was often the case that foreign cultures were depicted through a glass darkly in the form of the perceptions of missionaries.[51]

Britain was in an especially unique position in encountering forms of religion that were affiliated with "savagery." As the supreme colonial power, one of its tasks was to sell natives on a better, and more properly British, way of life. This intention was primarily motivated by economic considerations, but the advancement of Christianity as the sanctifying power behind the British way of life was instrumental toward that end. Indeed, as far as "acts" of colonialism were concerned, English Protestantism and the imperialism of British culture were virtually inseparable at the time of the Great Exhibition.  When reports of the complex process of colonial interaction between missionaries and heathens reached home, it was not so difficult to conclude that British evangelism was indeed sanctioned from on high and that natives were in desperate need of the gospel. The mutual interdependence between religious ideology and politics in the colonial context can be seen clearly by observing that religious valuations of foreign cultures echoed the more general cultural assessments:

But who are those who convene on our shores? Here you have the disciples of the Veda, the Koran, the Zend Avesta, and the Bible. Moving amid the temperate climes you see some on whom the hue of Africa is stamped. What a difference between the birthright of two men—the one having an English, the other an African birth. Think of that wide continent and all the woes under which it weeps and withers; of the cold, harsh Islamism. Men will tell you that the law of human society is progress. Yet look at Africa. Men worship the Fetish and kings dwell in palaces with walls of human skulls. You see some [peoples here in] Asiatic costume. In these lands letters were cultivated when England was a wild. They calculated eclipses when the first book by a Briton was unpenned. Yet while we sit here queenly amid states, bright among the lights of religion and of science, binding bonds of brotherhood with all mankind, the people of those magnificent Asiatic Nations are being ruled by a handful of strangers. Years alone have not made England a land of quiet homes . . . of freedom . . . and domestic happiness. No! No! England, it is not time that has made thee what thou art. It is Christ's good gospel.[52]

Religious assessments of foreign cultures did not merely reflect the economic structure of the world, but in fact they explained it.

Civilized nations were not immune to being placed in a religious hierarchy either. The same interpretive lenses that saw a world peopled with savages, colonies, and semicivilized Islamic and Oriental countries brought into focus on the same general basis religious hierarchies within the West itself: "Italy wants what England enjoys—a better inspiration than that of art and a better guide than that of priestcraft." Similarly, of the Spaniard, "How splendid his nation was" before it "rejected the dawning light of the reformation." Again, religious predisposition is aligned quite directly here with a lack of industrial success.[53]

The Protestant-dominated countries of northern Europe and the Anglo-based United States were all but ignored in specifically religious commentary. The reasons for their subordination to Britain were less about religion and more about politics, though the basis for political difference—the means of assessing political adequacy—was still industrial capacity. Yet such technicalities mattered little. Religious commentators on the whole were content to muse lazily about the spiritual unity of the world at large, imagined through the eyes of a British Protestantism, which was being further sanctified by the increasing global success of British commerce. The Great Exhibition might have appeared as an excellent opportunity for the insular island nation to rethink some of the colonial presumptions about the precise nature of the intercultural world that were beginning to emerge rapidly from armchairs across the nation, but for the most part this opportunity was missed. Instead, the Crystal Palace was employed to reinforce existing fantasies about the amorphous world beyond British shores rather than to reinvent them.

## A Quickly Fading Dream: Drawing the Curtain on the Great Exhibition

The final word on the results of the Great Exhibition was given during a series of lectures to the Royal Society of Arts and was appropriately reserved for the person who best qualifies as its founder—Henry Cole. Cole's principal concern was to call attention to the advances in international relations marked by the meetings of the international juries. For Cole, the jury meetings and their reports symbolized a novel historical event—a world congress on commerce, the arts, and the sciences:

> Thus, for the first time in the world's history, the men of Arts, Science, and Commerce, were permitted by their respective governments to meet together to discuss and promote those objects for which civilized nations exist. A new principle was introduced by the Great Exhibition of 1851, and questions of Art, Science, and Commerce were permitted to be discussed in a Parliament of Art, Science, and Commerce. I believe the recognition of this principle is of the first importance for the progress of mankind. Before we introduce war steamers . . . apply the principle of international discussion. I believe the Great Exhibition has opened the way to this kind of treatment—more reasonable, more civilized, less costly . . . and more consistent with religious convictions.[54]

The commissioners had every reason to be proud of their effort. Some self-congratulation was in order. The Great Exhibition had done what no later exposition would: it made a tremendous profit. The £186,000 profit would be invested wisely and used for creating museums for the purpose of public education—a legacy that is still unfolding in London to this day. The overall organizational success of the event, led by the indefatigable Prince Albert, was undeniable. The international juries completed their tasks in an admirable manner by issuing greatly detailed reports about the state of production in each of the exhibition's thirty categories. As far as the dilemma posed by animosities arising from the jury awards, the commissioners could at least fall back on the fact that the juries had followed the prescribed rules. In the years to come, there would be a virtual consensus that the event was partly responsible for the increase in international trade for the island nation in the years following. All in all, the Great Exhibition could be counted as a smashing success.[55]

The actual judgments of the juries on the particular displays at the Great Exhibition caused great controversy, however, and raised serious doubts about the value of the event as a whole. In retrospect, it is frightening to observe how the peace and goodwill that marked the opening of the Great Exhibition was transformed into some monstrous jealousies after the jury awards were read at the closing ceremonies. This development was to cast a pall over the closing of the first international exhibition. In addition, given the vast number of exhibitors and the limited number of prizes, there were ten times as many losers as there were winners: "The original mistake of the prize system has, somehow or other, pervaded and spoiled everything within its reach," concluded *Fraser's Magazine.* "The outcry, both on the part of the exhibitors and the public, against the awards of the juries continues unabated: it may be said to be universal." The article concluded by noting that "the great enterprise which, two years ago, was so well begun" thus ends "in ridicule and disappointment and angry contention."[56]

The jury awards had gone according to plan, but there were a handful of glaring discrepancies that left numerous individual exhibitors up in arms. There were bitter complaints from the French about an unjust overall assessment of their progress in manufacturing. The entire state of Tunis, which sent a large display, somehow came away without a single award. Displaying commodities in unison was one thing for newly formed nations, but making judgments about those commodities was entirely another. It was in the judgments of the jury committees that this problem came unavoidably to the fore.

By the time of the Great Exhibition, it had become difficult for British analysts to separate production potentials from nations and cultures and their religions. For the British, these were made predominantly through a quantitative, as opposed to qualitative, assessment of industrial prowess. Religious assessment had become usurped by the economic competition between nations, even if unconsciously, in the attempt to make determinations of ultimacy. The sophisticated debates between Britain and France about the subtlest forms of industrial philosophy were the most refined discourse within which this equation between religion and culture was made. The process of categorizing the remaining Western countries was made on a similar basis, if not one that was as fully differentiated. At the next lowest rung on the Western hierarchy, Spain and Italy were dismissed as industrially retarded due to the fact that Catholicism had become outmoded and nonprogressive in the context of a modernizing world. From that point downward, religious distinctions came more to the fore in completing the global hierarchy, but with the central focus still bearing direct reference to developing a proper understanding of, and relationship to, the material world. Cultural demise resulted from a misguided understanding of the proper relationship between religious sensibilities and the necessary participation in the material world. Idolatry was the milder form of this degradation and applied mostly to the "exotic" countries of the Orient; fetishism was the extreme form and was affiliated with savagery. The separation between the divine and the material—so long considered a critical aspect of religion in Britain—was collapsing, and it was doing so most specifically in the quest to define the world interculturally. Implicit religious ideologies had become largely inseparable from the way the material productions of the attending nations were assessed at the Great Exhibition; hence, judgments about those material productions carried deeper implications. The door was being opened for a material-based, secular analysis of cultural difference to supplant enduring religious presumptions about the reasons for Western social superiority.

As is true with all broad generalization, there is always something that does not fit well into any given schematic, such as those emerging out of the Great Exhibition commentary. The Islamic countries could not be classified effectively within the global hierarchy based on industrial ability. Muslim peoples were denigrated mostly on the basis of a perceived inclination toward violence, which in the end was a result of long-standing antagonisms with Christian countries rather than anything to do with industry or the worship of matter. It was simply difficult to disentangle Muslims from Christians altogether given the extent of their collective history.

At ensuing international expositions, the ideological bases behind the participating countries' material displays would become increasingly detached from their material contexts. Direct debates about international issues in the form of intellectual congresses would supersede the intellectual significance of the jury awards for the nations involved. Some forty-two years after the Great Exhibition, the first discussion of intercultural issues inclusive of extensive representation from beyond the Western bloc of nations would take place around the topic of religion at the first World's Parliament of Religions. The Parliament would discuss globally based issues that the expositions, as much as anything else, were making apparent.

The phenomenon of the Parliament would raise an intriguing question, however, which was anticipated by one of the commentators on the Great Exhibition. Writing about the possibility of cross-cultural unification presented by the Great Exhibition, contemporary observer H. W. Burrows emphasized that peoples will come together on the basis of secular concerns but never on the basis of religion: "The [Crystal] palace is for man rather than for God. It is easier to get men to combine for what is of this earth than for what concerns God's glory. If men are united for science and commerce, how sadly are they divided on religion. Never more divided than now; nowhere more than in our own land. In order to unite, men leave out religion; they exclude it because that which ought to bind them together keeps them separate. Some recognition of religion was felt to be necessary, but one act of religious consecration was not sufficient to hallow the scene."[57]

If Burrows is correct, the process of comparative religion would represent the most implausible arena for intercultural interaction. But in the early literature related to the extensive contact between cultures in the modern period, we find religion to be very much toward the center, if not the actual center itself, of cross-cultural representation and discourse. This much granted, it is even more important to ask *why* religion found its way into this exalted position. If the motivation for advancing intercultural interaction was not primarily intellectual edification but rather economic advancement, as I have argued, the early predominance of comparative religion may point to a recognition that an understanding of another people's religion is the most effective step toward ultimate control of them. The question to be addressed in relation to the World's Parliament of Religions, then, is this: is the subject "religion" an effective forum for uniting peoples across cultural boundaries, or is it in fact the most closely guarded of cultural possessions and the element of a culture about which it is the most difficult to communicate?

# 3

## SOCIAL EVOLUTIONISM AND INTERNATIONAL EXPOSITIONS
### A CULTURAL HISTORY

EVEN MORE CONTROVERSIAL than putting up the Crystal Palace was taking it down. London had taken the enamoring glass spectacle into its collective heart, and it was not going to let it go easily. After the event closed, numerous apologetics calling for the retention of the building at its Hyde Park location were set forth. The most recurring argument was that it could be a winter garden providing amusement for Londoners through the dreary English winter. But commissioners of the Great Exhibition had promised to remove the building when the exhibition ended, and since opinion was not unanimous for retaining it, a compromise was reached. It would be allowed to stand for one year, at which time it would be dismantled and reconstructed—bigger and better—at Sydenham, just south of London.

The Great Exhibition had sparked considerable interest in foreign cultures—especially in the most exotic of them. Once the so-called eighth wonder of the world had been reconstituted in 1852 about twenty miles to the south of Hyde Park, it housed replicas of peoples such as Inuits that were set up in elaborate displays of make-believe villages of cavemen. Dinosaurs were strategically placed in mock prehistoric parks set up over several acres inside the building, evoking visions of long-forgotten worlds only recently rediscovered by the blossoming science of archaeology. The idea of a lengthy human prehistory and the hypothesis that the earth may be of a truly ancient origin were quickly becoming sources of great public fascination in Britain. In the decades to come, this deepening inquiry into the earliest terrestrial and human history would challenge the authority of the Bible and cause a transformation in religious consciousness throughout much of Western society.

Traditional religion was still firmly in place within both popular and ecclesiastic circles throughout the 1850s, but science—still called "natural philosophy"—had cast a growing shadow of doubt over many biblical presumptions about nature. The coming religious transition in Britain and the United States toward a predominantly evolutionary rather than biblical explanation of history and human origins would exert a profound influence on ensuing international expositions. When evolutionary theory proper began to be reimagined in the form of social evolutionism—the idea that human societies formed a great chain of being comparable to the one that could be observed in nature—all of the world's cultures began to be constructed into comprehensive hierarchies marking a specifically human evolution. The rise of comparative religion at the expositions was equally affected by the social evolutionary vision. Presumptions about the relative degree of people's religious evolution followed assumptions about the extent of their cultural evolution almost verbatim.[1]

As the international exposition tradition developed, international expositions and social evolutionism became engaged in a process of dual reification. The social evolutionary paradigm was reified by the blatant hierarchical arrangement of cultures at the expositions, which provided a living example of what the theory proposed: that some human groups had evolved further than others from a common source, based on the demonstrated ability to dominate their natural surroundings. Similarly, the cultural hierarchies that developed at the expositions became reified through the growing acceptance of the doctrine of social evolutionism in the surrounding culture as a scientifically authoritative explanation of cultural differences. The arrangement of cultures appeared increasingly scientific rather than arbitrary. While the connection between evolutionary theory and the rise of a field of religion has already been noted, what has not received enough attention is the extent to which the scientific and the comparative aspects of evolutionism combined to reinforce one another and promote the success of each. Social evolutionism included attractive possibilities for the interpretation of human cultural differences, and this provided an additional impetus for the acceptance of evolutionism's strictly scientific tenets, which were theologically problematic. Conversely, as evolutionary theory gained scientific credibility within the West itself and began to undermine the authority of scripture, it facilitated the growth of comparative religion, which began to appear as a less blatantly sacrilegious endeavor than it had been in the past.

The doctrine of social evolutionism can be described as a bastard child of evolutionary theory proper, because it involved such a distortion of the original scientific tenets that it gradually became all but impossible to tell what had given birth to it. To understand the widespread influence of social evolutionism within the international exposition tradition and its impact on the formation of a field of religion, it is necessary to trace its development up to the time of the Great Exhibition. So pervasive was its influence that although we risk a digression here and a facile review for readers well acquainted with the field, it is one that is nonetheless unavoidable.

What I will argue is that the widespread popular acceptance of evolutionary theory in general was primarily due to the fact that it could be used to interpret cultural differences in a way advantageous to the West. The logical certitude of the evolutionary argument was of only secondary importance to its success. The precise form of evolutionary thought that was most widely embraced in the nineteenth century—neo-Lamarckian as opposed to Darwinian evolutionism—reinforces this claim. Neo-Lamarckism pictured evolution as marking inevitable progress toward a goal. The goal of evolution within nature had been the human being. With this natural model firmly in place, there was little difficulty in imagining that human life was evolving toward a more complex goal—and that some human groups had made more progress toward it than had others. By contrast, Darwinian evolution, which worked more conscientiously from the hard science behind the theory, was forced into acknowledging that the term "evolution" described merely the possibility of random transmutation among animal species. The idea of human social progress could be linked to this essential scientific foundation only with great difficulty.

Neo-Lamarckism not only upheld the assumption that adaptation, change, and evolution implied inevitable progress; it also promoted the idea that *volition* was an important part of the evolutionary process. It was the specific idea that some human groups were more evolved than others due in some measure to their own effort that allowed neo-Lamarckian evolution to gain favor over the Darwinian version in the nineteenth century. The idea of evolution through volition was what gave evolutionary theory its driving force. It was what made people interested in the idea.

The really intriguing aspect of evolutionism was its broad acceptance as a fact of popular culture. This was the reason for its real import. It was never the *idea* of evolution that was significant in the nineteenth century. That had been around for some time. What was of compelling interest was that evolutionism caused a cultural revolution rather than a merely intellectual one. The popular embrace of evolutionary theory forced traditional religious institutions to adopt some form of the idea into their theological structures. As much as anything else, it was this that allowed evolutionism to become an enduring feature of Western religion. The popular acceptance of evolutionism greatly facilitated the advance of all the human sciences, including a field of religion. These came to coexist alongside, and often supersede, traditional biblical religion as a means of cultural orientation. Evolutionary theory was the primary theoretical development that allowed a field of religion to gain clear definition. What this chapter seeks to show is that the widespread popularization of evolutionism was greatly encouraged by the international exposition tradition.

## *The Historical Background of the Concept of Social Evolutionism*

To understand how evolutionary theory gained acceptance to the extent it did through the latter half of the nineteenth century, one must trace the cultural history of the general theory and note the broad social resistance it had to overcome as it was emerging. The advance of evolutionary theory involved a complex interplay between theoretical science, cultural mores, and religious presumptions (all of which, as stated earlier, could only be separated with great difficulty before the latter stages of the nineteenth century). Evolutionism threatened Western society with such a fundamental reorientation that it was not possible for its theoretical aspect alone to instigate a "Darwinian Revolution." Certain changes in Western culture in general were necessary for the more technical aspects of the theory to be taken in full seriousness. It is only by exploring both of these aspects of the rise of evolutionism—cultural context and scientific theory—that the whole of the "revolution" can be assessed as the enveloping cultural phenomenon it became. The Great Exhibition proved to be pivotal in providing an example of how evolutionary theory could define intercultural relations in a way that would be fortuitous for Britain. As much as any other single event, the Great

Exhibition opened the door to the social acceptance and eventual reification of evolutionary theory.²

The real threat of evolutionary thought was that it ran counter to a number of fundamental biblical assumptions about the nature of the external world and the place of human beings in it. The question of the human being's origin and relationship to nature was always at the center of evolutionary theory, but that question proved so volatile in the early stages that debates about it were played out at subsidiary levels—such as hypotheses about the age of the earth. Evolutionary theory had actually been more popular in the latter part of the eighteenth century. The early decades of the nineteenth century in Britain saw a renewal of that pietistic form of religion that is most hostile to naturalistic explanations of human life. The tide began to turn, however, when Sir Charles Lyell published his *Principles of Geology* in 1833, which gave strong arguments for extending the dating of the age of the earth. This made the idea of "transmutation" more viable: if animal species had the necessary time, it was more likely that they could have "evolved" from a common source into the myriad forms found in nature. However, Lyell exempted human beings from his search for a grand uniformity in nature. He was unable to comprehend how rational thought could arise from strictly natural processes. Nevertheless, there were others who could imagine such a possibility.

In the years leading up to the Great Exhibition, when politics took a swing to the left and evolutionism was resurgent, it became increasingly apparent that the argument about evolution was not primarily about nature, as Lyell had suggested. It was about humanity, its relationship to the natural world, and the efficacy of the sacred scriptures of Western civilization. Charles Darwin would eventually take up the torch for the group who wanted to radicalize the evolutionary argument about the grand uniformity of nature by incorporating human beings into the great chain of being. He and his mentor Lyell would split over this issue. With humans placed at the center rather than at the periphery of the evolutionary debate, the discussion took on a new intensity. The way in which the whole of the argument finally played itself out in Victorian England would say as much about that particular society as it would about the scientific theories being debated.

The general tenor of religious sentiment in Britain in the decade preceding the Great Exhibition made a general acceptance of evolutionary thought inconceivable. The fundamental challenges the theory presented for traditional religion were insurmountable. There had been several developments, however, that had begun to chip away at a religious orthodoxy whose basic principles had long been carved in stone. One of those developments was that a growing number of thinkers began siding with Sir Charles Lyell and against literal interpretations of the Bible regarding the creation of the world. Another was the translation of David Strauss's *Leben Jesu*, originally written in 1835 and translated into English in 1846 by George Eliot as *Life of Jesus*. Strauss's work gave historical specificity to the life of Jesus, and the translation of his work marked the advent of the "higher criticism" in biblical interpretation in Britain. This development would undermine the literal approach to interpreting the Bible even more than the new geological evidence and would open the door to challenging the Bible's absolute authority.

The long-developing relationship between Britain and cultures outside the West also contributed to the relativization of the biblical-based worldview. The ethnological researches of James C. Prichard had given some concrete definition to the growing popular interest in "exotic" peoples by 1850 and—especially given the quantity of such people discovered across the globe—provided another radical counterpoint to basic Western presumptions about human culture and religion. And in 1849, F. Max Müller published the first of a four-volume translation of the *Vedas*. Translations of various Eastern religious classics had begun to appear more than a half-century earlier, but advances in comparative philology made such translations archaic. Müller's work placed the comparative project on a firmer footing and contributed to the growing question of whether the Bible was the sole legitimate repository of spiritual knowledge.

Still, even with these various developments, the structure of religious understanding at the time of the Great Exhibition was very much as it had been for the past century. Charles Darwin's theory of evolution was conceived, as is well known, in the late 1830s, some twenty years before it would be published as *The Origin of Species* in 1859. Darwin held back the theory from publication because he realized that what he had tucked away in his study held truly revolutionary implications. His fears proved well founded when in 1844 Scotsman Robert Chambers anonymously published his *Vestiges of the Natural History of Creation*. Chambers's work, which anticipated Darwin's but was missing the key notion of transmutation through natural selection, brought an outcry from the scientific establishment as well as much angry speculation about its author—results no doubt not lost on the secretive Darwin.

Nearly all persons responsible for assessing the plausibility and value of evolutionism during this period were themselves religious in the traditional sense and to a significant degree. Even Darwin struggled early on with the religious implications of his scientific theory of evolution. The fact that the scientists of the time were predominantly religious points out that no clear division between science and religion in the mid-nineteenth century can be forged. It also accounts in part for the great difficulty intellectuals had in attempting to take evolutionary theory seriously. Theorists were reluctant to adopt a new theory of the origin of the world and its inhabitants that would necessitate their having to reorder their own spiritual lives just as it would everybody else's. The scientific evidence had to be perceived as definitive; in the cultural climate of the Great Exhibition, it was nowhere near that.

It is only by recounting some of the relevant aspects of British cultural history from the first half of the nineteenth century that the Great Exhibition can be definitively placed within the old-world religious environment in which it occurred. Inside the Crystal Palace, Britain at last came face-to-face with distant worlds it had known primarily through travelers' tales and the accounts of missionaries. The encounter with the rest of the world at large and its material culture stimulated interest in many of the issues related to evolutionary theory; in short, it piqued the collective curiosity about the apparently vast differences between the many human beings who made up an expanding world. Analyses of the event reflected a heightened fascination with actual so-called savages, prompted questions and answers about why cultures differed, and fueled speculation in the decade to come about the possible validity of evolution and the nature of the first human beings.

The social significance of the Great Exhibition is undeniable: an estimated 20 percent of the English populace visited the Crystal Palace. Herbert Spencer, who was a more famous evolutionist than Darwin in the nineteenth century, was indelibly intrigued by the building and made countless trips through its many aisles. General Augustus Pitt-Rivers modeled his famous anthropological collection that is now housed in Oxford on the same classification system as that employed in the Crystal Palace, with specific classes of objects being organized from simple to complex. Banker Henry Christy, who was E. B. Tylor's companion on his trip to Mexico where he formulated the key tenets of the field of anthropology, began his study of primitivism as a result of his visit to the Crystal Palace. Whether the nineteen-year-old Tylor himself visited the Great Exhibition is unknown. The intercultural world became more directly tangible inside the Crystal Palace, and this lent increasing relevance to the many intercultural classification schemas such as social evolutionism that abounded in the decade following the event.[3]

The Great Exhibition significantly contributed to breaking down the insularity of an island society that from time immemorial had been more closed than other European countries. To encounter natives in their own lands and send back orderly reports about them was one thing. To believe that all of the world's cultures had been gathered together and were represented in one's capital city was entirely another. The fantastic worlds and peoples reported by the travelers and missionaries were actually real, and they had come collectively to London.

The Great Exhibition made more flexible the social barriers formed by centuries of tradition. To some degree, the event has to be viewed as contributing to the willingness to accept new modes of thought such as evolutionism, which offered a scientific explanation of how such radical differences between peoples came about, and especially why some had succeeded over others. The international exposition tradition started more or less immediately following the Great Exhibition, with a major event in Paris in 1855 and then another in London in 1862. These helped keep issues of cultural and religious comparison before the public eye.

Evolutionary thought in general—and social evolutionism specifically—could never have gained ascendancy as quickly as they did without shining examples such as the Great Exhibition and the ensuing international expositions of how the idea might be useful in making sense of a frighteningly diverse human world. Although Sir Charles Lyell exempted human beings from his evolutionary inquiry, for most scholars and others who had an interest in the matter the question of how evolutionary theory might affect traditional religious understandings of the nature and origin of human beings was always the central question of evolutionary theory. When the cultural consensus began to shift toward an acceptance of the evolutionary explanation and the proposition that human beings had a natural rather than strictly divine origin, it was natural to question how this new vision could explain the differences between human groups that seemed to be at enormous variance with one another.

It can be legitimately argued that theories about the origin of human beings (evolutionary theory proper) and theories about why human groups differ (social evolutionism) were never entirely separate from one another. Before the hard scientific inquiry into the possibility of the transmutation of animal forms had even commenced in any serious manner, an increasing need had developed for explanatory models to account for differences between apparently distinct groupings of human animals. These two aspects of evolutionary theory—the hard science and the human science—emerged as a dialectic that in certain times and places appeared to be composed of unrelated discourses but by the end proved to be a single discussion. The level of general interest in the hard scientific inquiry into the possibility of evolution, as well as the eventual triumph of evolutionary theory, owed a considerable debt to how evolutionism could also be made useful as an anthropological explanation of human cultural differences. Evolutionary theory and social evolutionism were part of a comprehensive theoretical breakthrough, which seemed to solve more unanswered riddles at once than any new theory ever had. At the level of pragmatic application, however, the "truth" of evolutionary theory proved to be much more difficult to establish—most especially in its social applications. The problem of cultural and even personal bias in the interpretation and application of evolutionary theory marred the manner in which it was initially introduced and caused it to be viewed as a "softer" science than Darwin himself would have hoped.

In the decade following the Great Exhibition, Britain saw a rapid growth in public fascination with evolution-related subjects such as ethnology, archaeology, paleontology, geology, and the possibility of a lengthy prehistory filled with innumerable, bizarre forms of life. The public acceptance of social evolutionism would eventually be reflected at international expositions by the popularity of evolutionary-minded displays of cultures designated as "savage" or "primitive" that cast modern, "evolved" civilization in a positive light. The representation of a great clash of cultures in an arbitrary spatial arrangement inside the Crystal Palace began a movement toward, and a desire for, the creation of more abstract theoretical models that could neatly define a comprehensive global hierarchy.

Evolutionism was instigated to a much greater degree in Britain than in any other country. The Great Exhibition appeared at a crucial stage in the advance of evolutionary thought and provided a case study of the many ways the general theory might be applied and utilized as a tool for interpreting intercultural differences. At later international expositions, the pragmatic application of social evolutionism would grow exponentially as it became the principal concept around which intercultural hierarchies were formed. Yet the precise form of evolutionary theory that proved to be triumphant was not Darwinian evolutionism but rather a neo-Lamarckian version that, in one of the great historical anomalies, was more akin to the evolutionism that existed prior to Darwin. Neo-Lamarckian evolutionary theories allowed more room for the idea that those cultures that had evolved the furthest had not done so due to mere random processes but at least partly through their own accord.

## The Darwinian Revolution and International Expositions

By the time of the Paris Exposition Universelle in 1867, Darwin's theory of evolution, based on the key concept of transmutation through natural selection, had permeated the intelligentsia of every Western country. The rapidity with which evolutionary thought infiltrated the Western intellectual world indicates that by the time Darwin formulated his classical statement of the hypothesis in 1859, the general concept was widely known. As stated earlier, in Britain by the middle of the 1850s, the idea that the diverse forms of human culture were the possible result of vast prehistories had been placed before the public eye repeatedly. In 1858, a key archaeological find made on British soil at Brixham Cave turned up human skeletal remains at the same site as the remains of animals known to have been long extinct. This indicated that they had perished coterminously and that human prehistory must be much more vast than most before that time believed.

The day had been largely won regarding an extended dating for the age of the earth, but it was still necessary to establish separately a lengthy *human* prehistory in order to include humanity within the total evolutionary vision. The find at Brixham Cave cemented the notion of a lengthy human prehistory in British archaeological circles. Comparable discoveries had been made in the 1840s in France but had been dismissed in Britain as not being definitive—partly due to the simple fact that they occurred in foreign territory. Making a similar find on British soil, where questions about human antiquity had come to the fore and in a slightly different historical context, changed everything. The general consensus turned: a crucial obstacle, possibly *the* crucial obstacle, in the quest to overthrow the ancient biblical myth of human origins as an act of special creation had been overcome. As much as the scientific explanations, it was the vogue of prehistory as a subject of growing interest that contributed to this sea change.[4]

The Darwinian "revolution" must be seen primarily as the result of a long series of cultural developments in Britain. Historians have taken two primary tacks in attempting to explain how something like a Darwinian revolution was made possible. On the one side is the "internalist" explanation. Internalists maintain that it was the theory of natural selection specifically that was primarily responsible for initiating a more general cultural revolution. The mass acceptance of evolutionism is seen here as having followed in the wake of, and as being a kind of byproduct of, the strictly scientific breakthrough. Those who emphasize the internal explanation are primarily intent on countering radical alternative claims that Darwin's theory is strictly hypothetical and that it cannot be definitively proven to any significant degree. What the internalists seek to discredit above all is the idea of the Darwinian revolution being exclusively a product of a wider cultural movement to which the science involved made only a nominal contribution.[5]

On the other side is the "externalist" explanation. Externalists maintain that Darwin's theory would never have gained the hearing it did prior to the time it was published, because the historical context of his culture was not yet suitable for its reception. That is, a change in cultural attitudes was imperative for a Darwinian revolution to become even conceivable, and if true, this fact renders considerably less important Darwin's specific theory of evolutionary processes. Further, and to reiterate, externalists have noted that once Darwin paved the way for a general acceptance of evolutionary thought, his specific explanation of evolutionism fell out of favor toward the end of the nineteenth century and was replaced by a form of neo-Lamarckism. After the 1930s and the rise of what is known as the "modern synthesis" with Mendelian genetics, a modified form of Darwin's theory of natural selection would again come to be the explanation of evolution favored by most biologists. Nevertheless, in the nineteenth century, the "internal" aspect of Darwin's theory—the scientific explanation—was largely discarded. This leads externalists to conclude that it was not Darwin's selection theory specifically but rather a more general cultural willingness to accept the basic structure of evolutionary thought that best explains how what is known as the "Darwinian" revolution came about.[6]

The rapid rise of evolutionism is thus a curious historical phenomenon, because the theory with which it began and on which the "revolution" was built was discarded in favor of evolutionary theories more similar to those that existed prior to the emergence of Darwin's theory. How can any sense be made of such anachronistic occurrences? The externalist approach to the Darwinian revolution is more revealing on this account. Alvar Ellegård has observed, "The majority of the general public, and a good many scientists, refused to accept [Darwin's] Natural Selection theory, while allowing themselves to be converted to evolutionism. The ideological development [of evolutionism] was evidently more deeply influenced by traditional attitudes and beliefs than by logical considerations." The success of evolutionary theory—assessed strictly in its nineteenth-century manifestation—thus reflected the growing predominance of a specifically neo-Lamarckian evolutionism. Neo-Lamarckism was concerned with evolutionary theory as a potentially attractive explanation of cultural differences more than it was with any exact theory of how transmutation itself might occur.[7]

There was never a question of evolutionism creating a basis for cultural hierarchies, but merely of building them on a new foundation. Cultures had long been subjected to value judgments in the process of Western expansion, but the basis for these had been within a theological rather than scientific framework. From at least the middle of the sixteenth century through the Enlightenment, foreign peoples deemed either "exotic" or "savage" were imagined to have "fallen" further from an original state of grace than Christian peoples. It was the committing of sinful acts without any means of redemption that explained how "savages" had fallen so far into the degraded material world and lost all contact with the saving spirit of the Christian religion. Evolutionism succeeded in creating a new hierarchical system based on progress rather than on degeneration. This made it possible to regard less industrially inclined societies as simply having failed to develop to the same extent as industrially sophisticated cultures. What evolutionary theory was able to accomplish that no earlier model had was to convince a large enough percentage of the populace that the new basis for intercultural hierarchies was now grounded in the apparent objectivity of hard science rather than in the cultural subjectivity of religion.

While the cultural history of evolutionism demonstrates that its success was dependent on many factors, there can be no doubt that the actual publication of *The Origin of Species* was the focal point of the evolutionary phenomenon. Still, the popular success of *The Origin of Species* resulted more from its implications for religion than for science, calling to mind again the idea that the Darwinian revolution was not primarily a scientific revolution but rather a cultural one, in which changing attitudes about religion played a pivotal role. For instance, *The Origin of Species* paled in comparison to a more famous publication during the period, *Essays and Reviews*, published in 1860. This latter work was the first major application in Britain of the higher criticism emanating out of Germany. Britain had remained largely insulated from theological movements on the continent, and the publication of *Essays and Reviews* touched off a firestorm more controversial than Darwin's theory of natural selection for the simple reason that it dealt more directly with the question of the ultimate authority of sacred scripture.[8]

As the 1860s progressed, increasing numbers of people jumped on the Darwinian bandwagon. They did so in a variety of ways, however. The many evolutionary positions were based on the degree of divine involvement—or the complete lack thereof—in the evolutionary process. Another issue was whether the theory of the mutability of species applied only to the lower forms of life or to humankind as well. As a rule, the lower the educational standard of a particular group, the more likely they were to take a conservative position on evolutionism. Evolutionary conservatism meant an increased role for the Deity regarding the precise manner in which the transmutation of species occurred and a rejection of any application of the general theory to humanity.

From the beginning, there was significant resistance to Darwin's specific theory of evolution. Darwinian evolutionism revolved around the troubling notion of transmutation through natural selection, which maintained that change occurred in a random rather than directed and rationally identifiable way—a difficult proposition to entertain in theological circles. In 1870, St. George Mivart published his *Genesis of Species*, the first credible scientific attack on Darwin's theory of natural selection. This work initiated a trend away from the Darwinian version of evolutionism and toward more orderly neo-Lamarckian ones, a trend that would continue throughout the nineteenth century. Despite the decline of Darwinism, however, evolutionism continued to gain ground steadily in Britain such that, as Alvar Ellegard has observed, "Among the educated . . . the battle for it was virtually over by 1870."[9]

The religious response to the evolutionary phenomenon following the publication of *The Origin of Species* was divided. The one thing that religious groups in Britain shared in their initial responses to evolutionism was the rejection of the application of the theory to humanity. The Church Fathers had drawn a sharp line between humanity and the animal world, and especially for the Roman Catholics, this was a line that could not be crossed, even if parts of the evolutionary doctrine were acceptable. As the century progressed, however, there would be continual compromises in churches on both sides of the Atlantic as evolutionism permeated popular culture in a way that made its existence impossible to dismiss in any context. As the churches acquiesced to remain in step with popular sentiment, evolutionism gained in authority and social evolutionism increasingly became an accepted means of interpreting cultural differences.

## *Darwin, Spencer, and Neo-Lamarckian Social Evolutionism*

There were several reasons for the decline of the specifically Darwinian version of evolutionism in the later nineteenth century. The explanations are telling in analyzing the particular manner in which evolutionism developed and how it influenced international expositions. Although Darwin's theory of natural selection is subtly complex in that it brings into interrelation numerous relatively simple ideas, the reasons why it presented a fundamental threat to the religious and cultural order of the time are more easily summarized. Darwin saw change in species coming about in a random rather than directed way, and he saw the goal of species as being mere survival more than evolutionary progress. Applied to humanity, these scientific data could be easily translated into visions of a godless, undirected universe hoping only for survival in a struggle of all against all.

In the beginning, Darwin avoided any direct application of his selection theory to humankind, such as depicting human beings as extensions of the animal world. The argument of *The Origin of Species* was aimed almost exclusively at demonstrating the mutability of animal species and began with forty painstaking pages about pigeons. His conclusion to the study contained only a cryptic comment on the ramifications of the work for humankind: "In the future I see open fields for far more important researches. Much light will be thrown on the origin of man and his history." He knew the study would be controversial and that readers would read into his careful analysis of pigeons and mutability the implications of his ideas for human beings and their relationship to nature. Hence, he chose not to needlessly provoke what would no doubt be a somewhat hostile reaction.[10]

As evolutionary theory gained ground through the 1860s, it became much less controversial to discuss the implications of the theory for humankind. By the time he was writing *The Descent of Man*, published in 1871, Darwin made it clear that his evolutionary theory had a very definite meaning for the interpretation of differences between human cultures. A revealing passage at the end of *The Descent of*

*Man*, quoted below, leaves little doubt that the evolutionary paradigm demarcated a firm boundary between so-called primitive and civilized peoples for Darwin. Darwin had spent five long years aboard the *Beagle*, and needless to say, in the 1830s it was still quite possible to have anthropological experiences that were transformative and psychologically profound—experiences demonstrating that there were truly important ideological issues to be addressed in the bizarre new world of intersocietal relations. Darwin's language indicates a distinct connection between his cultural anthropological concerns and his scientific ones:

> That man is descended from some lowly organized form will, no doubt, be highly distasteful to many. But there can hardly be a doubt that we are descended from barbarians. The astonishment which I felt on first seeing a party of Fuegians on a wild and broken shore will never be forgotten by me for the reflection at once rushed into my mind—such were our ancestors. These men were absolutely naked and bedaubed with paint, their long hair was tangled, their mouths frothed with excitement, and their expression was wild, startled, and distrustful. For my own part I would as soon be descended from that heroic little monkey, who braved his dreaded enemy to save the life of his keeper . . . as from a savage who delights to torture his enemies, offers up bloody sacrifices . . . and is haunted by the grossest superstitions.[11]

In part, Darwin's task had been to make some sense of the many human animals he encountered in his lengthy travels, along with accounting for the existence of so many animal species. While his scientific project talked in terms of randomness and survival, his anthropological conclusions were more definite and evolutionary. Darwin sought to ground his own vision of a primitive/civilized dichotomy in something genuinely scientific and objectifying like the hard science of biology. This methodological approach might prove capable of transcending the subjective cultural observations of ethnographers and hold true for all cultures everywhere as an immutable natural law. The problems with the theory arose when Darwin sought to give specificity to the original doctrine of transmutation—in short, to make it humanly meaningful. The more sensitive considerations of his theory—those that had to do with its implications for human societies—could only be approached subjectively from within Darwin's familiar cultural context. In the end, this method proved decisive: criticism leveled at the ethnocentrism and cultural subjectivity Darwin displayed in attempting to make his own theory of evolutionism relevant for a mass audience undermined the credibility of its more scientific aspects as the nineteenth century progressed.

Darwin's theory of evolution did stress the element of randomness in the process of transmutation and change, but the most useful random changes that survived in a given species still had to be "naturally selected," a phrase that Darwin never explained adequately. While random new traits were constantly being introduced into human societies, the precise means by which the best of them were "selected" to provide the greatest chance for survival remained obscure. The structure of his theory certainly left room to assume that any species (read *race*, or *society*) that had "naturally selected" the greatest abundance of those useful changes was the fittest, and that it may be in some small part responsible for its own success.

If the reigning metaphor was adaptation to nature in Darwin's evolutionary vision, the race or society demonstrating the greatest capacity to transform the raw materials of nature into useful cultural commodities through industry would have to be considered superior. The problems with defining progress on the basis of the adaptation to, or of, nature has been more obvious, collectively, to those writing outside the West than within it. The East Indian scholar Ashis Nandy, writing about Rudyard Kipling, observed, "Kipling correctly sensed that the glorification of the victor's violence was the basis of the doctrine of social evolutionism and ultimately colonialism, that one could not give up the violence without giving up the idea of colonialism as an instrument of progress." Following Nandy, the concept of human "progress" could certainly be defined by something more definitive than the capacity to build industry. An assessment of the relative propensity for violence exhibited by different cultures might be one alternative. If a measure such as this were adopted as a barometer for cultural success, then the determination of degrees of "progress" demonstrated by different cultures becomes more difficult to establish.[12]

Nonetheless, while Darwinian evolution to some degree lends itself to fantasies about human cultural progress, it was never able to entirely shake the perception that it emphasized random change far more than it did evolutionary progress. The reason for the definitive movement away from Darwinism and back to a nominally reconceived Lamarckism is best illustrated in the work of the other famous evolutionist of the period, who focused almost exclusively on the human part of the evolutionary equation. Herbert Spencer was little concerned with Darwin's fundamental problem of proving the transmutation of species—an endeavor that only subtly implicated the human animal within its overall agenda. For the less patient and mostly self-educated Spencer, the biological underpinnings of human social evolution were more or less irrelevant. Through Spencer's eyes, it was plain to see that some human groups had evolved and progressed further than others. His concern was not with hard science, but to define something called civilization in opposition to something that was less than that. For Spencer, civilization proper was founded on a very British laissez-faire utilitarianism, and he wove abstract evolutionary notions together with that social philosophy to promote a very particular form of British society both at home and throughout the world.

The combined elements of the randomness of change and the goal of mere survival in Darwin's evolutionary vision explain why it proved so difficult to incorporate it into existing theological hermeneutics. If the Bible's explanation of natural processes had to be adjusted, that was one obstacle to be overcome. If human beings had evolved from animal forms and were not specially created by a benevolent deity, that was another much more difficult problem. To argue, however, that the whole of creation was fundamentally directionless and engaged in an eternal struggle with itself for survival was a proposition that could not be interpreted theologically in any meaningful way. Thus, the nineteenth-century solution to the problem of Darwinian evolutionism was to go with the evolutionary tide but to adjust some of the specifics of its ebb and flow so that it would not wash over a theological view of the world altogether. It was Spencer who was primarily responsible for accomplishing this aim.

Also integral to the gradual rejection of Darwin's theory of evolution throughout the nineteenth century was the fact that it was not as easily applied within the sphere of social evolution as were neo-Lamarckian evolutionary theories. If it was to be accepted that human beings did develop out of the world of nature, it became critical to establish that some human groups had evolved more fully beyond brute creation than others and to offer an explanation as to why. Scripture had always been interpreted as conferring special status on those who believed in its authority. To gain success socially, evolutionary theory, with its ability to undermine traditional religious authority, had to offer something similar. The randomness of Darwinian evolution made it exceedingly difficult to neatly adapt the theory to an interpretation of differences between human groups, and especially to show how the human actors involved might have had a hand in the process. Spencer's neo-Lamarckism began with a social philosophy that promoted just this aim—a republican utilitarianism whose focus was self-responsibility—and it worked backward in as convenient way as possible from this point to the original science behind evolutionary theory.

In contrast to Darwinism, Lamarckism emphasized the inheritance of acquired characteristics. For Lamarck, new traits did not emerge randomly. Instead, they were acquired through the process of adapting to the external environment. Those new traits were then inherited by offspring. The inheritance of acquired characteristics could be interpreted as follows: human beings, through willed acts of their own, can acquire preferable traits in adapting to nature (or for the adapting of nature) that can then be inherited by their offspring to create a better society. Applied to the realm of social evolution, Lamarckism allowed a much greater role to the possibility of human volition in the act of evolution than did Darwinism, which viewed evolution as being incontrovertibly connected to randomness. This was why Spencer, with his interest in equating evolutionism at large with certain specifics of social policy, remained a Lamarckian to the end.

As evolutionary thought progressed throughout the nineteenth century, it gravitated more and more to the kind of neo-Lamarckism reflected in the work of Herbert Spencer. Darwin's own theory of evolution was to fall short of the scientific revolution he had hoped for it to become in his lifetime. It was a return to neo-Lamarckian evolutionism and the wider cultural embrace of this more palatable form of the theory that spelled traditional religion in nineteenth-century Britain. Evolutionary thought was seen as being useful primarily to the extent that it could explain differences between human societies. Darwin's scientific mechanism of natural selection was merely a symbol for this wider movement.

The early theorists writing more directly within the context of a field of religion in this period were not as deterministic as Darwin and Spencer in their attempt to apply the doctrine of social evolutionism to explain every facet of religious differences among cultures. With his strong focus on East Indian culture, F. Max Müller, often heralded as the father of the history of religions, was more concerned with conducting linguistic comparisons between the major civilizations of India and the West than with appropriating evolutionary theory within religious comparison. Müller completed most of his major works in the decade of the 1860s, when evolutionary theory was still dawning.

This much granted, by the time of Müller's foundational lectures on the science of religion, which he delivered in 1870, he observed,

"Though the belief of African and Melanesian savages is more recent in point of time, it represents an earlier and far more primitive phase in point of growth, and is therefore as instructive to the student of religion as the study of uncultivated dialectics has proved to the student of language." Further, the work of the Dutchman C. P. Tiele, who was seven years Müller's junior, was influenced even more by the evolutionary hypothesis. It seems that almost no one remained untouched by the sweep of evolutionary thought in the period. On the whole, however, it is fair to say that the dogmatic application of evolutionary theory to the interpretation of cultural differences was more earnest in anthropological circles and at the level of popular culture than it was among the early theorists in the field of religion.[13]

It was only after the broader sweep of evolutionary theory had managed to undermine the authority of traditional biblical religion on the most important human concerns that a scientific approach to religious phenomena in general had a chance to gain real influence. The religions of other cultures, and increasingly even Christianity itself, could now be partly understood through the emerging categories of the human sciences. What mainly took the place of traditional religious authority in the interpretation of cultural differences, albeit gradually, was the heuristic device of social evolutionism, which still granted Western—even Christian—supremacy, but now on an entirely different basis: the demonstrated ability to transform nature as opposed to claims of revealed truth.

The secular dominance of Western civilization would increasingly define the way the world at large was imagined, both interculturally and interreligiously, at ensuing international expositions. Still, the authority of religion was not lost altogether. The international exposition tradition narrowed the established gap between the divine and the material world such that material concerns were becoming less distinctly antithetical to a proper relationship with the divine. Christian apologists were clearly emboldened by the newfound economic success of their countries within the emerging modern world system—a fact that would be brought home forcefully at Chicago's World's Parliament of Religions at century's end. Equally, Western material orientation became ever more sanctified by Christianity itself—a development that would have been unthinkable in an earlier epoch due to the extreme ambivalence Protestant cultures had toward the material world. The eventual result of this growing division between religion and culture would be a sense of Western superiority that was simultaneously grounded in the religious and the secular.

## Social Evolutionism at European International Expositions, 1867 to 1889

The first international exposition at which evolutionary themes can be seen as having a decided influence was at the Paris Exposition Universelle of 1867. There were several facets of the Paris exposition to which evolutionism contributed. Frederic LePlay, the organizer of both the 1855 and 1867 French expositions, created an exhibit at the latter event depicting the history of human labor extending back to the Stone Age. The display was organized by country, enabling each country to trace its national identity back to a hypothetical point of origination and observe the evolution of its interaction with the material world. For some countries, the trip from the Stone Age to the present was portrayed as being brief, while for others it marked an epic journey.[14]

Also at the 1867 Paris exposition, the practice developed of setting up areas marked off as "Turkish Bazaars," and later, the "Street in Cairo"—concession areas that would become a hallmark at expositions. These concessions were peopled by natives who would hawk their national goods and serve unusual food and drinks. The 1867 exposition was the first instance of what would come to be called a "midway" by the time of Chicago's exposition of 1893. Midways were the places where societies that were deemed "primitive" and equated with Western prehistoric societies would be displayed most extensively at expositions.

The theme of evolution was also reflected indirectly in the display of photographs of foreign peoples, which was an emerging art at expositions in the period. The basis for photography, the daguerreotype, invented by Louis Daguerre of France, whose passing during the period of the Great Exhibition was greatly lamented, dates back to 1829. The process had been slow to develop, however, and there were only a handful of photographs of the Crystal Palace, mostly of a very poor quality. Refinements in this emerging art allowed extensive exhibits of photographs to make a pronounced debut at the 1862 exhibition in London. By the 1867 Paris exposition, entire displays devoted to photographs of little-known peoples were a source of great fascination for the public. Photographs made more immediate those contemporary peoples who were perceived as being the most different from modern Western norms. It brought them one step closer to real life and heightened interest in them. Coupled with the advance of evolutionary theory in the period, these photographs pro-

SOCIAL EVOLUTIONISM AND EXPOSITIONS            83

vided multiple examples of what evolutionary theorists of the period believed the earliest human cultures must have been like.[15]

The theory of social evolutionism became reified at international expositions most directly through the display of peoples who were themselves the principle "entertainment" offered by the exhibits of which they were a part. The history of exhibiting human subjects is long and complex within European history, as noted in chapter 1, but there was one particularly noteworthy instance of this practice that lent some impetus to development of such exhibits within the international exposition tradition. The Jardin d'Acclimatation, established in Paris in 1859 and originally filled with displays of exotic plants and animals, was suffering from lagging attendance by 1877, which left the museum in danger of closing. The Jardin thus sought to capitalize on an emerging cultural phenomenon: the fascination with "savage" peoples that had become evident at the 1867 Paris exposition. In 1878, fourteen Nubians were formally presented in a museum display that caused great excitement among patrons. Attendance increased markedly as a result of the display and guaranteed the institution's future. This original exhibit had the backing of the Parisian academic community, but the anthropological value of similar displays over the next ten years became more dubious. The theme of education became a background to the circus atmosphere surrounding the exhibits.[16]

The first international exposition to display actual peoples in a significant way was the small-scale Colonial and Indian Exhibition held in London in 1886. This exhibition was the first of many that exhibited dominions and colonies exclusively. Outside the exhibition buildings in South Kensington, a compound housed Hindus, Muslims, Buddhists, and Red Indians from British Guiana, among others.[17] Model natives were dispersed around courts designed to emphasize the diversity and nobility of the British colonies. Specific natives were selected to represent a wide range of skin colors and "every type of countenance." Natives at these events underwent the perplexing process of being represented as subordinates within the larger British worldview while simultaneously being held up as valued elements within the British Empire. As a token of respect, when Queen Victoria opened the Colonial and Indian Exhibition, the first verse of "God Save the Queen" was sung in English and the second in Sanskrit, specially translated by F. Max Müller himself.[18]

The art of objectifying human beings as potential sources of entertainment at international expositions commenced in full force at the Paris event of 1889. Despite the moral complexity of such displays, the organizers of the 1889 Paris exposition showcased several groups of human beings at once in commercially minded displays that made a shambles of the principle of "education" upon which such displays were originally founded. The display of mock native villages erected on Chaillot Hill along the Champs de Mars stood immediately adjacent to the impressive imperial pavilions of the "civilized nations." By the time of the 1889 event in Paris, it had become clear that expositions were attempts to display the modern nation in its totality. It was no longer a matter of creating a strong national display in contrast to other national displays. It had become necessary to present the nation as an empire, whose boundaries were not confined to national borders.

The interests of the modern nation had come to extend throughout the whole of the world, or as far as a country's military, economic, and ideological capacities had proven capable of carrying it. The displaying of colonial interests was an integral part of the complete promotion of a nation. The small settlements of French minions were extensive at the 1889 exposition: Senegalese, Congolese, New Caledonians, Gabonese, Dahomeans, Cochin-Chinese, and Kampong-Javanese were the main attractions. The exhibits were composed around the family unit as much as possible, with the different groups made up of a half-dozen or so families. Such an arrangement indicates that the intention was to present a picture of social harmony in native life within its larger colonial context. The reality of the peopled displays was not quite so orderly. The Senegalese families came from several regions, did not have a common language among them, and belonged to three distinct ethnic groups—the Peulps, Goloffs, and Bambaras. Thus, whatever rituals were performed for the crowds had little to do with the customs of the majority of the people in the display.[19]

This beguiling tradition at international expositions would be repeated in various settings in the decades to come, with varying actors playing the role of the "primitive" depending on the location of a particular event. Western observers proved eager to behold native peoples set up in displays where they were doing nothing more than acting out, in a minimal way, a stereotypical vignette of native life. The effect of this practice was to institute a more differentiated intercultural hierarchy based on the actual observation of several of these peoples at once, albeit in the artificial exposition setting.

The influence of social evolutionism in the process of legitimating human hierarchies would be endowed with a greater degree of urgency at international expositions in the United States due to its being applied directly to the immediately surrounding society. The global hierarchies resulting from the armchair anthropology of the Great Exhibition in London had entirely different connotations in the ethnically diverse United States and involved a different set of consequences. Displays of the cultures of Native American peoples at the first major international exposition in the United States at Philadelphia in 1876 were intended to be educational, but instead resulted in objectifying the generic Indian as a race whose passing marked the closing of the frontier and the opening of the museum. Education-minded displays of Native Americans appeared more fully at the 1893 Chicago exposition, but here the educational displays of the fair's official organizers became confused in the mind of the average fair visitor with the potentially similar but commercially motivated displays of peoples along the midway. The net result was that peoples deemed "exotic" were understood as being either relics of the past or freaks of the present, whose proper place at international expositions was along a fair's carnivalesque midway and not within the main fairgrounds.

When the World's Parliament of Religions took place as a part of Chicago's Columbian Exposition, the category of "religion," conceived as a newly objectifiable phenomenon distinct from culture, appeared as a mostly empty concept that was almost wholly defined by the interpretive categories of the exposition in which it took place. The inclusion and exclusion of particular religious groups at the World's Parliament of Religions was based almost exclusively on the esteem in which the various cultures of the world had come to be held within the unfolding international expositions tradition.

# 4

# EXHIBITIONISM, AMERICAN STYLE

**W**HILE EUROPEAN international expositions followed the successful Crystal Palace with major events in 1855 (Paris), 1862 (London), 1867 (Paris), and 1873 (Vienna), the tradition was slow to develop in the United States. When it did, it took on a tendentiousness in its portrayal of cultural differences that was unmatched in the European context. The American expositions were distinct from the European events because of the marked difference in social context. Representatives from many of the modern nations and distant cultures that occupied the press coverage of the European events shared a single social context in the vast cultural experiment that America had become. And it was in the United States that the subject of religion first began to appear in earnest as yet another means through which the widening circle of intercultural relations might be both represented materially and even discussed among participants. Exhibitionism in America thus represents a separate case study altogether from its European counterparts.

For the most part, international expositions were always grand carnivals and were never meant to be taken as literal descriptions of the integrating world. But in the American context, delusions of grandeur about a global cultural hierarchy proffered by the exposition tradition contained immediate political ramifications for the American social order. Because of this, the events lost much of their sense of fantasy and become more indistinguishable from reality. Expositions in the United States were turned into political exercises in which the country became defined through the metaphor of the carnival. The American events made it appear as if it was only in fun that the hierarchies of the races of the world portrayed along exposition midways just happened to be synonymous with the broadest outlines of the classes of American society. This allowed a clear message to be sent about an implicit social order but prevented that message from seeming overtly political due to the context in which it was being delivered.

At the time of the Columbian Exposition, American historian Henry Adams wrote that "Chicago was the first expression of American thought as a unity." Adams went on to construct his famous essay "The Dynamo and the Virgin" around the theme of world's fairs as a novel form of modern education. Without world's fairs, Adams claimed, the education of the masses would be impossible. Indeed it was the case that the American public was introduced to numerous facets of modern culture, both domestic and intercultural, through the world's fairs. In an era when human scientific understanding was replacing much of what previously had been regarded as revealed knowledge, the world's fairs—as they came to be known in the American context—illustrated some of the creative possibilities this new mode of human understanding could provide. While it fashioned itself as an objective critique of the biases of traditional religion, this new secular-based vision arising out of the international exposition tradition made its own set of political assumptions about the emerging global village. The Columbian Exposition did lead Americans to imagine modernizing America as a unity for the first time, but the Enlightenment-based morality on which that new vision was founded was distorted by the chaotic atmosphere of the carnival. The structure of the fair indicated that some of America belonged in the freak show along the exposition's midway, while the rest dreamed of an empire inside the "White City" of the main fairgrounds.[1]

The focus of this chapter is to consider all three of the major nineteenth-century American international expositions in an effort to place the Columbian Exposition within its American context. When "religion" made the unprecedented and multidimensional appearance it did at the Chicago fair—a phenomenon that proved to be unique to the American context—it did so because of numerous cultural factors that had appeared in embryonic form at the earlier American fairs.

## *A New York Crystal Palace?*

The earliest major exhibitions in the United States centered not on industrial production as they did in Europe, but rather on agrarianism. Suzanne Hilton has traced the tradition of American exhibitionism back to the Berkshire Cattle Show of 1810, hosted by Elkanah Watson. As the country continued to spread throughout the west and distances between farms increased, a number of "mechanics institutes" emerged as forums at which farmers could gather in major cities to share the newest technological discoveries in farming.²

Another source of the exhibition tradition in the United States was parades, which during the same period began to take place in major cities, most notably in the early national center of Philadelphia. One of the distinguishing features of American international expositions as compared to the European events was that they were conceived regionally rather than nationally. The events were identified with the cities in which they occurred as much as they were with the whole nation. London symbolized Britain and Paris symbolized France more than any one city in the United States could comparably represent the entire country. Given this distinction, the early American parades, which were eminently local affairs, can be viewed as more direct precursors to the later international expositions than they otherwise might be.

The most significant of the early parades was the Washington Centennial parade, which took place in Philadelphia on February 22, 1832, and commemorated the centenary of the birth of George Washington. As with the later international expositions, the parades were carefully orchestrated events that identified implicit presumptions about the country's social order. Specific cultural groups were invited to march in the parades, while others were excluded. Philadelphia's black population, for instance, which by this time included many free blacks with strong hopes for equal rights in the North, honored the day among themselves but found no place in the public drama. Despite protests, women were also excluded from the Washington Centennial parade.³

These specifically American precedents of the parade and the agrarian-based mechanics institutes aside, the tradition of international expositions in the United States emerged predominantly out of the European—and especially British—exposition tradition. The American events are generally regarded as having begun with Philadelphia's "Centennial Exhibition" in 1876, which clearly set the tone for Chicago's Columbian Exposition in 1893. Prior to Philadelphia, however, the first official international exposition in the United States took place in New York in 1853, following on the heels of the Great Exhibition in London. The United States was so taken by the grandeur of the Great Exhibition two years earlier, with its glamorous Crystal Palace, that it somewhat shamelessly attempted to replicate the event. In an enthusiastic letter to the *New York Tribune* during the first month of the Great Exhibition, Horace Greeley had proposed that New York hold a similar event. When that proposal reached the table, the initial location designated for the event was Madison Square. Just as at Hyde Park, however, local residents and businesses complained and in this case were successful in halting plans.

The eventual site selected was Reservoir Square, between Fortieth and Forty-second Streets and Sixth Avenue. The site was unfortunate in many respects. In 1853, Reservoir Square (which is now Bryant Park and home of the New York Public Library) was a long way from the center of the city. Worse yet, the space was not large enough to accommodate one of the originally proposed buildings—nothing less than an exact replica of London's Crystal Palace, to be designed by Sir Joseph Paxton himself, architect of the original building. The final choice of building design was the plan of Georg J. B. Carstensen and Charles Gildemeister, the former being the designer of the famous Tivoli amusement park in Copenhagen. Dubbed the "New York Crystal Palace," the building emulated London's Crystal Palace in construction but was shaped in the form of a Greek cross with a one-hundred-foot-diameter dome at the intersection of the arms.[4]

Omitting only the "Great" from the title of the London exhibition, the event was officially entitled "The Exhibition of the Industry of All Nations." From the beginning, the event was more of a profit-seeking enterprise than a genuine, nationally based exhibition. It was organized by a group of New York businessmen seeking to reap some benefits from the success of the original Crystal Palace. As the event took shape, the New York press took pains to express its disgust with the capitalist enterprise. Dubious, entertainment-minded concessions, which would become a pronounced feature of all American international expositions, made a notable appearance at the New York Crystal Palace even before it opened its doors. While the building was under construction, enterprising parties built shanties out of spare materials lying around outside the construction site and set up businesses of the least desirable kind. Classic exhibition sideshows included the French bearded lady, dancing bears, and "rattlesnakes with a tender and loving disposition."[5]

The rise of the shanties provided a rude shock to event organizers and fueled the ire of the press. Entrepreneurs promoted their wares using any means possible. After a presidential parade had been scheduled for the opening ceremonies, one advertisement promoting cockfights noted that "the President probably will attend the performance."

A local boardinghouse plastered ads for cheap rooms all over the tombstones of a nearby cemetery. By the time of the opening, business at the shanties was brisk.⁶

Despite the sham elements and the debunking by the press, the event finally got under way. On July 12, two months behind schedule, President Franklin Pierce, accompanied by Secretary of War Jefferson Davis, led an opening-day parade that drew some twenty thousand spectators. The crowd cheered as a band struck up "Yankee Doodle Dandy." Inside the exhibition building, however, the New York version of the Crystal Palace bore little resemblance to the British original. No concessions were opened for the first two months; there were no seats on which to sit; and tardily varnished banisters remained sticky all summer from the heat. The number of exhibitors varied but hovered around the four thousand mark (compared to seventeen thousand at the Crystal Palace). About one-third of the displays were American and two-thirds were foreign, which proves the extent to which the event was legitimately international in its scope.⁷

The prize exhibits were the same as those shown at the Great Exhibition. McCormick's reaper and Colt's revolvers were chief among these, but Samuel F. B. Morse's electromagnetic telegraph stole the show. The first telegraph line was set up between Washington and Baltimore in 1844, with fifteen thousand miles of line having been laid after that time. Demonstrations of the fascinating discovery impressed visitors, many of whom had never even been near a large urban center. The ubiquitous P. T. Barnum organized a large museum inside the building and did quite well with events such as a play of Harriet Beecher Stowe's *Uncle Tom's Cabin*. Barnum's play featured "emotional scenes and a happy ending" and remained more popular than a competitor's version.⁸

There was little that was educationally redeeming about the New York Crystal Palace, but what lessons were being offered in analyses of the event focused on the problems of nouveau riche Americans. A recurrent theme within exposition literature was that the accumulation of wealth with no refinement of aesthetic taste or philanthropic sensibility was the essence of cultural corruption. Some small measure of success may have been achieved in the area of aesthetic awareness at the New York Crystal Palace, as one of the few lasting legacies of the event was that it included the first exhibit of paintings at an international exposition. Nevertheless, the cautious approach adopted at London's Great Exhibition, which sought to avoid having that event degenerate into an exclusively commercial spectacle, was all but absent at the New York exhibition. This inclination toward unchecked commercialism would mark all future American expositions and mitigate their attempts to offer strictly educational exhibits. It would prove difficult to take educational exhibits seriously in an excessively carnivalesque atmosphere.

Women's organizations, which would become a pronounced feature of American expositions as compared to European ones, made their presence felt at this initial event by hosting informal meetings that were not directly affiliated with the event.[9] The biggest surprise of the exhibition, however, was the large number of working-class people who were willing to pay fifty cents for admission when they would have been lucky to make ten dollars in a week. Thus, a family of four entering twice would have spent half a week's wages for their exhibition experience. Hackneys charged a dollar fifty and up for a ride to the grounds, compared to the twenty-five cents paid by Londoners two years earlier. Nevertheless, a surprising number of older people from the country used the occasion as an excuse to visit the big city or their relatives. There were no public art museums in the United States in 1853, only one national museum—the Smithsonian—and the few libraries that existed were the domain of the elite. Thus, despite its drawbacks, the New York Crystal Palace made a significant contribution to American awareness of high culture within the social context in which it occurred.[10]

The strict class organization of the New York exhibition also reflected what would become an unmistakable feature of American international expositions. At the opening ceremony, Horace Greeley, then editor of the *New York Tribune*, remarked that none of the exposition's architects were up on the stage with the president and officials.[11] The president was accompanied during the parade by six conspicuously placed British commissioners from London, which as one writer surmised "was still America's spiritual capital." Exhibitors were told to stay in their designated sections rather than crowd the ceremony. The proceedings were tightly controlled to present a calculated image of the country to its inhabitants and the negligible numbers of foreign visitors. The event was viewed by President Pierce, among others, as "a possible means of welding the States of America together once more." Unfortunately, the exhibition "suffered from inter-State jealousies and no official government backing."[12]

The United States was not a tightly constructed political entity in 1853. Civil war was an increasingly realistic prospect. The country's international image was ambiguous after its marginal performance at the Great Exhibition, and now a poorly organized inaugural world's fair was taking place with embarrassing commercial spectacles set up outside it. All of these elements made the calculated formal ceremonies appear superficial. On the one hand, organizers of the New York Crystal Palace promoted the advancement of humanistic and purportedly "national" agendas, but on the other they displayed the willingness to give free reign to commercial enterprise at the event. This phenomenon pointed to sharp disparities in the nation's collective intentions and would leave a definitive stamp on later American expositions as well.

While the New York Crystal Palace was ostensibly set up to run interminably, it gradually dissolved without so much as a closing ceremony. Some seven hundred thousand visitors passed through its gates between July 15 and November 30, shelling out more than three hundred thousand dollars, but attendance fell off dramatically in the winter months. Exhibition president Theodore Sedgwick resigned; the original stockholders sold their interests, leaving all losses to a second tier of investors; and the reins were turned over to the greatest showman of them all—the infamous Phineas T. Barnum. Barnum tried a number of remedial measures to revive the exhibition, the most unfortunate perhaps being the hosting of musical performances in a hall so vast and lacking in acoustics that patrons in the back could not hear anything at all. Barnum resigned on July 10, 1854. The "Exhibition of the Industry of All Nations" officially closed on November 1 of that year, leaving a debt of three hundred thousand dollars. The exhibition site was destroyed by fire on October 5, 1858, which prompted one writer to declare it "the most celebrated day in the history of the Crystal Palace."[13]

What the New York Crystal Palace revealed about international or intercultural conceptions of religion in the evangelical-dominated and pre-evolutionary United States of 1853 was something that had already become clear in London two years earlier. The only significant intersocietal awareness the country had at mid-century was of its troubling subordination to Britain in nearly all matters of deep cultural and religious significance.

## The Centennial Exhibition, Philadelphia, 1876

The disappointment of the New York Crystal Palace coupled with the onset of the Civil War led to any grand ideas about staging international expositions being placed on hold for a longer period than would otherwise have been the case. During the Civil War, however, the flexible exhibition tradition found a surprising forum in what were called "Sanitary Fairs," which were held in tents in various cities. They offered odd entertainment and curios in attempts to raise money for the Northern army. Proposals for a Philadelphia centennial exhibition in 1876 actually got under way as early as 1864 when Professor John L. Campbell suggested the idea at an address delivered at the Smithsonian, where it received only a lukewarm reception in the heat of the war. By 1871, an act of the United States Congress provided for "celebrating the One Hundredth Anniversary of American Independence, by holding an International Exhibition of Arts, Manufactures, and Products of Soil and Mine."[14]

Depending on how it is compared and who is comparing it, the Philadelphia Centennial is described as either relatively successful or a decided failure. When placed next to the European international expositions, a number of the national failings that had become apparent in the brief history of American international exposition performances to date came to light. Style was a significant problem with most of the 249 buildings, many of which *still* looked a lot like the original Crystal Palace in London. The consensus was that the complex of buildings was architecturally unimaginative. The immense, 1,880-foot-long Main Building was described as excessively droll. The exception to the drudgery was Memorial Hall, where the art exhibits were housed. The fair was half over before the flowers, plants, and grass arrived. The inevitable shanties rose up along Elm Avenue outside the main fairgrounds—an unfortunate stretch of commercialism known as "Centennial City."

The Centennial was also one of the more somber world's fairs, taking place in the era of reconstruction and after the economic collapse of 1873. The press attempted to emphasize the orderliness of the crowds at the decorous opening ceremonies, but one contemporary noted that Turks, Egyptians, Spaniards, Japanese, and Chinese "were followed by large crowds of idle boys and men, who hooted and shouted at them as if they had been animals of a strange species." The Philadelphia Centennial also lost nearly two million dollars, all of which the government insisted be paid by the mostly local stockholders.[15]

Still, viewed within an exclusively American context, it is possible to paint the Centennial as a cultural success. It was in many respects a historical leap forward for a nation still younger in 1876 than it might seem from a contemporary perspective. The fair began in dramatic fashion on May 10. President Ulysses S. Grant, along with the popular Brazilian emperor Dom Pedro, who was brought in to shift some attention away from the beleaguered president, turned a wheel to start the seven-hundred-ton Corliss steam engine designed by George Corliss. The world's most powerful machine to date provided energy for the whole of Machinery Hall and staked a claim for the United States as an emerging international industrial power. The Corliss engine ran in silence, with its boiler set away in a separate building, and was the fair's most popular exhibit. The expression of raw power fired the imagination, stimulated national pride, and became a central entertainment, though it had not been conceived as such. Walt Whitman sat for half an hour in silence in front of the "great, great engine."[16]

There were other aspects of the fair that lent prestige to the Centennial and helped put the country on the international map. Throughout the event, the Centennial's administration gained a solid reputation as a just and dignified body, thus restoring some lost national confidence after the scandals endured by the Grant administration. Presidential candidates Rutherford B. Hayes and Samuel J. Tilden spoke before large crowds on the fairgrounds. The classifications and subclassifications within the exposition's eight categories developed by William Phipps Blake were so well conceived that they were adapted by Melvil Dewey to revolutionize the organization of books in public libraries in the form of the Dewey decimal system. The most famous living composer, Richard Wagner, had been handsomely commissioned to write a Centennial march for the opening ceremony, lending some international prestige to the event. Unfortunately, the composition itself was panned, prompting Wagner to admit, "The best thing about it was the money." The art exhibit was on a serious scale and boasted many international contributions. The forearm, hand, and torch of the eventual Statue of Liberty, created by the French sculptor Frédéric Bartholdi, stood next to Machinery Hall. Foreign trade received a definite boost as well. If the United States stood on shaky international legs at the Philadelphia Centennial, there could be no doubt that it was indeed standing and would soon be off and running.[17]

Especially noteworthy within the American exposition context was the dramatic debut of American women, whose formidable organization resulted in a separate Woman's Pavilion at the Philadelphia Centennial. European events had set no precedent whatsoever for the highly visible presence of women at the Centennial. At London's Great Exhibition, for example, women were represented almost exclusively by a series of articles in the *Illustrated London News*. The series was comprised of a female author's drifting reflections on classically feminine exhibition items such as clothing, styles of design, and gems. The Woman's Pavilion emerged at the Centennial when the demand for a separate women's section in the Main Building was deemed inappropriate. Commentary on the displays in the Woman's Pavilion hovered between acknowledgment and condescension, since so many of them were based on themes at that time affiliated exclusively with women. Nonetheless, the unique status of women at the Centennial opened a new chapter within the history of international expositions.[18]

In the international context of expositions, what became clear at America's first significant event was that unlike Britain and France, which boasted colonies abroad and presented them in a calculated manner at their expositions, the United States was living in its colonies.  Paul A. Tenkotte has drawn attention to the manner in which "cultures," as distinct conceptualized entities, became identified with geographical regions at early international expositions in the attempt to develop comprehensive intercultural taxonomies. This phenomenon underscores the complexity with which American fairs were imbued since various cultural representatives from disparate geographical regions had come to inhabit a single geographical locus called the United States. Hence, American events displayed indigenous peoples much as the European powers displayed their colonies. The events were intercultural without necessarily having to involve peoples with different geographical orientations.[19]

Native American cultures, imagined as a unified cultural entity, were set up in displays in the U.S. Government Building primarily through the offices of the Smithsonian. The attempt to promote the assimilation of Indians into Euro-American civilization was full of ambiguity at the Philadelphia Centennial. Part of the display focused on an archaic Native American past and part on the place of the Indian in the future. The level of concern about the "Indian problem" was reflected clearly in the fact that nearly half of the massive Government Building, which was centered on the theme of "A Century of Progress," was devoted to displays of various Native American cultures.

The attempt to incorporate Indians into Euro-American society was an obligatory theme at an event attempting to unify the nation. As Frederick E. Hoxie put it, "It seemed that a nation devoted to progress could promise nothing less." Ironically, in the context of the Centennial, at a point when it had become clear that the "Indian problem" was no longer a serious long-term threat, General George Custer made his last stand at Little Big Horn in the hills of South Dakota during the Centennial's run. Occurring as it did during an event that called for national reflection, Little Big Horn renewed the dying legacy of the uncontrollable "savage" Indian and would be manipulated to justify later, lopsided conquests.[20]

There can be little doubt that as the numbers of the many "savages" to be found across the world by Western explorers declined throughout the nineteenth century, scientific interest in them grew exponentially. This dynamic was especially evident during the period between the first two international expositions held in the United States. While Native Americans were generally deplored, their now certain subordination allowed for them to be imagined more safely within Euro-American ideological constructions. This tension between the "dangerous Indian" and the "fascinating Indian" was fully apparent in the organizing of the Native American displays at the Centennial. On the one hand, the Indian problem appeared so well under control that consideration was given whether to create actual displays of living Indians as veritable museum pieces. This did not happen, but only because of the lack of a government appropriation. On the other hand, the Bureau of Indian Affairs was so concerned about potential Indian problems at the event that it expressed hesitancy even to allow Native Americans to journey to the Centennial as visitors for fear of an uprising. Was the Native American a museum piece representing a vanishing era of ancient history, or a "savage" whose full destructive potential was still an unknown quantity? In the context of the Philadelphia Centennial, the answer was clearly the former, but Euro-American fears in the United States were deeply ingrained, and caution proved preferable to overconfidence.[21]

The concept of race was so foundational in the United States, with its conjuncture of widely varying ethnic peoples from northern and southern Europe, Africa, Asia, and the Americas, that even the displays of Western societies in the Main Building were meticulously divided along racial lines. The exhibits of the Latin races (France and colonies), Anglo-Saxon races (England and colonies), and Teutonic races (Germany, Austria, and Hungary) were each arranged separately. The ethnicities left out of the fair's categorical equations were those emanating from Africa, both in their American as well as their African forms. Similar to their position at London's Great Exhibition, African societies were represented to a much greater extent by raw materials than by material culture.[22]

African Americans were excluded from nearly every aspect of the fair. The problems presented by this "race" were entirely different from the problems posed by Native Americans. There was no indication whatsoever that African Americans were on the decline in the

America of 1876. Indeed, African America was clearly destined to grow and become a force, and the contemplation of that inevitability fell entirely outside the scope of white ideological projections about progress and a rose-colored future. The main representation of blacks at the fair took place in a concession called "The South," or the "Southern Restaurant," which was run by a white businessman from Atlanta. Jovial blacks were commissioned to act the part of the happy and capricious Negro, engaged in acts of conjure and strumming banjos. In the context of Philadelphia's Centennial, there was only one realistic solution to the African American problem: ignore it as completely as possible. At the Chicago exposition seventeen years later, black involvement could scarcely be seen to have advanced beyond this point at all.[23]

Religion at the Philadelphia Centennial was still decidedly pre-evolutionary and traditionally biblical. The very same year as the Centennial, in fact, the National Reform Association gathered thirty-five thousand signatures in an attempt to propose to Congress a Constitutional amendment that would officially declare the United States a Christian nation. The interregnum of the Civil War resulted in evolutionary thought getting off to a late start in the United States; religion was only beginning to be separated from culture in general and to proliferate into the many new forms that would appear by the end of the century. The idea of religion as something that could be effectively isolated from within numerous cultures at once and engaged in a highly nuanced process of comparison had gained a small foothold in the intellectual history of the period, but scarcely at all within religious circles or as a matter of popular culture. James Freeman Clarke's *Ten World Religions*, published in 1871, sold well to an intellectual elite, but the embrace of evolutionary thought within the pulpit, which began to occur throughout the 1880s, was still in its embryonic stages. As such, social evolutionism and the notion of a global hierarchy of cultures that would follow on its heels were still relatively remote to the American public in 1876. What would become a definitive field of comparative religion in the decades to come in the United States was confined to the process of comparative culture at the Centennial, with the Native American displays and the arrangement of European cultures by "race" providing an anthropological basis out of which religious comparison could emerge.[24]

If the Philadelphia Centennial was still predominantly pre-evolutionary and comparative-minded only in the most obvious of ways, it nevertheless must be viewed as a significant event in stimulating intercultural awareness in the United States and advancing the idea of religion as a culturally relative phenomenon. More than any prior international exposition, the Centennial paved the way for the popular embrace of various conceptions of social and religious evolutionism, with its deterministic categorization of cultures along racial lines coupled with the fact that it was broadly international.

The Centennial also included extensive religious gatherings. Baptists and Presbyterians held national meetings at the Centennial, along with numerous other groups with some degree of religious affiliation, such as temperance organizations.[25] The American Bible Society began a long series of Bible displays at the Centennial, and keeping in line with the commercial inclinations of American expositions, the Centennial marked the first international exposition at which Bibles were actually sold for profit. Over a hundred intellectual congresses convened at the Centennial, many of them international in composition. The next step would be the merging of the theme of internationalism and the ambitious gathering of religious bodies, both of which were becoming pronounced features of international expositions.[26]

By the time of the Chicago exposition in 1893, the notion of the relativity of religion—a combined result of the irresistible attraction of evolutionary thought and an increasing intercultural awareness—would begin to initiate a sea change in the relationship of religion to culture within Western society as a whole. These themes were made manifest only nominally at the Philadelphia Centennial, but the extreme emphasis on racial demarcations at the event promoted their increasing visibility in the years to come. With the gradual triumph of an evolutionary way of thinking in the United States, cultures would be located more clearly and with greater theoretical precision within schematics designed to account for all human culture. Once this occurred, it was but a small step to classifying "religions," as hypothetical essences of those cultures, through the use of comparable theoretical models.

## Columbus Has an Anniversary in America

The impending anniversary of the arrival of Christopher Columbus at a Caribbean island some four hundred years earlier proved to be just the occasion for hatching plans for the most ambitious international exposition to date. What would come to be called the "World's Columbian Exposition" developed as a tripartite structure, with each of its three elements making unique contributions to the whole of

the event. In the central and normative position was what was known
as "White City," a series of immense white buildings constructed
out of a perishable material that were set along the southwest shore
of Lake Michigan adjacent to the University of Chicago, which had
opened just the year before. The main buildings of White City consisted of several pavilions erected by foreign nations, a United States
Government Building, a Manufactures Building, a Woman's Building, and several buildings devoted to various areas of commerce, the
arts, and science. For buildings not meant to last, these were built on
a preposterous scale. The Manufactures and Liberal Arts Building was
the largest enclosed structure constructed to date. At a half-mile long,
it would have taken perhaps thirty minutes simply to walk around
the outside of it. The central part of White City was constructed
around a water basin that was connected to Lake Michigan and held
a gaudy statue of Columbus aboard a ship, as if discovering America.²⁷

Extending west, and set apart distinctly from White City by a dividing rail-bridge beneath which visitors had to walk in order to move
between these two areas, was the "Midway Plaisance." The term "mid-
way" originated at the Chicago exposition. The difference between
the Midway Plaisance and White City was pronounced and created a
more distinctly dichotomous hierarchical arrangement of the world's
cultures than had been apparent at earlier events. Inside White City
were the aesthetically pleasing and often costly buildings devoted to
various branches of industry as well as the foreign pavilions that
served as operating headquarters for the fair's "civilized" foreign
nations. The midway, on the other hand, was a chaotic assembly of
commercialized cultural exhibits comprised of a disparate array of
amusements, both human and inanimate. Everything from the 250-
foot-high Ferris wheel designed by George Ferris himself—which
cost a stunning $350,000 to construct—to what were known as "ethnic villages," peopled by natives from less-industrialized foreign cultures, could be found along the midway.

The third component of the Columbian Exposition was the massive
Congress Auxiliary, which had been conceived in 1889 by Chicago
lawyer and Swedenborgian Charles C. Bonney. The Congress Auxiliary
was envisaged as a part of the fair that would rise above the event's
commercialism by bringing together learned persons from across the
world and allowing them to engage in constructive international discussions. The Congress Auxiliary's meetings covered a vast range of
subjects. The most pronounced themes related to the hard sciences
(including medicine), the rapidly emerging human sciences, women's
issues, and finally religion. The World's Parliament of Religions was

conceived as the crowning event of the whole of the Congress Auxiliary. A meeting among the world's religions was seen as being capable of producing a grand synthesis of what was most essential about human culture as a whole. The congresses met some eight miles north of the chaos of the fair at the Art Institute in downtown Chicago. The Art Institute was a permanent building and had been constructed for the specific purpose of hosting the Congress Auxiliary.

All international expositions were concerned to varying degrees with offering quality educational exhibits. These amounted to acts of philanthropy designed to offset an exposition's predominant focus on commerce. At the Columbian Exposition, planners advanced this theme in two predominant ways, and in no particular order: first, through the Congress Auxiliary, with its serious-minded discussions of the arts, sciences, and human problems; and second, by the Department of Ethnology and Archaeology, which set up extensive displays of peoples native to the Americas as part of an attempt to illustrate their countries' history since the arrival of Columbus. Both of these educational features received considerable governmental appropriations to carry out their respective tasks, and they were united by this common theme.[28] The Anthropology Building, which housed the exhibits of the Department of Ethnology and Archaeology, cost $125,000 alone, while the Art Institute cost $200,000, with another $80,000 being set aside for the organization of the congresses. In being set apart geographically from the general fair, some have interpreted the location of the Congress Auxiliary symbolically as indicating a desire on the part of organizers to create some distance between its altruistic aims and the unbridled secularism of the main fair.

Given the peripheral status of the Congress Auxiliary, the Department of Ethnology and Archaeology, known as "Department M," became the principal focus of the fair's educational theme within the exposition grounds. What was important about Department M in a religious sense was that it was the only serious forum within the fair that represented peoples who fell into the exposition's category of the "primitive." With negligible representation throughout the Congress Auxiliary, the way in which Department M represented cultures it deemed "primitive" would emerge as the primary means through which fair visitors and analysts would be able to consider the religious inclinations of those peoples.

Since the fair was a celebration of the arrival of Columbus in the Americas, those who were concerned with the fair's educational function argued that it only made sense to develop displays designed to demonstrate all that Columbus's arrival had meant to the continent. Clearly, such displays would have to be overseen by America's fledgling anthropological discipline, the only body with adequate expertise and resources to create a display of four hundred years of material culture in the Americas. The task of organizing a display of Columbian consequences was handed to Frederic Ward Putnam, curator of Harvard's Peabody Museum in Cambridge. The task was immense and indeed proved too big for Putnam to handle. The eventual result was that anthropological exhibits became divided between the educational Department M and the commercially driven Midway Plaisance. This division ended up having unfortunate results for the theme of serious education at the fair. Exhibits of actual peoples that were originally conceived with similar educational themes in mind came to be alternately presented either just outside the serious-minded Anthropology Building inside White City or in a carnival atmosphere along the midway.[29]

It was Putnam who first suggested that the fair incorporate an educational theme centered on the ethnology of the Americas. His article in the *Chicago Tribune* on May 31, 1890, read, "American Ethnology; an interesting suggestion for the Columbian Exposition. Why not a collection of habitations of dwellers in the three Americas from primitive savages up to the present time? This would give the best possible accounting of the continents reclaimed." The imperialism and evolutionary theme of Putnam's plan were predictable enough as 1893 intercultural conceptions, but what is more interesting is the programmatic nature of Putnam's vision—its level of ambition and naive confidence in imagining the possibility of a complete material representation of the entire history of the "three" Americas.[30]

There is perhaps no better example of the lengths to which Department M was willing to go in its quest to provide "education" at the fair than the early preparatory tasks it set out for its phrenology section. Professor Frederick Starr, who had just been appointed to the department of anthropology at the University of Chicago, recalled that the phrenology section was told that to carry out its duties some "20,000 Indians must be measured" by the beginning of the fair.  Starr went on to recount some of the many difficulties in carrying out the measurements on some Cherokee in North Carolina: "In order to accomplish our work it was necessary to hunt for the people. Our outfit consisted of a pair of sharp-pointed steel calipers and a sliding compass. Some of the measurements were not pleasant to the subject; to have the head firmly gripped with the points of the calipers, or to have the sharp tips of the slide compass placed one above the roof of the nose and the other below the point of the chin was not delightful." Clearly, Department M was taking in earnest the task of "educating" fair visitors about the history of the three Americas.³¹

Putnam went on to argue for the importance of encompassing anthropological displays by noting the interest aroused by similar exhibits at the 1889 exposition in Paris. The argument for an anthropological display as the fair's educational offering was more beside the point than to it: data on "primitive" cultures, it was argued, had to be gathered quickly because it was fast disappearing. Of course, this did not speak to the specific meanings of the displays themselves or to the plight of those being represented.

The educational value of vast exhibits of Native American material culture was very much a matter of dispute, in fact, with many complaining that only specialists could really appreciate it. Later on during the fair, the *Chicago Sunday Herald* would write: "Be it known in the first place that the Anthropological building is the most serious place on the face of the earth. Before you study anthropology you must have learned all about history, physiology, geology, zoology, and all the other topics ending in *y*. Your hair must grow long and your tongue must caress with the familiarity of an old love words of fifteen syllables. You must know at a glance the touching history of a piece of flint, and you must become familiar with the tales expressed by a long buried image." The *Chicago Tribune* also gave a vote of no confidence to the proposal early on by observing, "For such a proposition as this the directors have not a dollar which they can spare. If the archaeological enthusiasts think the public has a wild, yearning desire to see skeletons from the glacial gravels or detritus from the cave floors and shell heaps, let them spend their own money." Nonetheless, the plan went forward with a sizable budget.³²

The other division of Department M had originally been planned as a display of the world's cultures to extend along the Midway Plaisance —conceived as a more ambitious reprise of the ethnic villages found at the Paris exposition of 1889. As planning for the fair progressed, Department M lost control altogether of the displays along the midway, and commercially based exhibits of foreign peoples would come to coexist with the more official anthropological displays in White City. As early as January of 1892, about a year and a half before the fair was set to open, the midway became the focus for concerns about the financial viability of the exposition. It was well known by this time that the commercial potential of international expositions was to be found in their carnival sections. With Putnam overwhelmed by his duties of organizing the displays inside White City, the fair's architect—the well-known Daniel H. Burnham of Chicago—

placed a twenty-three-year-old man named Sol Bloom in charge of the entire midway, including the exhibits that were supposed to be educational.

Bloom had made a name in San Francisco in the entertainment business and was known for being able to produce profitable shows. He recalled that when he arrived on the scene, the midway was in chaos and appeared as if no one was in charge of it. He began his project almost from the ground up to make the midway the greatest entertainment spectacle ever seen. Unfortunately, his efforts would cause the elements of commercial entertainment and educational anthropology to clash markedly along the midway. Much has been written about the Columbian Exposition's midway as representing a great hierarchy of cultures constructed along evolutionary lines by anthropologists, but in the end, the structure of the midway was not scientifically minded. Bloom had been a promoter at the Paris exposition of 1889 and wrote of perceiving a hierarchy of cultures there, but Bloom's hierarchy was based on entertainment value rather than on an anthropological assessment of "races." If the "lower races," based on contemporary presumptions, were placed at the end of the midway farthest from White City, the more plausible reason was that Bloom believed the commercial viability of their concessions warranted a less advantageous position farther away from White City.

In its commercial appropriation of numerous foreign cultures, the midway would bring great dismay to people involved in the exposition project at numerous levels. The fair's educational displays inside White City were never able to be clearly demarcated from some of the embarrassing, commercially based cultural spectacles along the midway. As a result, peoples who fell into the category of the "primitive" within the fair's structure became largely affiliated with the circus of the midway and were thus perceived as freaks. This practice of representing cultures considered "primitive" primarily along exposition midways and not in the main fairgrounds certainly contributed to their being viewed as generally unworthy of participating in the more serious discussions at the events' intellectual congresses.

## *White City Culture*

Within the main fairgrounds at the Columbian Exposition, many of the traditional exposition exhibits and much of the commentary about the more overt aspects of the event that had been novel and significant at London's Great Exhibition had become tired and predictable. Chief among these was the element of competition between Western nations. The foreign presence at international expositions was more of a formality or obligation than it was a source of compelling interest by 1893, save for isolated exhibits. Foreign "pavilions" were generally large houses, constructed in some representative cultural style, the function of which was as much to serve as an operating headquarters for the country's commissioners as to be a genuine exhibit. The competitive aspect of expositions had come to take place as a competition between entire events more than within particular categories of displays.

Adding to the lack of international drama was the fact that Britain and France had taken to downplaying the display of their colonial interests at foreign international expositions, even though colonial displays were centerpieces of expositions in their own countries.[33] It was thought best to let colonies display themselves on neutral territory to whatever extent they wished. Similarly, the work of the juries assigned to give out awards, while still fully capable of stirring hostilities, was greatly diminished in its intellectual significance from earlier expositions. The patient assessment and chronicling of commodities accomplished by earlier juries had been superseded by the burgeoning phenomenon of the expositions' intellectual congresses. The latter had become a traditional feature of international expositions and was taken to a new height at Chicago.

Particularly noteworthy at Chicago's fair was the number of displays featuring peoples thought of as "primitive" or "exotic," which had begun in earnest in Paris in 1889. These displays appeared inside White City and along the midway, with decidedly different consequences facing the cultures represented in each locale. The most notable cultures represented inside White City that would have been considered genuinely "exotic" in 1893 were India and Japan. Representatives from these regions were also the same ones who would  enjoy the greatest degree of prestige among foreign participants at the World's Parliament of Religions at the end of the fair.

India was technically a colony of Britain and thus not a "nation" proper, but its sense of independence had grown considerably since London's Great Exhibition of 1851, especially in the sphere of private commerce. East Indians were in an advantageous position primarily because their displays had a number of attendants at them who spoke impeccable English. The lengthy British occupation of their country had made India the non-Western country most cognizant of Western culture and the ways in which it differed from its own. India was an old hand at international expositions, having been originally put on display by the East India Company at London's Great Exhibition.

EXHIBITIONISM, AMERICAN STYLE 105

Figure 3. The East Indian Palace inside White City. This building enhanced Indian credibility throughout the fair and at the World's Parliament of Religions. (Courtesy Chicago Historical Society, ICHi-23586; photograph by Harrison, courtesy of Harrison)

Merchants from India knew the value of the expositions as venues for advancing commercial aspirations. As a result, India had a credible pavilion inside White City financed by private interests and modeled roughly after the Taj Mahal. Inside, there were ornamental tearooms, which were one of the more popular exhibits inside White City. The hosts at the Indian concessions took great pride in lecturing visitors on the facts of their country and their religion, as well as on Western misconceptions of them, and they did so in a paternal British accent that captured the attention of visitors. With so little known about the people of India, the Indian displays and English explanations impressed fair visitors and drew generally favorable press.[34]

It was Japan, however, that cemented Asian credibility inside White City. Japan, too, had taken an interest in Western international expositions, most notably at the Vienna exposition of 1873, from which its commissioners produced a staggering ninety-six-volume report of the proceedings.[35] The Japanese made a grand gesture at the Chicago fair, erecting the three buildings of the beautiful Ho-o-den Palace at a cost of one million dollars and offering ahead of time to donate the palace to the city of Chicago at the end of the fair.

A prestigious site was accorded the Japanese, appropriately located on a wooded island just behind the center of the main fairgrounds. Tucked away in a place of respite from the chaos of the fair, the building allowed visitors to marvel at the subtlety of both Japanese painting and interior decorating brilliance. Because of its calculated design, a bonsai garden outside appeared to be more extensive than it actually was. The Japanese handed out more pamphlets than any other foreign country; these too were tasteful and elegant. The pamphlets described Japanese history, culture, and most importantly, the booming commercial industries in Japan, which were most definitely open for business. The entirety of the Japanese approach to the fair was eminently cautious, understated, and concisely executed. This covert approach to commercial enterprise could not have been less American. The collective image presented by Japan was not that of a competitor challenging a much too powerful American opponent; rather, it was a lesson in understatement that piqued the American

Figure 4. Japan's million-dollar Ho-o-den Palace. The palace stood in stark contrast to its architectural surroundings and cast the emerging nation in a favorable light. (Courtesy Chicago Historical Society, ICHi-31718; photograph by Glessner, courtesy of Glessner)

curiosity and led viewers to wonder if they might not have forgotten something important within the total picture of what human culture might be.[36]

While the colony of India and the nation of Japan were conspicuous presences inside White City, the absence or inadequate representation of other groups that fell into the general, if ill-defined, category of the "primitive" was glaring. Through a scheduling quirk, one group that would have been considered by general consensus to be "primitive" was actually located inside of White City instead of along the midway. This was the village of Inuits, called "Eskimos" in the press, who were brought to the fair a year early so that they could become slowly acclimated to the Chicago environment. The village encountered numerous problems from sickness to fights with the village promoter, who apparently reneged on several promises made to the group. The disputes drew considerable press in the days before the fair, since the Inuits were the only foreigners on the exposition grounds early on.[37]

The Inuits were an excellent example of how much "life" really occurred for some of the villagers at the fair who, after all, were brought in to live "as usual" for the lengthy six-month period. After the fair opened, a young boy named Degoulick drowned in a pond near the Inuit camp. In an article entitled "Weird Funeral Rite," Chicago's *Daily Inter-Ocean* reported: "Several hundred persons paid the necessary admission fee in order to witness an Eskimo funeral service. Curiosity was stretched to the highest tension when it was learned that the boy who met untimely death was an avowed heathen. Following in a grotesque procession came the entire village population. Tears ran down the faces of the foster parents of the boy. Reverend Mr. Atchison offered a simple but earnest prayer. The rest at once resumed their games for the entertainment of visitors in the village." The Inuits were one of the many "ethnic villages" that did not really have much of an entertainment act, save for a few relatively simplistic dances and songs. Their "act" was the simple reality of their lives, a fact that sometimes had unfortunate consequences, as the one described in the passage above.[38]

The exposition's cultural category of "primitive" had the most unfortunate effects on the American domestic groups who fell into it: Native Americans and African Americans. Blacks had been systematically excluded from nearly every aspect of the Chicago fair through a series of maneuvers that never required the omission to be acknowledged directly. They were barred from all phases of the fair's planning as well as from its more gainful forms of employment. The few blacks who were hired performed menial labor of the lowest order. Fannie Barrier Williams, who would later speak at the World's Parliament of Religions, held the only black clerical position within the whole massive enterprise of the fair, and even that position was eventually eliminated due to "lack of funding." Out of hundreds of commissioners appointed to the exposition commission from the separate states, there was only one black appointed—St. Louis school principal Hale G. Parker—and this was only as an alternate and after much complaining. The situation was the same as it had been at the Philadelphia Centennial seventeen years before, indicating the near absence of progress in the incorporation of blacks into the general fabric of American society during this period.

The black community was sharply divided about how to answer to the collective snub by the fair's commissioners. The central issue was whether to argue for the right to have separate black displays, or to go through the appropriate channels to submit separate black exhibits that would be incorporated with white exhibits in their respective categories. Black alternate commissioner Hale Parker called the idea of separate black exhibits "both offensive and defensive." Nevertheless, requests for separate black exhibits were eventually denied, and the submission of exhibits by individual blacks to the separate state commissions brought little acceptance and negligible black representation throughout the fair.[39]

The main meeting ground for blacks at the fair was at the restaurant inside the Haitian pavilion. Haiti and Liberia were the only countries with significant black populations to host pavilions inside White City. Haiti had appointed Frederick Douglass, the best-known black spokesperson in the United States, to its organizing committee. It was from here that a protest pamphlet was distributed by the famous antilynching crusader Ida B. Wells, who was originally from Memphis, where she had been driven out of town. Some one hundred thousand copies of "The Reason Why: The Colored American Is Not in the World's Columbian Exposition," which included a lengthy introduction by Douglass, were handed out to fair visitors. The pamphlet provided historical background on the plight of blacks in the United States and offered racial explanations for their lack of visibility at the fair.

Apart from the fair's Haitian pavilion, the black presence was minimal. Two blacks dressed as slaves sold cotton for the Brinker Cotton Company inside the Manufactures and Liberal Arts Building, but such representation was unfortunate to say the least. On a more positive note, trumpeter Herbert Clarke and trombonist Arthur Pryor played for John Philip Sousa's band along the midway. The most noted black exhibit was an oil painting by George Washington Carver called "Yucca Glorioso"; the painting was from the State of Iowa collection in the Palace of Fine Arts and won an Honorable Mention award.[40]

A major controversy arose among African Americans when it was announced during the course of the fair that there would be a "Colored Jubilee Day" on August 25. Special "Days" devoted to particular nationalities were primarily designed to boost fair attendance, and with the lack of respect shown to blacks throughout the fair, many felt it to be wholly inappropriate that blacks support the fair as visitors. Wells and Douglass split over the issue, with Wells refusing to participate and Douglass seeing it as a concession by fair organizers that could be utilized. Despite the dubious context, the events of the day added up to a significant moment in recorded African American history, which had been negligible to that point. The guest of honor was Harriet Beecher Stowe's sister, Isabella Beecher Hooker, who recited poetry. The rising young poet Paul Laurence Dunbar also recited his poem "The Colored American." Musical selections performed by concert singers Harry T. Burleigh and Madame Delseria Plato were well received. The quality of the overall program was debated, but the music, by most accounts, was a "glittering success."[41]

That evening an estimated three thousand people packed Festival Hall to see a reluctant Frederick Douglass speak. This was to be the last significant public appearance by the seventy-six-year-old Douglass, who would die in 1895. Douglass mainly spoke about the injustices of racism and drew repeated applause from the audience. The peak of the talk came toward the end when Douglass turned to address some white hecklers in the crowd. "There is no negro problem," the aged Douglass told the youths sternly. "We negroes love our country. We fought for it. The only problem is whether American people have loyalty enough, and patriotism enough to live up to their own constitution." Douglass returned to his seat amidst a stone silence that soon erupted into thunderous applause.[42]

The various Native American groups represented at the fair probably stood in the most complex relation to it. Viewing the event as a commercial opportunity like everyone else, a number of indigenous peoples agreed to be set up in mock villages inside White City near the Anthropology Building. The status of Native Americans inside White City was perfectly mirrored by the fact that while other social groups constructed their own displays, Native American cultures were displayed by American anthropologists.

Native Americans were the principal set of ethnic groups utilized to legitimate the evolutionary hierarchy of cultures that dominated all aspects of the fair. The *Daily Inter-Ocean* ran a cartoon of the fair's opening that showed several Native American figures in headdress looking over a wall at the fair, with the caption, "The past looks upon the present." The *Chicago Tribune* described a group of Indians looking down at the opening ceremonies from the rotunda of the Administration Building and giving an aggressive battle cry as it began. This was followed by a report of a scene in which a Major Burke of Buffalo Bill Cody's "Wild West Show" elicited another war cry from his hired hands, causing "gayly-uniformed diplomats [of foreign countries] to shrink to the protection of the big pillars" of the administration building's courtyard. The Indians were then said to have been "drawn up in a saluting line" to meet President Grover Cleveland, who "came out and bowed to them."⁴³

This studied representation of vanishing indigenous peoples obviously contained the covert implication that it was necessary to subdue them given their inherent propensity for violence. Any outbreak of violence among Native Americans—which was inevitable in a chaotic, six-month-long fair incorporating several cultural groups—received sensationalized treatment in the press, who missed few chances to denigrate Native Americans. The arrival of sixty-one Winnebago, Potawatomi, and Sioux—purportedly descendants of the original inhabitants of the Chicago area prior to European influence—to staff a concession on the midway was greeted by the headline "Return As Freaks." There was always the odd exception, however. One article, which allowed an Apache chief lengthy space to speak for the plight of native peoples, made clear that the handsome and articulate gentleman had caught the female writer's fancy as a rare example of nobility among "savages." One of the great lessons of the fair was that the large number of separate encounters between individual personages caused the theme of the "noble savage" to appear as a permanent feature of those interactions. When interactions became personal, they took on a very different hue.⁴⁴

The central issue involving the Native American presence at the Chicago fair was how they would be represented. Should indigenous peoples serve as authentic anthropological specimens in displays portraying their cultures as they most probably existed prior to the arrival of Columbus? Or were they to be exhibited in their capacity to adapt to white culture and as peoples on their way to becoming productive citizens? The answer was predominantly the former, though there was an Indian school located in White City—the Carlisle Indian

School, run by Richard Henry Pratt. Pratt organized groups of Native American schoolchildren to be brought in to attend the school for a couple of weeks at a time. Photographs show schoolchildren in neat uniforms standing before the school with Pratt in front of them. These images contrasted sharply with the pictures of encampments of various tribes in front of the Anthropology Building—so much so that Pratt, a staunch defender of the Indians, had the school moved a goodly distance away from the encampments to the east gallery of the Manufactures and Liberal Arts Building.

Exhibits of actual Indian groups designed to reflect pre-Columbian Native American life were set up in a series of encampments outside the Anthropology Building. Reports vary somewhat regarding precisely which groups were on display there. One of the more reliable chroniclers of anthropological data, Frederick Starr, lists Arawak of British Guiana, Iroquois from each of the Six Nations, Penobscot from Maine, Algonkin, and the central focus of the indigenous groups—fourteen Kwakiutl from British Columbia. The Kwakiutl had been recruited specifically under the direction of F. W. Putnam, and they performed rituals and dances that were studied by Franz Boas, who had been handpicked by Putnam to head the Ethnology section of Department M.

Interpretation was a significant problem in analyzing the Kwakiutl rituals. One dance, dubbed the "torture dance" in dramatized press reports of the activity, appeared to involve an enactment of ritual violence in which members of the group apparently beat each other on the head with clubs until blood was visible. In fact, the clubs were made of sea kelp and were filled with red paint. Ira Jacknis has observed that for the Kwakiutl the line between religious ritual and theatrical performance was not sharply drawn at the end of the nineteenth century. Reenacting rituals in the context of the fair involved the creation of new rituals and caused a transformation of existing ones. The fluidity in the Kwakiutl's internal understanding of the ritual events combined with the relativizing influence of the exposition makes religious interpretations of their activities difficult if not impossible.[45]

There can be little doubt that the Kwakiutl themselves agreed to engage in the enterprise partly as a commercial venture, but it was not the best of business investments. While midway organizer Sol Bloom made a remarkable one thousand dollars per week for his services, the fourteen Kwakiutl were paid just twenty dollars per week—collectively—for living at the fair for six months. After some debate, the Kwakiutl were finally allowed to sell native crafts from their village, but only half of the nominal proceeds went to them, while one-fourth went to George Hunt, the village promoter, and one-fourth to Department M. In the end, there was considerable haggling about whether the Kwakiutl's twenty-dollar-per-week fee included their transportation home.

Given the status of African Americans and Native Americans throughout the exposition, it can come as little surprise that they played virtually no part within the intellectual congresses that formed the other half of the educational aspirations of the fair. It would have been ludicrous for Native Americans especially to be set forth as museum pieces designed to educate fair visitors about the rapidly vanishing American past and then to be invited to take part in discussions within the intellectual congresses as ostensibly equal partners. With the structure of White City at the Columbian Exposition growing as it did out of the international exposition tradition, the possibility that African Americans and Native Americans would take part in such congresses in a manner similar to other non-Westerners was virtually nonexistent. The World's Parliament of Religions would reach beyond traditional boundaries and out to the rest of the religious world in the quest to host a global congress of religions, but in this case, its reach exceeded significantly its grasp. In excluding Native Americans from the event and inviting African Americans only as converted Christians, the religious images emerging from the fair of these domestic outsiders from within the United States had to be constructed almost exclusively on the basis of their presence across the exposition itself. Unfortunately, as minimal and inappropriate as the representation of Native Americans and African Americans was inside White City, their collective image would reach new depths along the fair's midway.

## *Midway Culture*

Midway culture at Chicago's fair was mostly just that: a hodgepodge of diverse cultures presented in a commercialized manner that was indicative of their "primitive" or semicivilized "midway" status in the developing Western vision of a hierarchy of world cultures. Following Robert W. Rydell's early portrayal, the midway has been repeatedly perceived as representing an evolution-minded "sliding scale of humanity." In reality, however, several cultures were out of place along the midway from what would have been the anthropological assessment of that scale in 1893—a fact indicating that the arrangement of cultures was primarily commercial and not anthropological as noted earlier. Still, even if the arrangement of cultures

# EXHIBITIONISM, AMERICAN STYLE

along the midway was chiefly commercial rather than anthropological, the result was largely synonymous with the reigning evolutionary conceptions of the day.

The more prestigious part of the midway began nearest to the main fairgrounds in White City. It then descended away about a mile from that point to where the peoples resided who were thought to be least desirable as carnival displays. The Western countries represented along the midway avoided making parodies of their present-day societies by erecting villages of bygone European eras. Two Irish concessions revolved around famous, ancient castles—the Blarney and the Donegal. The German village was based on a four-hundred-year-old era of German history, while the Austrian village represented a typical city from two hundred years earlier. Such exhibits diminished the chance that any direct connection would be made between the contemporary realities of those cultures and the more sham commercial exhibits of cultures deemed "primitive" located farther down the midway. In many cases, the midway concessions were quite elaborate commercial endeavors. The German village cost $267,000 to build and employed about four hundred people.[46]

After the historically based Western villages, the midway's hierarchy descended to the Asiatic and Islamic countries. While the major Asian nations of India and Japan forged their way onto the global stage inside White City, the Chinese had the most difficult time among the Asian principalities that would later be represented at the World's Parliament of Religions. There was no Chinese pavilion inside White City, because the Chinese government boycotted the event in protest of the series of Chinese exclusion acts beginning in 1882 that stifled Chinese immigration. The Chinese concession set up along the midway featured goods in a museum called Joss House that was primarily cluttered with religious objects. There was a theater, but the Chinese theatrical performances suffered from difficulties of artistic cultural translation. In particular, the Chinese music was aesthetically incomprehensible to the untrained Western ear.

The image of the Chinese at the fair was affected by the fact that of the three identifiable groups of Asian peoples to be represented at the World's Parliament of Religions they were the only one whose presence had already been felt within the United States. Over the prior few decades, Chinese workers had been immigrating to the United States at an increasing rate, until the new laws finally slowed the influx. They had been employed largely in the undesirable occupation of building railroads and did not enjoy a favorable reputation—a fate to which all newcomers to the American scene in the period were doomed. There was a Chinese "work display" that was as strange as all the rest. It consisted of a single room inside Joss House—supposedly structured like a typical middle-class Chinese domestic situation—with a woman and child in the room occupied with common tasks, there to be gawked at by visitors. The woman was one of few Chinese women in the United States in 1893 and drew considerable attention. On the whole, though, the image presented by the Chinese along the midway was filled with ambiguity. So little was known about the culture that the displays were hard to interpret meaningfully, and the country did not enjoy government backing that would have allowed for more appropriate and effective representation of the culture.

By contrast, the private Indian merchants who erected the Indian Pavilion inside White City had considerable experience with international expositions; hence, they were cautious to avoid projecting images of their country that might lead to false and unfortunate impressions. As an example, there was not a single official Indian display along the midway, where the commercial competition virtually demanded that cultures make unfortunate compromises. After the start of the fair, Hindu jugglers dazzled crowds at the Indian Pavilion with odd feats and magic tricks that had never been seen in the West. Before long they had set up a small booth on the midway. The activities of these fakirs were written off by some, but others took the shows seriously as possible examples of occultist manipulations of matter. Stories of Hindu magic from travelers and colonialists visiting India were beginning to be taken more and more seriously. As with all magic tricks, some of the feats of the Hindu magicians defied apparent explanation, but because they had originated in a foreign cultural context, judgments about such acts were suspended a little longer than would normally have been the case. The possibility of real magic being performed only added to the general Indian mystique throughout the fair.[47] The ability of the East Indians to avoid presenting an unfortunate national image along the midway would certainly help its representatives at the World's Parliament of Religions to be taken as seriously as they were.

The Japanese presented a conservative midway exhibit that was not a village and did not feature any entertainment. A bazaar dominated the exhibit and featured only Japanese national products. In fact, the closest thing to a Japanese entertainment concession was an exquisite teahouse set up by the Tea Merchants Guild across from the Ho-o-den Palace in White City. The Japanese did not exactly enhance their reputation with their midway performance, but they did no harm

Figure 5. "Hindoo" booth. The East Indians, cautious not to become caught up in the hoopla of the midway, were represented by only this small booth displaying "Hindoo" magic. (Courtesy Chicago Historical Society, ICHi-25102; photographer unknown)

to it either. As Japanese luck at the exposition would have it, the only Japanese performance at the fair was the "No" drama, staged in the much more elegant setting of the Art Institute, where the World's Parliament of Religions would later be held. As part of a program put on by the Congress of Folklore, "No, a Japanese ceremonial dance, with song" marked the first performance of this drama in the United States. The program was very well received, so much so that an encore performance was arranged at a private Chicago home a short time later. Similar to the East Indians, the Japanese speakers at the World's Parliament of Religions, buoyed by six months of generally positive press coverage about their culture's performance at the fair, managed to garner a great deal of respect for Japan as a legitimate modern nation with a venerable and ancient religious tradition.[48]

The most popular concession along the Midway Plaisance was probably the "Street in Cairo." This concession was a well-practiced act, having appeared in continually refined forms since the Paris exposition of 1867, where it featured Middle-Eastern waiters serving

Figure 6. The Islamic-based "Street in Cairo." "Cairo-Street" was the highest-quality non-Western concession on the midway and clearly differentiated Muslim-dominated countries from the peoples involved in the lesser midway exhibits in the eyes of analysts. (Courtesy Chicago Historical Society, ICHi-02431; photographer unknown)

espresso at a restaurant. What was especially attractive to the fair's visitors on the Street in Cairo in its Chicago incarnation was an evocative dance called the *Danse-du-ventre,* nicknamed the "belly-dance" by the press. The dance conjured up images of the "primitive" that drew male fairgoers like a magnet. Versions of the *Danse-du-ventre* were performed at various locales—including inside the Algerian village, which was promoted by the head of the midway, Sol Bloom. The dancers from the Middle East were perhaps the best example of the fact that some top-flight entertainment appeared along the midway. Experienced showman Bloom marveled at their "choreographic perfection" and exclaimed enthusiastically, "What artists they were!" The high quality of the Street in Cairo dictated that Islamic countries be taken with a seriousness not accorded other countries who appeared along the midway but had no headquarters inside White City. From the sheer quality of the entertainment and services they offered, it was clear that this was a formidable collectivity of peoples.[49]

What really drove the midway commercially were the many images of the "primitive" it offered, even though many of these had been located farther away from White City in less commercially attractive locations. These exhibits proved to be much more popular than was originally anticipated. For peoples who fell into this category especially, their work as human entertainment did not end inside their villages. Whenever they left their villages, the extent to which they were treated as objects became magnified; they were regularly followed around by small crowds as if still on display.

The bottom, most "primitive" part of the midway ladder was reserved for Native American groups and the Dahomeans from West Africa (who were actually the Fon people, though this was never noted in the contemporary literature). The Dahomeans were viewed as symbolically—and just as often, literally—representative of African Americans. Both fairgoers and the commentary of the time treated them with a degree of disdain that only the recently freed African American slaves could inspire. Native American groups encountered a largely similar fate. Numerous other cultural groups considered to be "primitive" and who had similar entertainment displays to the Native Americans and Dahomeans were placed in closer proximity to White City, even though there was no clear reason why they should be. African Americans themselves found no place along the midway; however, it is highly questionable that they would have participated even if they had been permitted to do so.[50]

The cultures that would have been considered "primitive" along the midway varied among themselves in the quality of entertainment in their villages. By far most well-off among these groups were the South Seas Islanders, mainly Javanese and Samoans, who were part of a concession called the Dutch Settlement. The Dutch Settlement was actually closer to White City than either the German or Austrian villages. The concessions were well run, the people were well treated, and apparently they were not altogether unhappy to be taking part in the festivities. The Samoans were especially revered for their placid countenances and physical beauty. They called to fairgoers' minds fantasies of the ultimate tropical vacation. The Javanese were tiny people, unthreatening and considered cute, like children. They performed clever pantomimes and puppet shows that amused audiences, even if they were not considered high art in the Western sense.

From there the quality of entertainment fell off sharply, and the people themselves—Laplanders from Scandinavia, Bedouins from the Middle East, Dahomeans from West Africa, and Native American groups—became the primary focus of the exhibits. The very structure

Figure 7. Victorian ladies admiring Samoan gentlemen. When members of the "ethnic villages" were not actually performing, they were gawked at by fairgoers. (Courtesy Chicago Historical Society, ICHi-25237; photographer unknown)

of this odd "entertainment" based on simple gawking did not bode well for those who were observed. After all, who would watch other Western people simply living as they would at home, occupied exclusively with mundane tasks? An element of the grotesque and savage was necessary to make these exhibits work, and that element was played up systematically. Two primary themes governed the fascination of visitors when encountering these cultures deemed the most "primitive" of primitives: rumors of their innate violence, and fantasies about the extent of their purported practice of cannibalism. In fact, the great myth of cannibalism grew to such epic proportions on the midway that signs had to be posted in front of several villages, including those of the peaceful Javanese and Samoans, asking fairgoers not to ask the natives about their practice of cannibalism as "it annoys them."[51]

Beyond the nominal entertainment these groups provided, their primary "act" was to engage in mock combat. Countless photos of the midway show one or another of these cultural groups holding spears above their heads as if readying for battle. An exception to this was the Laplanders, who had been a part of such Western cultural entertainment longer than any other group. The Laps brought nine reindeer with them and engaged in the activities of their homeland by incorporating the animals into their daily routine. The village also featured the legendary King Bull, who was rumored to have been 112 years old but was probably a weather-beaten 42. On occasion the ancient-looking patriarch would come to the gates of the village and implore fairgoers to enter the village, joining in the spirit of commerce like everyone else.[52]

Bedouins from Syria and Lebanon were also located at the end of the midway with the Native Americans and Dahomeans. Known as the "Wild East Show," the name of the Bedouin "camp" was conceived in contrast to Buffalo Bill Cody's "Wild West Show," which took place four blocks away from the official fairgrounds, having been refused a space along the midway because of the unfortunate light in which it cast Native Americans. Members of the Bedouin troupe enacted a mock attack on a desert caravan, among other things, but as a whole, the camp was not well kept and did not do well commercially. The Bedouins were held up as a "primitive" form of Islamic culture. This did not bode well for them, but the manner in which they were represented had the indirect advantage of allowing the other displays of Islamic culture at the fair to appear more sophisticated.[53]

The least fortunate of all of the cultural villages along the midway—and the ones that received the worst press—were the Native American encampments and the Dahomean display. There were three Native American villages on the midway by the end of the fair, although the Aztec village did not arrive until September and received little press. Halfway through the fair, a replica of Sitting Bull's cabin was transplanted from the Wild West Show and was occupied part-time by Chief Rain-in-the-Face, who was alleged to have been at the battle of Little Big Horn. One of the activities that took place in this village was a stereotypical attack on a settler's cabin, where visitors could see reenacted the frightening scene they had heard about—and had feared—all their lives. The third village was a disorganized encampment of various Native American groups, whose activities were sporadic and not particularly entertaining. Alcoholism was a significant problem in this camp, and its disorganization generally reflected the cultural decimation that the peoples inhabiting it had suffered during the prior centuries.

The village that drew the worst press by far was that of the Dahomeans. The sixty-nine persons inhabiting the village were popularly rumored to be the subjects of Behanzin, the king of the mythical land of Dahomey, which had been explored in the middle of the century by the famous English explorer Sir Richard Burton. In fact, the Dahomean villagers were from a French settlement in Benin, and a French flag flew above the village. The promoter of the village was Captain Zavier Peneé, who would show up at later American expositions as well. Peneé had exhibited a comparable camp at Paris in 1889 and was an old hand at the trade, but the village was still poorly run. The villagers were virtual slaves, receiving only their room and board, with their small share of the profits going to their settlement back home.[54]

Music performed in the village was generally derided, but on occasion it was given some degree of acknowledgment. The dances were uniformly cast as barbaric. The principal attraction of the village was its claim to house Amazon warriors—unique female warriors who were no doubt part fact and part fiction. Photos of the camp do not show any excessively unusual-looking women who might have filled the role, and this was corroborated by most observers. War dances and mock combats were the village's chief attraction. The ominous reputation of the female Dahomeans allowed the enactment of ritual violence to become a significant draw for the village. Despite the generally poor quality of the entertainment and bad promotion, the Dahomean village was so genuinely "exotic" in the eyes of fairgoers that it did quite well commercially, a fact that, as noted above, did not personally benefit the participating Fon whatsoever.[55]

The truly unfortunate development relating to the Dahomean village was that with African American representation in White City virtually nonexistent and no African American concessions appearing along the midway, the village became an irrevocable symbol for the cultural status of African peoples in general, including African Americans. When Frederick Douglass saw the village, he was incensed, claiming that the Dahomeans had been brought to the fair to "act the monkey." Press coverage of the midway made it abundantly clear that "primitives" with whom the West had had extensive interaction, such as Native Americans and African Americans, fell into an entirely different conceptual category than did the potentially "noble savages" from distant lands, whose lives had been embellished over the centuries by marvelous fictions.[56]

Given their negligible representation inside the main fairgrounds in White City or in the intellectual congresses, perceptions of, and judgments about, the more peripheral ethnic groups at the exposition had to be formed predominantly on the basis of their midway appearance. If the midway was all in fun, it nevertheless provided the fair's visitors and the press with enduring images representing a large part of the rest of the world. In the absence of being able to enthrall audiences with drama, dance, or music, many of the peoples deemed "primitive" had only one real function along the midway: to provide living examples of the lessons of social evolution and the unquestionable value of modern civilization. Amidst amusing entertainment like Carl Hagenbeck's animal shows and the "World's Congress of Beauties," the groups lacking a definitive entertainment act were assessed as they sat in a dusty space killing six months' time until they could return home. The acts of war they feigned to commit and the rumors of cannibalism that surrounded them served as recurring lessons about the dangers of "savagery."

Obviously, far less is known about how the peoples inhabiting the ethnic villages felt about the exposition experience than about how they were perceived by Western people. The fact that almost none of the villagers spoke or understood English made any extensive and meaningful interactions difficult and increased the extent to which they were objectified. Gertrude Scott's analysis indicates that there is little reason to believe that the villagers had any keen awareness that they were being denigrated to the extent they actually were, especially when the situation is viewed in retrospect.[57] Indeed, many of the same Native Americans showed up at subsequent fairs, though the precise reasons for this remain to be determined. Burton Benedict has noted that there were a variety of motivations for the villagers' participation in expositions, which cannot by generalized.[58] Such observations allow villagers to rightfully appear as more than the puppets of ruling-class organizers.

The religious existence of peoples deemed "primitive" at the fair was a virtual nonexistence in the eyes of Western analysts; fantasies about the extent of their savagery largely superseded any serious consideration of their religious inclinations. To the extent that such peoples represented at the far end of the midway were viewed as having religion, their religions were perceived as such obscure superstitions as to scarcely qualify as religion at all. Their ideological function was to reify the values of Western civilization rather than to take up places as genuine conversation partners about those values. The right of "exotic" peoples to engage in a genuine dialogue with the West would be reserved for the religious representatives from the more glamorous lands of Asia at the World's Parliament of Religions. The "primitives" of Native America and Africa would be part of that conversation. The function of peoples considered "primitive" at the

Chicago fair was not to engage in discussion with the civilized, but rather to act as a tabula rasa onto which all of the less fortunate aspects of Western civilization could be projected.[59]

What was true of the earlier trade fairs was true of later international expositions as well: the fairs *distorted* standards of value. When peoples regarded as "primitive" took up places along exposition midways within the context of the expositions as a whole, the value of modern civilization appeared to be beyond question. The only appropriate place to exhibit the alternative to civilization was within the comical context of the carnival. This sent a message that reverberated throughout all levels of Western society, implying that peoples deemed "primitive" had been all but excluded from the more serious aspects of Western civilization. Their role was to act as entertainment, or to deliver an "educational" message that taught that they were representatives of cultures whose time was now passing. In the exposition literature, the emerging concept of religion had come to represent that which was foundational, essential, and central to any given cultural setting, and hence, one might assume, something that was fundamentally serious within a culture as well. By aligning "primitive" cultures with the potentially comical, carnivalesque portion of the Columbian Exposition, the implicit organization of the event indicated that such peoples were not important enough to have their religiosity taken seriously.

# 5

# EXHIBITING RELIGION AT CHICAGO'S COLUMBIAN EXPOSITION

When the first "World's Parliament of Religions" took place as a part of Chicago's Columbian Exposition, a golden opportunity appeared for the developing field of religion. The Parliament might have emerged as a truly remarkable event, where religious categories were employed as a means of transcending the political and economic ones that had surfaced from within the international exposition tradition. As it happened, the Parliament ended up contributing to the colonial myths the exposition tradition was developing. Instead of shattering colonial illusions about the nature of the intercultural world, the Parliament appeared as a reflection of them. The Parliament organizers deserve credit for reaching out beyond the confines of the West itself to solicit global religious representation, but as we will see, their reasons for doing so were partly to insure that the many factions of Christendom would attend the event. The Parliament became noteworthy historically not primarily because of the vision of its organizers, but because of the remarkable performances of some of the peoples it invited.

At the Columbian Exposition, analysts began to imagine the grand conjuncture of cultures through religious categories far more than at previous events. In the literature pertaining specifically to the analysis of cultural differences at the Columbian Exposition, a conceptual category that could now legitimately be called "religion" was utilized by the vast majority of writers at the event. Religion was perceived as the center of any given society and the most obvious aspect of culture through which the essence of a given people's cultural orientation might be understood. Religion was a category of display for material culture, a subject for discussion within a number of the exposition's intellectual congresses, and the focus for the first globally based intellectual congress to include extensive participation from representatives outside the Western bloc of nations.

Although one might mark the birth of a field of religion somewhat earlier in Britain and some of the other European countries, the Columbian Exposition is as good a point as any to mark its rise within the United States. As much as any other single event, the Chicago exposition served to introduce the idea that religion could be viewed as simply one concern among many within the rapidly diversifying modern lifestyle. It contributed mightily to the defining of a relationship between religion and the wider world of human culture, and this occurred even at the level of popular culture.

When an objective approach to religion is viewed as a phenomenon emerging everywhere during the period, the position of the World's Parliament of Religions as a landmark religious event in and of itself becomes diminished. Because of the extent to which it reflected the Columbian Exposition, the Parliament is best viewed as an epiphenomenon that mostly applied the strategies used to define "cultures" to identify "religions." Nonetheless, the Parliament was without question the fair's most powerful symbol for the extent to which the idea of religion as an intellectual concept had developed. Without the Parliament, the profusion of religious material culture and the discourse surrounding it at the Columbian Exposition would have gained considerably less notice than it did.

The World's Parliament of Religions has been explored primarily as the first significant meeting of religious representatives from East and West. As such, it has been heralded as a foundational global religious event and a symbolic point of departure for the formal study of religion, which owes so much to the East/West interface. The more historical question of how and why the event first occurred on American soil is at least as pertinent, though, because during the period, it would have been implausible for a congress of world religions to meet in any other country.

Consideration of the Parliament as a specifically American phenomenon requires a wider methodological lens than the event itself would lead one to imagine. Because of the manner in which the event was conceived by its Protestant organizers, the many faces of religion that appeared at the Chicago fair and Parliament were not nearly as representative of the religious world of the time as was believed. Some of the faces that should have appeared more clearly at these events were shrouded in darkness. In the context of the Columbian Exposition, it was all but inevitable that some cultural groups would be omitted altogether and others inadequately represented at the first global gathering of religious representatives. To grasp the import of the World's Parliament of Religions for the ongoing field of religion, it is necessary to consider specifically how those who were present at the scene of the Columbian Exposition either participated, were represented, or failed to gain representation at the Parliament itself. The Parliament's call for a meeting of the "ten great world religions" excluded by category all Native Americans and included African Americans only as converted Christians. The interminable religious histories of these peoples appeared largely opaque in the total context of the exposition. The way these peoples were represented at the World's Parliament of Religions says a great deal about aspects of the Parliament that have not been adequately explored previously. To suitably understand the religions of those peoples not effectively represented at the Parliament, along with Western attitudes toward them, the World's Parliament of Religions, the Columbian Exposition, and the international exposition tradition out of which they both developed must be considered as a single context.

The most plausible historical context for the World's Parliament of Religions is the other comparable intellectual congresses that surfaced from within the international exposition tradition itself. Exposition congresses increasingly focused on international and intercultural issues, and by the occasion of the Columbian Exposition, the emergent discourse about global issues for the first time had come to include religion as one of its subjects. What made the World's Parliament of Religions significant was that in an unprecedented attempt at genuine global inclusiveness, the event's organizers solicited participation from representatives outside the Western bloc of nations. The real intrigue of the event rose from the fact that foreign representatives were allowed to speak without interruption or rebuttal— an unthinkable format in Britain, and certainly an implausible one in France.

In actuality, the World's Parliament of Religions was but a semblance of a representative world congress on religion. With recent scholarship focused on the East/West encounter at the Parliament, it has been largely overlooked that only about half a dozen men (depending on how one counts) from what today is considered Asia actually addressed the audience in English. In this the Parliament can be plausibly compared with the Congress on Africa, where at least a few

Africans spoke and some others sent papers (discussed below). The assessment of the significance of the Western encounter with the Asians at the Parliament depends largely on the degree to which one perceives the presence of Eastern thought to be influential in the West today. For liberal Protestants who are empathetic or enamored with Eastern culture, philosophy, and religion, this early encounter with the troupe of Asians is laden with sophisticated meanings. For other religious groups, however, such as Jews, Catholics, and evangelicals, the East/West theme represented a curious sideline to much more crucial concerns within and about the American religious scene. Women could be classified as falling somewhere in the middle of the spectrum regarding their assessment of the significance of the Asians at the Parliament.[1]

On the other end of the spectrum, for groups within the United States who fared poorly at the Parliament, such as African Americans and Native Americans, the encounter with the Asians was inconsequential in comparison to the paramount concern with their own lack of religious representation. These peoples—especially Native Americans—had come to be identified more by ethnicity than by religion. Native American culture had been largely usurped by the new discipline of anthropology at the Columbian Exposition, and there was a much stronger inclination to focus on these peoples as representing culture—especially the history of culture and a link to antiquity—than as embodying a religion or religions. Under these circumstances, one would not readily expect native peoples to be among the first invited to participate in a highly intellectual religion congress. To understand the full range of issues related to the emerging distinctions between religion and culture at the Chicago fair and the Parliament, it thus becomes imperative to place these events and the peoples involved in them squarely within the sociopolitical context of the exposition. This was definitive in determining how the concepts of culture, religion, and religions would be interpreted and applied in relation to specific peoples at both the Columbian Exposition and the World's Parliament of Religions.

## *The Changing Status of Religion in America during the Gilded Age*

For many religions, the events of the Columbian Exposition and World's Parliament of Religions have been focal points within their histories of this period in America, commonly identified as the "Gilded

Age." The external opulence of the period, reflecting the first manifestations of industrialized wealth in the country, contrasted starkly with lower-class poverty, giving rise to the notion of a "gilded" surface disguising something less attractive underneath. As the country modernized and urbanized during this era, a more flexible and changing societal structure allowed objective-minded and less traditionally religious approaches to spiritual concerns to gain more influence. When this happened to a sufficient degree, the theory of evolution began to permeate the culture at every level, forcing the churches to incorporate some version of the theory into their official positions. Evolutionary thought was slower to catch on in the United States than in Europe, but once it did, social evolutionism especially enjoyed a more programmatic application throughout all aspects of American society than it did across the Atlantic. The fact that there was a less sophisticated grasp of the nuances and debates spawned by the theory only contributed to the many ways it was applied.[2]

Another crucial development within this transition, and one too seldom noted, was the impact of biblical higher criticism within the United States. Ferenc Szasz has claimed that the higher criticism was at least as powerful as Darwinism, if not more so, in undermining the authority of traditional biblical religion in the American context. When the impact of this criticism began to be felt toward the end of the century, Szasz argues, it provided the support that evolutionism needed to seriously challenge the Bible's authority and become accepted widely as a feature of popular culture.[3]

The question of when an evolution-based interpretation of religion came to predominate over traditional biblical religion in the United States cannot be answered definitively. One difficulty in making such an assessment is that even today a significant number of people in the United States would claim that evolutionism has not yet achieved indisputable victory in the debate. Nevertheless, a cross-reading of the sources on this historical issue indicates that the event of the Columbian Exposition itself, with its ecumenical and intercultural World's Parliament of Religions, is as good a point as any to mark the change. This immense epistemological transition made it possible to presume that religion could be studied objectively as a subject of science, regardless of the separate question of whether science was viewed as being capable of exhausting the topic.[4]

When foreign religions could be subordinated to Christianity at the same time that the cultures with which they were affiliated were being subordinated to the West in a secular sense, they became more fascinating than threatening—as objects to be played with in a game where the rules had been stacked against them. At the Chicago exposition, this transition-in-progress toward an appealing evolutionary interpretation of cultural and religious differences contributed greatly to religions being represented freely in a wide variety of material forms and to their being discussed openly in several of the intellectual congresses. It also affected how regularly foreign cultures were interpreted through religious terminology in the press. The ability to place religious, or potentially religious, artifacts from a variety of religious contexts side by side with one another notably contributed to the idea that religion could be represented through material data, and thus categorized and objectified scientifically.

The question that really needs to be asked in relation to the remarkable outburst of religion in its many forms at the Columbian Exposition is: why did such a phenomenon occur in the United States? Possible answers to this question are both simple and complex. In an ambitious attempt to "do the anthropology of America" and assess the United States as a distinct cultural unit, Herve Varenne begins in an odd place by asserting that an essential characteristic of life in the United States, as contrasted with Europe, is the automatic friendliness and openness that characterizes the region. Though a simple assertion, this commonsensical observation about the flexible nature of American society might be a plausible explanation for what allowed religion a relatively free reign at the Columbian Exposition that it never would have been given in Europe. Underlying such religious tolerance at the Columbian Exposition, however, was the tacit understanding that all religions were acceptable as long as they could be located clearly within the grand hierarchical schema of social evolutionism. Alternative, fledgling forms of human religion needed only to be nurtured along in the spirit of Christian charity in their often ungraceful attempts to exhibit progress toward Christian ideals. Openness to alternative forms of religion generally went just this far and no farther in this early period of evolution-based comparative religion.[5]

Another factor contributing to the cosmopolitan nature of religion in the United States was the fluidity of the American class structure. Immigration was increasing exponentially in the decades preceding the Columbiad, causing rapid urbanization and continual wholesale changes in the country's social structure. For instance, the United States took in 78,615 immigrants in 1844, whereas in the 1880s the number averaged around 700,000 per annum. The immigration figures are only half the story. Also in this period there was an unprecedented expansion of the print medium, which progressed at a much faster pace in the United States than in Europe. While 758,000 newspapers, periodicals, and books circulated in 1850 in a population of about 24,000,000, by 1893 that number had grown to 5,134,000 in a population of 66,000,000. In other words, print production had grown more than eight times, while the population had less than tripled. A burgeoning society was accompanied by a burgeoning discourse about that society. Average citizens had begun to read and become aware of what was going on in the social world around them to a much greater degree than in the past.[6]

In such a modernizing and diversifying society, a more cognitive and objective argument than some version of Protestant biblical interpretation was becoming desirable in order to legitimate a social hierarchy. The American social structure was a truly slippery slope with its profusion of religious and cultural ideologies. Since the Bible was rapidly losing its unchallenged authority, there needed to be some clear connection to the advancing world of science in constructing a foundation for an encompassing social philosophy. The theory of social evolutionism was employed to build such a foundation in an ever greater variety of ways, and with the strong sociological focus of his evolutionary thought, Herbert Spencer was becoming increasingly lionized in the United States.

In its religious adoption of social evolutionism, the United States was different from Britain in that the theory had to be projected into so many different denominational forms. Social evolutionism thus became a multifarious discourse adopted and adapted by numerous religious groups with slightly different interpretations of and uses for it. It was also seized upon with vigor by nontraditional religious groups and nonreligious parties as well, many of which were grouped under the irremediably vague conceptual category known as "New Thought."

Because of the chaotic social situation in the United States during the period—with immigrants pouring in from all over the world, millions of newly free ex-slaves on the scene, and yet another entire range of indigenous peoples having been seriously compromised in the preceding decades—social evolutionism was aggressively applied to nearly every branch of thought in America in a wide variety of ways. Secular applications of social evolutionism and the various religious adoptions of it worked together in producing a multifaceted discourse and contributing to the encompassing total effect it had in America during the period. The essence of social evolutionism's success was its usefulness in legitimating a social hierarchy.[7]

The urgent need for defining a basis for a social hierarchy resulted in part from the religious factions of the United States in the 1890s being forced into cultural interaction with one another, even if they may not have particularly wanted such extensive interaction. During the latter half of the nineteenth century, it had gradually become apparent to the Protestant centrum that the remainder of the social body could no longer be simply ignored. In the pre-evolutionary period, non-Protestant factions comprised of both ethnically and religiously identified groups—from Native Americans and African Americans to Jews and Catholics—were placed into lower classes more or less without discussion as the Protestant hegemony maintained its predominance unquestioned. That social model began to break down through the first half of the nineteenth century. As the movement of peoples between localities increased with the growth of the country, there was a constant redefinition of both rural and urban communities as well as commensurate changes in the country's ethnic makeup and class structure. In the half-century leading up to Chicago's Columbian Exposition, the influx of immigrants from eastern and southern Europe made it even more difficult to collectively exploit those outside the Protestant mainstream without more sophisticated apologetics about the nature and basis of the American social hierarchy. The growing numbers of Catholics, and to a much lesser extent Jews, for instance, had to be addressed more and more seriously as obviously permanent fixtures within the American cultural superstructure.[8]

Martin Marty has employed the image of religious "cocoons" to argue that different religious groups in the period made a determined attempt to keep themselves separate from one another. This approach reflects the predominant trend in the writing of American religious history of picturing the structure of society as being defined by the influence of the churches. The opposite argument can be made with at least equal effectiveness: that the structure of American society is defined by the forced cultural interaction between religious factions within a shared cultural setting. Connecting links between the differing religious denominations and ethnic groups of the United States do not have to be reduced to oppositions between "culture" and "religion." These twin aspects of specific social groups could only be separated with the greatest difficulty in the period in question, and both were influenced powerfully by their new American context.[9]

In view of the cultural and religious disparateness that was beginning to define what "America" meant, some authoritative point of departure in legitimating a comprehensive social hierarchy was becoming more desirable, at least at some ill-defined level. It was the "science" of social evolution that was used, albeit in an insidious and multifarious manner, to validate an American class structure. The idea was applied most directly and tendentiously to domestic religious outsiders such as Native Americans and African Americans, who by mere appearance could be identified as being clearly outside of the Anglo-Protestant center and thus placed automatically on the lowest rungs of the social ladder. Other foreign peoples from across the globe who could be distinguished by appearance, primarily the Chinese, were only a negligible part of the society in this period and did not figure into the evolutionary equation in any quantitatively significant way.

Once this first tier of a social hierarchy based on social evolutionism had been constructed, the complete social picture could be embellished with subtler attempts at social differentiation higher up. Social evolutionism was made to pertain to groups such as the Catholics indirectly because they were affiliated from within the international exposition tradition with the less industrially sophisticated countries of southern Europe (even if most were in fact Irish). The marking of cultural differences based on economic potentials was always connected, however subtly, with religious ideologies.

The Jews stood in an awkward relationship to the social evolutionary formula because they were not affiliated with any particular country in Europe, and they also were clearly industri*ous* if not exactly industri*al*. Still, their economic status as newcomers in the United States left them on the lower rungs of the social ladder and vaguely connected them with the idea that they were somehow not industrially adept and thus less "evolved."

The final piece of the evolutionary puzzle in America involved eastern European Protestants, primarily Germans, who could only be subordinated on the basis of their lesser, though much more comparable, degree of industrial success relative to the Anglo-Protestant population. While these slight evolutionary distinctions were affiliated with the drawbacks of Lutheranism in some of the Great Exhibition literature, there was no central church body comparable to the Church of England in the United States at the time, and the connection to religion at this level of the hierarchy remained in the background and was virtually invisible. If it seems that the influence of social evolutionism is being overestimated here, it needs only to be recalled that European peoples themselves were divided "racially" at Philadelphia's Centennial through the most intricate taxonomies, which points up the remarkable degree to which fantasies about race marked American thought during the Gilded Age. The affiliation of industrial capacity with intercultural status and religious orientation operated both overtly and covertly within the exposition tradition, but the effects of both were plain to see in the structure of the events.[10]

What was unique about the Chicago fair as compared to earlier events was that something called "religion" had become a much more indispensable aspect of the argument through which the global cultural hierarchy was constructed. The "science" of social evolutionism did not eliminate the traditional sense of religion during this period; rather, it incorporated it into an encompassing vision of Anglo-based dominance—one that was a combined result of divine ordinance and human effort. The new model of comparative-based, objectified religion did not lose the authoritative impact it had enjoyed in its traditional form altogether. It could still sanctify the more secular-based value systems in a way that comparison based strictly on industrial prowess could not. This inspiring vision of a new form of religion that was simultaneously of secular and divine origin is what would motivate the organizers of the World's Parliament of Religions to initiate the first global congress of religions to occur at the end of the fair. Although religion had become a separable aspect of culture within the exposition tradition, it was by no means possible to assess the status of any given "religion" apart from the particular culture with which it was affiliated. The confidence with which the Parliament's Protestant organizers would approach their first interface with other "world" religions owed much to the attractive secular position in which Protestants in general found themselves at the time.

## *Tracking Religion at the World's Columbian Exposition*

The use of creative combinations of social evolutionism and comparative religion in the interpretation of foreign cultures and non-Western Americans was the most fascinating—and pervasive—aspect of the Columbian Exposition commentary about foreign cultures. Religion was the principal mode of interpretation through which foreign cultures were ordered, compared, and made comprehensible by Western writers throughout the fair. This pronounced use of religious analysis as an intellectual tool at the Columbiad shows the extent to which something called "religion" was seen as being separable from its cultural contexts, objectifiable, and made useful as a mode of cultural analysis—even for the purpose of simple description within popular culture.

Displays of religious material culture appeared in distinct categories throughout White City. A religious exhibit from the Smithsonian under the guidance of Cyrus Adler found its way into the Department of Liberal Arts in the U.S. Government Building categorized in a section headed "Religious Ceremonials." The categories reflect the spare beginnings of religious taxonomies: "religious organizations—statistics and publications; religious choirs and music; missions; spreading religion through publications; Bible societies; religious instruction; the association for moral improvement; and charities." What was important about this exhibit was that Adler insisted that religion itself be the category of display for the artifacts, not geographical region, as had been the standard anthropological practice. A German Jew by background and an important figure for the Conservative movement in America during the period, one result of Adler's novel approach was that it provided a means by which Judaism in particular could be conceived as a distinct civilization, even if it was one with no identifiable geographical borders. Beginning in 1888, Adler's position with the Smithsonian involved him in a series of displays of religion around the country, and he had developed the approach used at the Chicago fair from that experience.[11]

Most of the displays of religious material culture were found inside the Anthropology Building and were connected to cultures deemed "primitive," though there were exceptions. Other religious categories included ancient Spanish crosses, idols from ancient Egypt, Buddhist sculptures, East Indian photos of ceremonial observances, characteristic religious objects from the Siamese government, and a collection of fetishes and amulets. Such nuance only demonstrates an awareness of how useful the conceptual category "religion" could be made to be.

Catholic Charities made a significant display of their work in the Government Building, and religious exhibits found their way into the Woman's Building as well. The content of each of these collections was relatively inconsequential. What is important is that each of these very different areas of the fair found some way of viewing religion as a separable section of their overall display, capable of being marked off and placed in a distinct category.

The American Bible Society offered a display of Bibles in 240 languages, but since translating the Bible was now an accepted and ongoing practice, the display did not draw nearly as much attention as did a comparable exhibit at London's Great Exhibition. Still, the breakdown by region of the 240 languages was revealing with regard to missionary activity, with 131 biblical translations directed toward Africa and 93 toward Asia, but just 25 toward North America and only 6 within Britain.[12]

The most extensive displays of religion inside White City, however, were exhibits of Native American cultures—both persons and material culture—along with other displays of peoples designated as "primitives." The Native American displays were set up mostly by the

Smithsonian in the Government Building and by the Department of Archaeology and Ethnology in the Anthropology Building. As noted in chapter 4, Native American groups camped outside the building and accompanied these displays. Religion was always central to the analysis of these displays and peoples, but it would be difficult to ascertain the precise form of religion that was intimated in the eyes of the display organizers. I noted earlier that the dances of the Kwakiutl were studied in a scholarly manner by Franz Boas. Their music was also recorded and analyzed at length. The complex relationship of such cultural phenomena to the emerging concept of objectified religion from an anthropological perspective is beyond the scope of the present study, but it was clear that any given people's possible religious activity was at the center of what was of compelling interest about them. Displays related to classical anthropological focal points, such as ceremonial dances, music, ceremonies surrounding death and marriage—in short, anything resembling a ritual act and the material artifacts related to those acts—were seized upon as in some manner indicative of native religion. Activities that bore some relationship to "religious" inclinations, like these or the material displays pertaining to such, also largely determined the degree of "educational value" they were thought to contain.[13]

For the principal "exotic" foreign cultures who represented themselves with some dignity inside White City—India and Japan—interpreting their religions also caused enormous problems of interpretation. Hinduism's polytheism was an unfathomable religious concept in 1893. Nevertheless, India was in a much better position than Japan to defend itself and its religion at the fair in that it offered natives who could speak with credibility about the surrounding scene and how it might relate to their religions. The Indian pavilion was staffed, for instance, by an articulate man named Purushotam Rao, who had extensive enough interactions with one observer to tell her that he was a Brahmin and to express disappointment at the low level of culture in the United States. Rao so impressed the female writer that despite his criticisms of her country, she concluded, "These Hindoos are a great people." Another Indian, Gobing Burshad, described as a "high Brahmin priest," was said to take pleasure in "explaining the traditions of his native land" in an authoritative British accent.[14] Reports of these direct interactions with articulate East Indians served to legitimate the general culture. This could only help to enhance the more positive popular religious perceptions of the people.[15]

Preconceptions about Japanese religion followed Japan to the fair, which accounted in part for the cautious behavior of the Japanese. A

Chicago magazine, the *Graphic*, ran a series entitled "Japan and the Japanese" in the months before the fair, displaying religious misunderstandings typical of the period:

> It is a curious fact that Japan cannot boast of an indigenous religion, or of much original or moral philosophy. "Shinto" is only a cult, not a system of worship, not a religion or a philosophy. Shinto is a system of mythology. It . . . has no moral code. Christianity alone is the religion of liberty and progress. Buddha may be the "light of Asia," but Jesus Christ is the "light of the world." The Japanese are by nature superstitious and sensual and they need moral and intellectual training. Superstition can be dissipated by science, and sensuality can be conquered only by spirituality.

It reflected a great wisdom on the part of Japan not to attempt to counteract such projections directly. Such actions would have been impossible since these ideas were so firmly grounded and since so few Japanese spoke English. Instead, the Japanese simply refused to add to them by maintaining a low profile.[16]

The inclination to organize foreign cultures through religious categories was most in evidence along the Midway Plaisance in Jackson Park. The chaos of the midway strongly challenged fair analysts to organize such unprecedented intercultural exoticism around a dominant theme. The rallying cry in this endeavor was: what better than religion to explain cultural differences? When a culture being analyzed was affiliated with a world religion, this strategy worked with some degree of success. In other cases it proved inadequate: the religious-based analyses of the least industrialized cultures were mostly indistinguishable from the lazy notions of social evolution that abounded throughout the exposition commentary and were mostly collapsed into them. Mock displays of violence along the midway, for instance, did not necessarily have anything to do with religion, but they were often put forth as representing inclinations toward human sacrifice and cannibalism, which were then interpreted as wayward expressions of religion.

One religion along the midway that actually benefited from analysis based on religion was Islam. Islam had a prophet and a sacred book comparable to the Judeo-Christian tradition, and Islamic cultures were clearly demarcated from cultures regarded as "primitive" by simple virtue of the quality of their concessions. Tunisia had put together exposition displays as far back as Britain's Great Exhibition and was well practiced at the art. The Algerians, under the management of

Sol Bloom, had appeared in Paris in 1889 and also knew the trade. And the Street in Cairo, with its exquisite dancers in the "Palace of Eros" and its fine restaurants, was more or less the cornerstone of quality cultural exoticism along international exposition midways. The combined effect of these concessions was to provide fairgoers with images of Islamic cultures that indicated a long and rich cultural history. Denton J. Snider, whose volume on the Chicago fair seems today a hopelessly deterministic use of social evolution to explain religious differences, nevertheless was surprisingly charitable toward Islam. Snider called Mohammed "one of the supremely great men of the world," who "composed one of the Sacred Books" revered by more than "one hundred million souls of today. Not sacred to me; but who am I in the presence of such a fact."[17]

The Chinese occupied a liminal religious position along the midway. Although their culture possessed the identifiable world religions of Taoism and Confucianism, little was known about these religions. Joss House, the museum dominated by religious objects, contained images familiar enough to be categorized as religious, but those images were still foreign enough as to be written off as expressions of idol worship, thus relegating Chinese religion as a whole to a position somewhere just beneath the religions of India and Japan.

The cultures that did not fare as well in the religious-based analysis were those represented only along the midway and not in White City as well. Beyond the Chinese and the Islamic cultures, the remaining non-Western peoples represented along the midway were made up only of cultures viewed as "primitive." Peoples falling into the category of "primitives" were viewed as religious in no more than the most nominal of senses, being seen as having just embarked on the long trip up the evolutionary ladder to civilized expressions of religion. For the evolution-minded Denton J. Snider, it was a moral imperative that the midway's "vast multitude of details . . . be reduced to order," so that "the event can become our intellectual property." The midway was "a long highway of human progress," a voyage "around the earth and down time." By 1893, it had become a commonplace idea within intercultural analysis—even among persons with nominal education—that social evolution could be projected spatially around the contemporary world as well as historically "down time" to explain differences between contemporary human cultures based on their respective histories.[18]

Snider set apart Asian religions from European ones as being typified by visions of "the lapse of the soul" falling downward into matter. He viewed European religion as being defined by the contrasting vision of steady, organic religious development—social evolution. The liminal religious world occupied by Asian religion was preceded on the evolutionary religious ladder by predictable foils: "At last we descend to the savage races, the African from Dahomey and the North American Indian. Now we are ready to go to the . . . monkeys, or . . . crocodiles." Snider concluded his vision by noting that the Midway Plaisance "keeps flowing forward to the Great Fair, into which it pours itself for its final fruition." The fair's latent "primitive"/civilized dichotomy could not have received a clearer explication than this. In Snider's vision, "primitives" were necessary because the beginning of human evolution had to be identified for the whole structure to fall into place. Thus, the Dahomean had in him "the infinite potentiality of mankind," though it "may take him a million years to reach the first mile-post."[19]

Hazy images of "primitive religion" were encapsulated within a few central themes in the fair commentary, such as human sacrifice and cannibalism. Any activities potentially related to these themes retained vague religious connotations in the eyes of many observers. They represented survivals of the bestial mentality of primitive humanity and its earliest attempts at religious expression. Beyond such obvious crudeness, however, there was one religious-based theme that appeared endlessly in the analysis of "primitive" religion: fetishism, which involved the apparent deification of material objects. Religious language surrounding the fetish often became vitriolic and positively irrational—a phenomenon that can indicate more about the observer than the observed. The idea of a hierarchical order of the world's religions spiraling downward to the abomination of fetishism was omnipresent in the fair literature. In one of the few authoritative publications chronicling the Columbian Exposition, William E. Cameron identifies that hierarchy as follows:

> [Buddhism] is not a religion, but a system of crude philosophy embodying the worship of an idealized type of manhood through idols and symbols. The Chinese have Joss House where their peculiar forms of idolatry are observed. The Zulus, Fijians, and Samoans have weird beliefs, and their ceremonials are such as to strike pity and disgust upon the minds of enlightened beholders. That gross superstition should maintain its existence in the midst of an occasion which shows forth the fullest flower of civilization and Christianity, intensifies the repugnance with which one views the mummeries and grosser rites by which these savages travesty the name of worship. But it is in the Dahomey Village that the grossest and most repulsive forms of fetichism [sic] hold sway.[20]

Such passages make it clear that the essential religious sin is the worship of matter through some form of idolatry or fetishism. The prevalence of such an assumption calls to mind the long history of this problem in Western society (explored in chapter 1), marked most definitively by the eradication of material representations of the divine in English churches after the Reformation. Cameron goes on to cite a number of horrifying savage sacrifices centered on the religion of the fetish. His analyses portray the worship of matter as inevitably degenerating into what perhaps qualify as the two most abhorrent human acts: ritual murder, in the form of human sacrifice, and cannibalism, as the conclusion of the ritual.

The paranoia about fetishism in the exposition commentaries presented a great puzzle indeed: how was it that the culture expressing such religious concern about the deification of material forms could be the same culture responsible for the most extensive displays of material culture in the history of the world? The preoccupation with the material world through the mass production of commodities was one of the central religious issues at London's Great Exhibition: how to justify the unparalleled materialism of an international exposition in a country whose church walls were unadorned. Such concerns were virtually passé by the time of the Chicago fair, however. The spectacle of technological advance had clearly won the day; thus, it must have been sanctioned from on high. Even the Reverend H. W. Thomas was willing to acknowledge that "[t]he merciful miracles of the Christ in feeding the hungry, healing the sick, and raising the fallen are more and more to be the realized powers in the divine life of man." If materialism did appear to have prevailed in Chicago, however, the return of the repressed became apparent in the dogged religious condemnation of cultures deemed "primitive" with their ineradicable fetishism.[21]

Ambivalence about the material world was, in fact, the focal point for the fair's main religious controversy. The final verdict regarding the question of Sunday openings should come as no surprise given the power of the material over the divine at the Columbiad. The fair was officially closed on the first Sunday of the fair, May 7, but a court injunction instigated by the actions of a group of the fair's investors dictated that it remain open on future Sundays. The most important decision that related directly to religion had gone the way of the secular and the material. The Columbian Exposition planners went to great lengths to create a division between the fair's educational aspirations, marked by the ambitious Congress Auxiliary and Anthropology Building, and the shameless commercialism that was the fair's overriding concern. In the end, however, the attempt to separate religious concerns from secular ones proved unfeasible. The secular encroached upon the religious determinedly in the exposition setting, finally leaving even the Sabbath in its wake.

## The Rise of Intellectual Congresses at International Expositions

The first events to display the whole of the world's industry at various sites across the Western world also produced a unique discourse about those displays and all they represented. Early on, it was recognized that the forums in which this discourse occurred were largely unprecedented, and noteworthy as such. In fact, the most relevant historical antecedent for all the exalted rhetoric describing Chicago's World's Parliament of Religions was the assessments of the significance of the jury meetings at London's Great Exhibition. Using similar terminology, commentators waxed eloquent about the world-historical significance of both the Great Exhibition's juries and the World's Parliament of Religions, alternately invoking the notion that both events represented firsts in world history. One publication from the Great Exhibition, which aimed at showing the extent of biblical translations, featured a sentence of holy writ in one hundred languages that reflected the event's deepest hope, that "God Hath Made of One Blood All Nations of Men," and ended by anticipating the World's Parliament of Religions' motto, asking, "Have we not all one father?" This comparison between two seemingly remote historical events indicates at the least that both gatherings were perceived as landmarks at the time because they were more genuinely global to a greater degree than any before them. Historical hindsight shows the limitations, and even the conceit, of the extent to which participants viewed the events in universal terms, but both events were nonetheless major breakthroughs in intersocietal relations.[22]

In the opening chapter, I briefly invoked the name of Herder, who is often identified as having pointed to the historical importance of the increasing use of the common languages of the masses as conduits for serious scholarship. Intellectual gatherings like the jury meetings at the Great Exhibition were not possible to any great degree prior to that time precisely because the languages in which serious intellectual exchange occurred were not accessible to a wide variety of scholars across international borders. Further, the use of numerous languages to explicate complex concepts itself contributed to the development of more narrowly specific fields of inquiry. The international exchange of ideas between several nations at once was largely an occult process before 1850, and preceding the rise of distinct human sciences as it did, it pertained to very particular spheres of technical scholarship. There was simply no context in which more general discourses involving several countries at once and covering a wide range of humanistic issues might occur. Thus, it becomes more understandable that in the interest of posterity, the organizers of the Great Exhibition were adamant about obtaining thorough reports from each of the appointed juries who analyzed their respective groups of exhibition commodities. The jurors donated their time to the cause of the Great Exhibition awards, and the exceptionally high quality of the reports they issued is the best proof that the individuals involved fully understood their historical significance.

International meetings at expositions immediately following the Great Exhibition of 1851 were confined to the work of the juries just as at the initial event. Nevertheless, those jury meetings changed with the differing emphases of ensuing expositions. After a few less significant attempts to duplicate the success of the Great Exhibition at Dublin and New York in 1853 (see chapter 4), the French came up with a significant challenge to the fable of the Crystal Palace by hosting a definitively French international exposition in 1855 that placed special emphasis on art and design. While Britain had listed raw materials first among its four principal categories—appropriate for a nation chiefly concerned with manufacturing and export—the French emphasized design and expanded the fine arts category considerably. French manufactures thus appeared in a more favorable light next to their clumsier, if more prolific, British counterparts, and the jury meetings were obliged to judge exhibits under a different set of criteria.

The next major British exhibition, in 1862—slightly larger than the Great Exhibition, though almost completely forgotten historically—would give considerably more attention to aesthetics in an obvious acknowledgment of the success of the 1855 French exposition. While the results of the jury meetings varied from one exposition to the next, all of these events were unlikely candidates to hold international intellectual congresses as distinct gatherings separate from the pragmatics of the events. Britain's cultural insularity was a stern preventive measure, and France was still too volatile a political entity in 1855 to propose egalitarian, humanitarian congresses that would inevitably cross over into politics.

It was at the 1867 Paris exposition where the first plausible instance of an international intellectual congress took place. The conjuncture of the world's productions at one setting had brought into sharper focus the disparities between the different nations' procedures in weighing metals and making coins. Hence, the Imperial French Government organized a scientific commission on weights, measures, and coins that was the focus for an international discussion of monetary value and the increasingly fine art of exchange. The symbolic structuring of the 1867 French exposition could not have been more appropriate to this inaugural international discussion. The exposition grounds were constructed in concentric circles representing different groups of commodities, with the smallest, innermost circle being a garden. In the middle of this circular garden was a display of weights and measures that took on the appearance of a veritable *axis mundi* within the context of what many perceived as the new "religion" of capitalism. As Arthur Chandler described it, "The placement of this pavilion [the garden and display of coins, weights, and measures] was a masterpiece of planning. After the vast collection of objects at the exposition—gathered from all over the world and from every era of human history—this exhibit invited the visitor to reflect on concepts and systems that bound them all together. Every country had a different kind of currency, it was true, but every country did have some medium of exchange."[23]

Commissioners from participating nations met on the matter of international values, and their efforts probably contributed to the signing of an international treaty and the founding of the International Bureau of Weights and Measures in 1875. This meeting can be distinguished from the international meetings of juries at earlier expositions in that it was not directly related to any specific exposition category, but rather discussed one theme in particular that related to the whole of the event.[24]

More significant international congresses would come into being at the Vienna exposition of 1873, at the Philadelphia Centennial in 1876, and at the Paris expositions of 1878 and 1889, with thirty-two and seventy congresses being held at these latter two events respectively. Evolution-related themes became a part of these congresses, with a separate congress being devoted to ethnology at the 1878 exposition and one on colonial affairs in 1889. In fact, a congress of religions might well have occurred at Paris in 1889 had it not been for an edict of the French government preventing any discussion of religion at government-sponsored events. It would be reserved for the Chicago exposition of 1893 to host the first international congress specifically devoted to religion at the World's Parliament of Religions.[25]

## Religion throughout the Congress Auxiliary

The Columbian Exposition's Congress Auxiliary was conceived by Chicago lawyer and dedicated Swedenborgian Charles Carroll Bonney. Of the origin of the Congress Auxiliary—by far the largest ever conceived—Bonney says only that the idea came to him while "thinking about the nature and characteristics of this great undertaking [of the fair]." Yet it can certainly be assumed that he was aware to some degree of the historical precedents for such an enterprise. The expansion of American culture in the decades following the Civil War, along with the impact of evolutionism and intercultural awareness, had allowed for a profusion of ideologies to develop, both religious and secular. Bonney's Swedenborgian vision of a massive Congress Auxiliary with its crowning achievement of a World's Parliament of Religions must be seen in part as a product of this religious diversification in the United States at the time.[26]

There was considerable discussion of religion throughout the Congress Auxiliary in congresses not devoted directly to religion. The Congress of Philologists heard a paper from Maurice Bloomfeld on Vedic Studies and one from Richard Garbe of Konigsberg on connections between Greek and Indian philosophy. The Congress of Women heard a sympathetic paper on Mohammed, while the World's Congress of Representative Women had three separately headed sections devoted to religion. The Third International Congress of Folklore mirrored the World's Parliament of Religions in that it proclaimed itself to be the first congress to which all nations were invited, boasting participation by thirty nationalities. As in the Anthropology Congress, folklore papers having to do with religion focused almost exclusively on cultures considered "primitive." These cultures were viewed as orienting themselves through mythology rather than religion, the study of the former being a subject within the field of folklore.[27]

Chief among the nonreligion congresses discussing religion were the International Congress of Anthropology, the Congress on Evolution, and in an indirect manner, the Congress on Africa. Papers on religions viewed as "primitive" dominated discourse on religion in the Anthropology Congress with themes including common symbols in primitive religion, Zuni mythology, and primitive thought in ancient Egypt. Cyrus Adler presented a paper that chronicled other recent displays of religious phenomena at various events from around the world, a number of which he had constructed. As for the World's Parliament of Religions, the event looked quite different through an anthropological lens as opposed to a religious one. Adler observed, "A Parliament of Religions has been called which, while conducted along church lines, and almost exclusively from the propagandist or philanthropic point of view, [still] enables the presentation of many creeds by their own professors." For the anthropologically trained, the first point to be made about the Parliament was its Christian agenda.[28]

Adler went on to recount why he felt a religious typological arrangement was preferable in the art of displaying religious artifacts in the museum setting. While the instance of Judaism was the most pertinent case in point, Adler also used the example that only a religious typology would be effective in allowing the different geographical regions practicing Buddhism to be grouped together. Professor Morris Jastrow Jr., on the other hand, sought to append Adler's typological construction by insisting that such a schematic was appropriate to "civilizations" but not to "primitives." In an otherwise well-conceived paper called "The Scope and Method of the Historical Study of Religions," Jastrow called for a study of the "*geographical* distribution of primitive doctrines and rites" (emphasis mine). With regard to civilizations, however, Jastrow said that "each religion is to be treated independently." Certainly one way of interpreting this methodological distinction is that for Jastrow and others along with him, "primitive" humanity is bound to the earth and is to be defined by its geographical locus, while civilizations and their world religions have to some degree extracted themselves from the terrestrial and become self-constituted ideological worlds. In a milieu where such sweeping theoretical divisions were the norm, Cyrus Adler's genius is obvious when one notes how he adopted a taxonomy based on "religion" rather than geography as a means of exalting Judaism in his display.[29]

The papers specifically about religion at the Congress on Evolution have been lost to posterity, but during this period, all discussion of evolutionism had such a profound effect on religious thought that the remaining papers are still relevant. The Congress on Evolution was initially slated to be held as part of the science and philosophy congresses. It became a part of the religion congresses only because it was late in being organized and there was no other place for it. This arbitrary placement of the Congress on Evolution allowed Bonney to seize the opportunity to hail the "coming unity between science and religion." In the place of the benign congratulatory address he gave at the other congresses, Bonney offered a distinct argument at the evolution congress. Taking a Swedenborgian perspective, he countered the materialism and randomness of Darwinian evolution by asserting that evolutionism defined as "creation by means of mighty laws" is "infinitely more rational" than "creation by the exercise of arbitrary power." In Bonney's view, because social evolution had the ability to organize the interreligious world around a Christian agenda, there was no reason to fear the idea. By moving away from the more threatening aspects of Darwin's evolutionism—materialism and randomness—Bonney, like so many others, was content with offering some lazy theology designed to incorporate the new theory into existing Christian doctrine to the advantage of all believers.[30]

The evolution congress began with a letter from Herbert Spencer being read to the audience. Spencer offered a hazy argument—a tired argument by this time—refuting the notion that the potential fatalism of evolutionary thought led to social apathy. He argued that social philanthropy was the highest stage of evolution and demanded a conscious involvement on the part of individuals. This was how far evolutionary thought had come by 1893: the focus of Spencer's evolutionary argument was human consciousness and conscience, while the original argument began as a biological study of the possibility of animals transmutating into new forms. The precise connection between the science of evolution and contemporary social philosophy had been explored and reworked so many times since Darwin published *The Origin of Species* that it had often become hard to tell fact from theory in the matter. By 1893, the idea of social evolution was widely enough accepted that the scientific underpinnings of the general notion had become less important. It had become a theoretical discourse unto itself, and one that had all but lost sight of the original propositions.

The evolution-based, primitive/civilized dichotomy that characterized discussions of religion throughout the congresses was evident in a different way in the Congress on Africa. While other congresses considered sophisticated intercultural matters such as museum display and the study of comparative religion, the statement of intention by the "African Ethnology Section" is ominous in retrospect. The statement observes, "The recent partition of Africa among the European powers has given a greatly increased importance to the question of the future of the African race, and its capacity to subserve the civilization of the age." However, as Christopher Robert Reid has pointed out, despite this initial intention the concerted efforts of both diasporan and continental Africans to make a powerful showing at the Congress on Africa were successful in staking a claim for a definitive African-based voice at international expositions.

At the Brussels exposition of 1888, discussion about Africa had broken down and ended in acrimony, with one observer doubting whether any future discussion of Africa could take place on the Continent. It was hoped that on the "neutral ground" of the United States the issues could be reopened and discussed amicably. Conceived by Frederick Perry Noble, the son of a Congregationalist minister in Chicago, the American version of the Congress of Africa took on a surprising vigor due to the credibility of the presentations by a number of key Africans and African Americans.[31]

Much as would be the case at the World's Parliament of Religions, the relationship of religion to the themes of the Congress on Africa begged a number of questions about the relationship of religion to culture. In any discussion of Africa in the period, there was bound to be discussion of both Christian missionary activity on that continent and the impact of Christianity on ex-Africans living in the American context. Notable diasporan Africans such as Benjamin W. Arnett (who would speak at the World's Parliament of Religions), Frederick Douglass, and Henry McNeal Turner gave forceful presentations about the cultural and religious plight of Africa on both sides of the Atlantic. In addition, both presentations by continental Africans emphasized the potential influence of religion on cultural realities. Each emphasized the concern of Africans when religious language became so technical that it took on the appearance of politics rather than spirituality. Prince Monolu Massipiou of Liberia noted that his people did not care for "theological speculations or the finely drawn distinctions between sects," claiming "no African would believe them." The Yoruba minister Abayomi observed, "What the Negro needs is Christianity, not Anglicanism or Americanism." Largely due to the nature of their interaction with European Christian societies, the distinction between religious orientation and cultural realities was so fine that it often appeared nonexistent for both continental and diasporan Africa. The cultural reality of colonialism and the religious reality of Christianity had encroached so thoroughly on African life that it had become difficult to tell one apart from the other and to distinguish an authentic Africanness that preceded their arrival.[32]

The importance of the Congress on Africa was extolled by countless observers, to a point where Reid could claim—though it would be very difficult to support—that it was more significant than the World's Parliament of Religions. About the Congress on Africa, the *Daily Inter-Ocean* claimed, "Of all problems coming before the Auxiliary none is so hard to solve as that which will engage the African Section." At the very least, the Congress on Africa was noteworthy for its willingness to fully engage both African Americans and Africans in a congress about a truly complex problem. The limitations of the World's Parliament of Religions are seen most clearly in relation to the Congress on Africa. The topic of Africa proved to be much more capable of incorporating "exotic" peoples into its discussion than did the perhaps more high-minded topic of "religion."[33]

The most significant paper delivered throughout the Congress Auxiliary of the World's Columbian Exposition dealt only indirectly with religion. It was left to little-known historian Frederick Jackson Turner, who would become the next president of the American Historical Association, to put the essential character of American culture into perspective by defining it in relation to an expanding frontier that was only now closing down. The paper could not have found a more appropriate setting. With the magnanimous Columbian Exposition occurring in the more central American location of Chicago, the United States, with or without Turner's thesis, was drifting westward in terms of the way it was being conceived as a whole.

The extent to which the fair may have served as impetus for Turner's idea is uncertain. It is certain, however, that the structure of Turner's frontier thesis was informed in a significant way by the ubiquitous theory of social evolutionism. For Turner, the frontier line was the ultimate symbol for his renegade vision of what defined a uniquely American identity. On the western side of Turner's frontier was the "primitive"; on the eastern side was the advancement of civilized Europe. His frontier thesis defined the "primitive" not only by the open land, and the ruggedness and individualism necessary to settle it, but also by the people living on that land:

> The United States lies like a huge page in the history of society. Line by line as we read this continental page from west to east we find the record of social evolution. It begins with the Indian and the hunter; it goes on to tell of the disintegration of savagery by the entrance of the trader, the pathfinder of civilization; we read the annals of the pastoral stage in ranch life; the exploitation of the soil . . . in sparsely settled farming communities; the intensive culture of the denser farm settlement; and finally the manufacturing organization with city and factory system . . . In this advance, the frontier is the outer edge of the wave— the meeting point between savagery and civilization . . . In this progress from savage conditions lies topics for the social evolutionist.[34]

In Turner's view, the necessity of having to constantly come to terms with the "primitive" is what lent the United States its unique character. Early American culture was suspended at the meeting point of the "primitive" and the civilized. As so often in the literature of the period, the "primitive" here takes on a positive role in its ability to inform the civilized world about its positive attributes.

Turner's thesis proposing a progression from savagery to civilization was the congresses' most recurring theme dealing with humanistic questions. In the context of the Columbian Exposition, the primitive/civilized dichotomy began to take on an increased tangibility as a legitimating foundation for the concept of social evolutionism in general. The American social context made urgent the need to answer questions about how to mark distinctions between cultures, religions, and especially "races." At base, the primitive/civilized distinction was more about "race" than it was about culture or religion. It created a human scientific distinction that had as much to do with physical anthropology as it did with cultural anthropology. The primitive/civilized dichotomy proposed blanket divisions between peoples based on the most general of perceptions regarding visible differences between human beings. Whether "primitives" represented other forms of human culture or some life form that existed just prior to what could be defined as human, cultural, and hence religious was an unanswered question in the nineteenth century. It was just this kind of confusion that led to the complete lack of representation of the "primitive" at the World's Parliament of Religions.

## *Religion and Culture at the World's Parliament of Religions*

Looking back on the first World's Parliament of Religions, Parliament president John Henry Barrows would write, "Matched with its significance and universality how provincial appear some of the greater events of the nineteenth century, even negro emancipation." Such sentiments seem infinitely skewed by the standards of today, yet they accurately reflect the feelings that prevailed for many at the time of the Parliament. Still, that "negro" emancipation could appear "provincial" next to the "universality" of the Parliament gives moment to pause.[35]

Despite Barrows's perception of the universality of the World's Parliament of Religions, for today's religious world, the event is as noteworthy for all the religions it excluded by its organizational rubric of "ten great world religions" as for those it included. The goal of the Parliament, as developed by Swedenborgian Charles Bonney, was "to unite all religion against all irreligion." Bonney acknowledged that what he was taught in his church about the thought of Emanuel Swedenborg included "the fundamental truths which made a World's Parliament of Religions possible." Bonney's vision, and Swedenborgianism for that matter, are good examples of a mode of American religious thought extending back to the Transcendentalists that sought to define a grand unity within all religions, but only by observing their differences. A unity defined on the basis of narrowly manifest differences would not be likely to produce the sense of grandeur worthy of true divinity. On the other hand, to allow the world's religions to be appreciated in the full range of their nuances and to identify the unity within that degree of differentiation might be the clearest reflection of the divine possible. Especially in the writings of Emerson there can be seen this thematic emphasis in his acknowledging nature as a phenomenally differentiated manifestation of the divine. The guiding theme of the Parliament, to promote the unity of all religions, has to be seen as owing some debt to this earlier movement within the history of American religious thought.[36]

For Emanuel Swedenborg, Bonney's guiding inspiration, "irreligion," meant "lack of religion." To be religious meant "to acknowledge God, and to refrain from evil because it is contrary to God." These two acts "make religion to be religion." In the context in which Swedenborg was writing, such generalizations were of course not proffered with any real awareness of their intercultural implications. At the World's Parliament of Religions, however, the art of "acknowledging God" was determined to be a possibility for certain cultural groups, while others were deemed incapable of it altogether. In effect, the Parliament organizers came perilously close to sanctifying themselves with the power to define religion and then uniting it against something they had identified as irreligion. If some of the foreign cultures attending the World's Parliament of Religions were victims of Christian triumphalism at the event, those peoples not invited to attend were worse off still, having the rest of the religious world united against them.[37]

The idea conceived by Parliament organizers was that something morally malleable called "religion" could be extracted from its historical contexts and engaged in high-minded discussions of global ethics and transcendental theology. By contemporary standards, such a notion represents a locus classicus of progress-minded, nineteenth-century thought. Complicating this picture was the fact that certain groups whose participation was sought by the Parliament's organizers refused to attend for political reasons, a fact that directly challenged the notion that religions could be ultimately separated from their cultural settings. Politics did get in the way of intercultural religious discussion; so did culture, with barriers of language and custom; and so, for that matter, did the more pragmatic aspects of religious activity. The increasingly controversial work of Christian missionaries abroad became a central focus among foreign delegates at the Parliament's meetings. The vision of religion as a globally defined phenomenon was implied by the very fact of a World's Parliament of Religions. However, this idea proved to be a different matter entirely as a matter of praxis; so intimately connected were the attending religions with their different political circumstances across the globe that it was this fact more than any other that defined the event.

Considering the ambitiousness of the event and the well-nigh impossible task of organization it involved, at a certain point one has to ask fundamental questions about the covert agenda of the World's Parliament of Religions. The first of these would be: why was it held at all? The second would be: why was it held in America? The first question is perhaps the easier of the two to answer. The growing awareness of intercultural issues that was promoted by the expositions themselves along with the inclination of religious groups to meet at international expositions made it quite plausible that these two themes would eventually merge. As noted earlier, commercially minded expositions always needed something to sanctify them, given their economic ambitions. The entire Congress Auxiliary, with its intention of promoting human progress as a whole, fulfilled this role at the Columbian Exposition, along with the "educational" Anthropology Building mentioned above.

Still, the extent to which a World's Parliament of Religions might sanctify the international exposition at which it was being held was hindered considerably by the fact that it was comprised of representatives from across the globe. In the place of a sense of social harmony and any consensus about what qualified as educational value, the Parliament was marked more by contestation and ideological dispute. One of the principle themes of the Parliament as advanced by its organizers and Protestant representatives was to show the essential unity of all religions. How the various religious parties in attendance perceived this goal varied markedly. To the Protestants who organized the Parliament, such an intercultural religious event appeared as the perfect setting for discussion of the unity of the human race. The theme of unity was connected in some obscure way to the idea that religion had shown great moral progress in the nineteenth century—presumably to the point where the unity of religions could finally be recognized. Given the organizers' sense of political and economic dominance, human religious unity meant the acknowledgment of a modern world system that was governed by the Protestant moral vision and sanctioned by the Protestant God.

In all other religious quarters, the goal of unity was highly controversial. In fact, the idea of religious unity as moral progress was not unanimous, even among Protestant groups, and dissension from the concept escalated from there. Catholics and Jews were much more suspect about the proposition of unity. Indeed, the Christian and Jewish denominational congresses were designed as a counterbalance to subvert the notion that participation in the World's Parliament of Religions was a compromise of one's "own peculiar faith." The many other religious representatives from lands being dominated by Protestant cultures proved even less interested in speculating about the religious unity of the race and focused instead on reestablishing their unique precolonial identities. For the colonized, moral progress meant recovering the important sense of cultural differences that had been seriously threatened by Western encroachment.[38]

The question of why a World's Parliament of Religions should occur in the United States is more difficult to answer definitively. The very fact of a World's Parliament of Religions on American soil makes clear that Protestants were at some level beginning to realize they were going to have to engage in serious intellectual discussions to maintain the predominance of their faith in the United States. Catholics and Jews were the most immediate religious groups whom the Protestants needed to acknowledge. It was not difficult to procure extensive Jewish participation, because the proud religious history of the Jews stood exalted over their social position in the United States at the time. It would have been difficult to see how their participation could do anything other than enhance their status within the American context. But securing Catholic participation was considerably more difficult. To some extent, American Catholics were in the same position as the Jews in their relation to the Parliament, but the history of the whole of Catholicism's relationship with Protestantism was more adversarial in that the two had posed genuine threats to each other at various historical junctures. There were, then, two sides to the question of Catholic participation that had to be negotiated separately and together—the American question and the larger question of the long history of Catholic-Protestant relations. At the same time, the Protestants needed to insure Catholic participation more than any other single religious group, because Catholics were such an integral part of the American scene. For that particular religion to be absent would have irremediably dampened Protestant hopes to host a universal religious gathering, along with the delusions of grandeur that accompanied them.

From a non-American perspective, reasons for an American-based World's Parliament of Religions are perhaps best explained by the sentiments of the planners of the Congress on Africa, which viewed the United States as "neutral territory." After all, nearly a half-century after the Great Exhibition, with the world having become far more of a global village than it was in 1851 London, the Archbishop of Canterbury had to regretfully decline an invitation to an American-based World's Parliament of Religions. Religion in Europe bore no real resemblance to what it had become in the American setting. For the Archbishop, the nature of religion in the Church of England was such that it belonged to "a region too sacred" for it to be merely one among many at a congress of religions. Whether that sacred "region" was defined more by England's insular politics than from on high is, of course, open to debate.[39]

Conversely, the United States of 1893 was still a largely unknown quantity—culturally, politically, and even religiously. It also boasted the world's most diverse domestic population. American social fluidity made a parliament of religions more feasible and even more desirable—especially to the organizers of the event, who had the advantage of being able to plan the meeting around their own preferred religious themes. European countries were unlikely candidates to host a parliament of religions for political reasons, given the enduring tensions between them. As important, their empires abroad, which the United States did not have, would have made extensive foreign participation untenable at intellectual congresses, because the hosts would have had no real desire for direct debate with their subordinates.

In the United States, however, the empire was a domestic affair. Broad foreign participation, such as from India, could be solicited without the interference of prohibitive political impediments. In addition, oppressed domestic peoples from within the United States—mainly African Americans and Native Americans, who were the American equivalent of the distant colonies of the European powers—were all but forced to become reluctant participants in the Chicago fair and the Parliament, since a limited role was generally preferable to no role at all. These members of the "internal colonies" were largely excluded from all serious discussion at the intellectual congresses—with the notable exception of the Congress on Africa—through the same covert means that they were excluded from any serious role within the exposition itself. Nonetheless, because they were already on the scene in massive numbers, these peoples were swept up in the flux and flow of the Parliament setting in a way that the European colonies could not have been. These were the factors unique to the American scene that caused the World's Parliament of Religions to be the broadly representative event it was, and one that could not have occurred in Europe.

The role of the Asians at the Parliament has been emphasized in recent scholarship, but it is at least as efficacious to argue that the primary significance of the event—at least in terms of the peoples who *were* well represented there—is that the Parliament was a landmark event in the history of American ecumenicism. The World's Parliament of Religions was made significant as much by the presence of the Catholic and Jewish delegates as the Asians, especially when it is realized that securing participation from the various world religions was not uniformly easier at home than abroad.[40]

The Jews were newcomers on the American scene to a greater extent than the Catholics, whose presence by mid-century had begun to be felt in a significant way with the influx of the Irish after the potato famine. The Jews stood in a strong relationship to the Parliament as the foundation of the Judeo-Christian tradition. In this they can be contrasted with Native Americans in that the latter, while being extensively represented at the Columbian Exposition—albeit as part of Euro-American exhibits—were absent at the Parliament. Jews, on the other hand, were prominent at the Parliament, while being virtually invisible at the fair and in the commentary about the exposition in terms of being represented or perceived as a separate culture. There were rare exceptions to the Jews not being represented as a religious peoples at the fair, though, such as the display of Jews as a distinct culture based on the category of religion accomplished by Cyrus Adler. Further, the general lack of Jewish visibility at the Chicago fair and even within the exposition tradition—at least after a certain point—is somewhat deceptive. Barbara Kirshenblatt-Gimblett has noted that Cyrus Adler, the Jewish head of the Smithsonian displays in the Government Building, was also appointed commissioner to five foreign countries from around the Mediterranean. In securing representation from those countries, Adler contracted for a large number of Jewish persons to be a part of those countries' exhibits. The Turkish Village along the midway, for instance, was perhaps as much as 80 percent Jewish in composition, and there were numerous other examples of a Jewish presence behind the scenes, as it were, throughout the Columbiad and at earlier international expositions as well.[41]

Still, the Jews did not occupy a distinct position of their own in either White City or along the midway, and this made their strong appearance at the World's Parliament of Religions even more noteworthy. Led by Emil Hirsch, a Reform rabbi of Chicago who was on the initial organizing committee and also spoke at the Congress on Evolution, prominent Jewish men and women participated in the Jewish Religious Congress and the Jewish Women's Congress, as well as in the World's Parliament of Religions. Jewish papers primarily emphasized the legitimacy of the place of Jews within the mainstream of the American community by pointing to the contributions of Judaism to the broad history of Western religion and theology.[42]

As far as the Catholic presence at the Parliament, Dennis P. McCann has observed that it was not the content of the papers delivered by Catholics that was most significant, but rather the symbol created by the mere fact of Catholic participation in the event. It was also the symbol of that participation, McCann argues, that was responsible for the conservative movement in the Catholic Church in America in the years following. The move to the right would prohibit anything like Catholic involvement in an ecumenical religious gathering for years to come. Regardless of future consequences, Catholic visibility at the Parliament was extensive. Without the fundamental religious symbol provided by the Catholic presence, the universality and grandeur of the event would have been sorely diminished. James Cardinal Gibbons of Baltimore sat at center stage at the opening ceremonies; Bishop John J. Keane, a liberal rector from Catholic University in Washington, D.C., was the most visible Catholic spokesman. Like the Jews, the principal focus for Catholics was to identify their place within the mainstream of American life. They did this by speaking on a wide range of issues and pointing out the extent of their collective immersion within American society.[43]

Extensive Asian representation produced the great irony that has been the enduring legacy of the World's Parliament of Religions. The Parliament president, Presbyterian minister John Henry Barrows, admitted that one of the principal motivations behind ensuring extensive Asian participation was in fact to diffuse the potentially insurmountable tensions of any meeting between Catholics and Protestants: "It required a parliament of all religions to bring together the first modern parliament of Christendom. An effort less ecumenical would not have brought together the disciples of Christ." Without their presence, the ecumenical gathering of American religious representatives would either not have happened, or it would have been a more politically restricted and less genuine exchange of religious ideas than it was. As it did happen, inviting the Asians and allowing them to speak without interruption had unfortunate consequences for Protestant evangelical aspirations globally, while it gave Asian culture a new credibility in the West. This is why, as Joseph Kitagawa has observed, the Parliament has been remembered much more fondly in Asia than in the West.[44]

There are two problems with the emphasis on the Asians at the Parliament. To begin with, Islam, a religion perennially on the borders of East and West, had no representatives from the Middle East because of the refusal of Sultan Abdul Hamid II, the Emir of Turkey, to endorse the event. As stated earlier, Asia proper was represented by only about half a dozen representatives, who nevertheless proved to be, collectively, the noblest "savages" ever to visit the West to that date. The presence of the Asians was enhanced considerably by the fact that many of them spoke several times, by the considerable press coverage accorded them, and by the fact that they were well received, especially by the women in attendance. The fact remains, however, that out of 183 delegates who actually spoke in English at the Parliament, only about half a dozen were from India and Ceylon, Japan, and China, or what are considered definitively Asian countries today. Nevertheless, it is fair to say that the actual content of the presentations by the Asian delegates, as opposed to the mere symbolic significance of their participation, which was also important, was provocative. If the presence of the Asians at the World's Parliament of Religions has been overemphasized in recent studies, the Asian delegates were still indispensable to the success and prestige the event enjoyed.[45]

The degree of influence the respective Asian cultures gained at the World's Parliament of Religions corresponded very closely to the impression they had already made in exhibiting themselves at the Columbian Exposition. There can be little doubt that most Parliament participants visited the Columbian Exposition and that it affected how they perceived the event of the Parliament and felt they would be perceived at it. It was at the top of the Ferris wheel, after all, that the Buddhist H. Dharmapala of Ceylon said to the Englishman Alfred Mommerie, "All the joys of heaven are in Chicago," to which Mommerie replied, "I wish I were sure that all the joys of Chicago are to be in heaven."[46]

The Chinese were represented only nominally by two papers on Confucianism from one author, Kwang Pang Yu, and a prize essay on Taoism. The Parliament committee solicited the Taoist essay with an advertisement in Chinese newspapers that drew forty-two responses. All of the Chinese presentations had to be delivered by

English translators, however, which greatly diminished their sense of authenticity and impact. It was acknowledged by Chairman Barrows in an apologetic tone when introducing Mr. Yu that the Chinese had been generally mistreated in the United States. At the closing ceremonies, Mr. Yu, who was adored by the crowds as an exotic foreigner, implored the audience to treat the Chinese who were living in the United States with the same dignity shown to him.

With their country behind them making strong overtures to the West, the Japanese generally found the Parliament to be a historical marvel by its end and celebrated the possibilities of interfaith enrichment it offered. Japan was represented by one Shintoist and five Buddhists. Japanese religious delegations had been divided on whether to attend and finally sent this relatively small contingent. One of the Japanese papers, "The Real Position of Japan Toward Christianity" by Hirai Ryuge Kinzō, was sharply critical of Christian missionary work in that country, and many of his declarations were followed by loud applause. Other more academic papers gained the solid respect of Western audiences, such as "The Law of Cause and Effect as Taught By the Buddha" by Shaku Soyen. Indeed, the tradition of Zen in America would begin at the hand of Soyen's student D. T. Suzuki, who was at the Parliament as an interpreter. Soyen's paper was read by Chairman Barrows, however, and only a few of the Japanese presentations were made in English by natives from Japan.

The strongest Asian voices at the Parliament came from India and Ceylon. Barrows observed that a World's Parliament of Religions was able to occur in 1893 because of the widespread use of English. However, this notion needs to be carefully specified historically, because it was really the exquisite English spoken, with a British accent, by the East Indian contingent that allowed the Parliament to seem legitimately international. Further, the Indians did not just speak English at the Parliament; they were sharply critical in the foreign tongue, using the West's own language to challenge Western culture as a whole on its own territory. The lengthy British occupation of India had caused deep animosities, and the foremost thing on the Indians' minds was not to enunciate transcendental truths, which they also did, but to talk religious politics. The Hindu Swami Vivekananda of India is the figure generally affiliated with this phenomenon at the Parliament, but the Buddhist (and Theosophist) H. Dharmapala of Ceylon and another Hindu, P. C. Mazoomdar of the reformist Brahmo Samaj sect, also spoke eloquently and critically about their respective traditions and Western involvement in their countries. The manner in which the Asians chose to participate calls attention to the cultural and historical significance of their presence as much as it does to the religious significance.⁴⁷

While the stated intention of the Parliament to define a unity among all religions was generally resisted by the Asian representatives as it was presented, they were not immune to making excessive claims of their own about the normativity of their own religious traditions and of their own particular sects within those traditions. The Asian participants were members of what would be considered liberal and reform-minded movements within their respective "world" religions and were thus in a position of trying to advance new religious movements within those traditions by displaying them on a world stage. Such nuances would have been entirely lost on the average Parliament participant but are important nonetheless in realizing that the Protestants were not the only ones trying to advance a specific agenda at the Parliament or to claim superiority. They were just the ones with the greater means to do so, given the power of the Protestant-based exhibition spectacle that was behind them. Swami Vivekananda in particular claimed that his specific form of neo-Vedanta was the true essence of Hinduism and that it was fully capable of containing all of the religious forms of the world under its generously liberal aegis. The potential of the international exposition setting was not lost on the young D. T. Suzuki either, who in the years to come would claim the Rinzai sect of Zen as the essence of not only Japanese culture but of all authentic religion as well.⁴⁸

An interesting way to understand the political dynamics that defined the relationship between the Asians and the Protestants at the World's Parliament of Religions is to recall the analogy between the potlatch ceremony and international expositions that was forged by Burton Benedict and discussed in chapter 1. In the potlatch ceremony, the only way for a party to reassert itself in the act of exchanging gifts is to return a greater gift than it has been given. Thus, entering into the act of gift exchange with a party who is in a far inferior position in regard to exchanging material gifts is ill-advised, because any victory will be a hollow one and the slightest giving of ground is amplified. This was precisely the faux pas the ambitious Parliament organizers made when inviting representatives from Asia to attend their event, while hoping to show the dominance of Christianity as a world religion. As a region, Asia was far inferior to the West economically, and at a congress promoting an even exchange of ideas, the underdog Asians essentially had nothing to lose and everything to gain. The Westerners were in just the opposite position. The very structure of the exchange that was taking place, based on the politics of the potlatch, placed them in a difficult situation.

The meaning of the World's Parliament of Religions can be legitimately summarized in either of the above two ways: as a landmark event in the history of American ecumenicism, or as the primordial East/West encounter for the history of religions. In terms of considering the relevance of the Parliament in the American religious world of today, however, I would like to recast the discussion of the event negatively—in terms of absence rather than presence.  When the Parliament is approached through its own general categories of religion, as it predominantly has been, those groups that were omitted, and their religions, become lost in the shuffle. Any analysis of the Parliament that does not take absence from the event as seriously as presence will fail to allow the Parliament to tell us all it can about the early development of a field of religion.

Both Catholics and Jews have become incorporated into the mainstream of American life and religion to a degree that would be viewed as representing adequate progress from the perspective of 1893. Asians in the United States have not fared as well as the Catholics and Jews but have still done better than the groups omitted from, or nominally represented at, the World's Parliament of Religions. It is significant that the domestic American groups who fared poorly at the Parliament now form a large part of the religious world in the United States of today. Native American groups of the period have lost large parts of their cultures or had them irremediably reconfigured since the time of the Parliament, and the sad reality is that contemporary Native American culture has become a quantitatively negligible force. Nevertheless, the ardent attempt to reconstruct and salvage what is left of those cultures, though a relatively recent phenomenon, has become a movement that far exceeds the quantitative presence of Native American peoples today. There can be little doubt that awareness of the historical significance of native cultures for the American society of the future has become firmly implanted and has made that collective group of peoples past and present more formidable than might otherwise be the case. This fact only makes the study of the manner in which Indians were represented at the Parliament all that much more relevant.

While Native American peoples proper are relatively few in number, other minority groups of today, such as Latinos and African Americans, who face greater struggles than Catholics, Jews, or Asians, are quantitatively significant forces in the contemporary United States. It is critical that the status of such groups at the Parliament be assessed, even if that assessment can only be made negatively—as part of an analysis of religious groups all but omitted by the very structure of this religious event.

Native Americans and African Americans faced fundamentally different obstacles in the latter half of the nineteenth century; the former groups were in their homeland, while the latter were in a state of exile. While Native American cultures were simply eliminated from the American scene, for the most part through countless oblique strategies, African Americans were commodified and utilized as a critical component within the vision of American empire. By the time of the Columbian Exposition, the African population had come to represent an immense social quandary for Euro-America that was hard to simply dismiss like the "Indian problem."

The manner in which these two groups were represented within the Columbian Exposition, as discussed above, reflected their social status. Anthropologists displayed Native American groups extensively, but the reason for the interest in them was historical and educational rather than a political matter pertaining to the present and future. There were nominal attempts to promote the actual education of Indians and adopt them into civilization, but this theme was minuscule next to that of the historical Indian as evolutionary link to human antiquity. Conceptually, Native Americans were reduced to the status of "disappearing races." They belonged to the earliest stages of the developing social evolutionary ladder. The Battle of Wounded Knee, which occurred just three years prior to the Columbian Exposition, was to be the last famous Indian battle. When the threat of the Indian left, so did his significance as a vibrant element of the present in the eyes of Euro-America. Frederick Jackson Turner's frontier thesis emphasized the demise of open land as the basis for the closing of the frontier. What he did not draw out was the fact that the land in question had people on it. It was never exclusively the process of homesteading that defined the rugged individualism of the American character; it was also the ruggedness of fighting off "savages" in the process. When the number of Indians declined to the point that the collective threat they represented dissipated, so too did the primitive/civilized frontier line and a defining theme for the American character.

The social context of the United States in 1893 made it highly implausible that Parliament organizers would solicit participation by any Indians. The event was much more focused on the future than on the past, and the Columbian Exposition had determined that the

Indian was a relic in the eyes of Euro-America. Further, Native American cultures had been usurped under the aegis of the field of anthropology at the Columbiad, and while religion was always a focal point for anthropological inquiry, more often than not it was focused on in order that it might be dismissed, or at least reduced. The result of this fact in the case of Native American groups is that they became defined predominantly on the basis of ethnic or cultural orientation rather than religious orientation.

The net result of these complex machinations surrounding the politics of exhibiting the collective Indian was that not a single presentation was made by any Native Americans at the first World's Parliament of Religions. The only word on indigenous American peoples at the Parliament was from a paper titled simply, "The Religion of the North American Indians," which was read by Harvard anthropologist Alice Fletcher. Fletcher did her best to detail common elements of Native American religions, but the paper was full of those blatant nineteenth-century value statements so indicative of the time. Fletcher began with an evolutionary notion, noting the "slow growth of society" in Native American cultures, and observed that "the vagueness of the Indian's metaphysics should never be lost sight of." About Indian religion she argued that "[the Indian's] mass of poetry" and often "incomprehensible thought" made systematizing his religion difficult. Finally, there was a reversion to moral judgment:

> The belief that everything [in nature] was alive and active to help or hinder man . . . prevented the development of individual responsibility. The Indian seldom thought of himself as being in the wrong, his peculiar belief concerning his position in nature having engendered in him a species of self-righteousness. The ethics of the race were simple . . . nothing excused a man who broke his word. Hospitality was a marked virtue in the race. This deeply rooted principle of giving is a great obstacle in the way of civilizing the Indians, as a civilization depends so largely upon the accumulation of private property.[49]

To her credit, Fletcher concluded by noting that "no American Indian told us how his people have sought after God" at the Parliament of Religions, despite the fact that "God's family is a large one." What is especially revealing about the above passage is the consistent use of the past tense to describe Indian culture and religion. Morality, or the lack thereof, becomes suffused with an evolutionary interpretation for Fletcher to imply that the Indian has contributed to his own demise: flawed ethics explain his inability to survive in the face of evolved civilization. The collective Indian is religiously confused and innately selfish. His potentially positive traits are used against him as well; honesty—the recurring focus of Native American complaints about dealing with whites—appears as an oversimplified ethics. Hospitality is simply uncivilized; it hinders the necessity of private property in a civilized society. Just as was the case at the Columbian Exposition, Native American groups were collapsed into the interpretive structures of early anthropology at the World's Parliament of Religions. The memory and reconstruction of their history had been reduced to a mere footnote within the evolving and triumphant narrative of Western history itself. More than anything, it was the Parliament's desire to entertain only the most inspiring of thoughts about comparative religion—to look only to the future and not the past—that eliminated the chance of there being any plausible place for Native American representatives at the event.[50]

The predicament of African Americans at the World's Parliament of Religions may well have perfectly mirrored that of Native Americans had it not been for the saving grace of that hallowed black institution, the African Methodist Episcopal Church. The AME Church was one of the more improbable nineteenth-century religious institutions. The two-decade struggle of Richard Allen, an ex-slave who had bought his freedom from his owner, was primarily what led to the appearance of the Church. It came into existence as a distinct African American Christian religious body on April 9, 1816, when several African American congregations from the areas surrounding Philadelphia met jointly to form a single denomination. By the time of the Columbian Exposition, the AME Church was a well-established Protestant religious body, and it would become the only black religious organization invited to the Parliament. Still, while the AME Church was represented as a Christian institution at the World's Parliament of Religions and secured a place for blacks at the event as such, blacks themselves understood their participation at the Parliament in ethnic terms more than religious ones.[51]

Dennis C. Dickerson has noted that black churches of the period must be demarcated from white churches in terms of the extent to which they functioned socially as well as religiously—as "black institutions more than salvific ones."[52] As Albert Raboteau has observed, one could also argue that the "ethnic bonds," though difficult to define, could be interpreted as a proper religious phenomenon in themselves. In 1893, African Americans lived in a kind of netherworld between various religious and cultural realities. It was the African American as converted Christian who was welcomed at the World's Parliament of Religions. True African religion was not represented. Though there was some argument about including some African representation in early Parliament planning, "world" religions, identified with major civilizations with long and identifiable histories, defined who was and was not to be at the event.

The AME Church's prominent leader, Bishop Benjamin W. Arnett, was an easy choice to represent the country's nine million African Americans at the World's Parliament of Religions. A local woman named Fannie Barrier Williams, mentioned earlier, also spoke at the Parliament as a member of Chicago's Providence Crandall Club, which was dedicated to breaking down the color line in America. In glaring disproportion, Arnett and Williams were the only African American representatives of a group that comprised about one-eighth of the United States.[53]

At the Parliament's opening ceremony, Bishop Arnett was the last religious dignitary called upon to make some introductory comments. In an address called "In Behalf of Africa," Arnett seemed to have no doubt about whom he represented at the Parliament. It was an ethnic group, not a religious body: "Through the partiality of the Committee of Arrangements, I am put in a very peculiar position this afternoon . . . I have been chosen as the representative of the negro race in this great Parliament . . . I am to represent on the one side the Africans in Africa, and on the other side the Africans in America." The difficulty here for Arnett, and for many other African American Christians, was defining the extent to which religious conversion—in this case from an African religion to Christianity—might take precedence in the definition of a peoples over perhaps more deeply ingrained cultural or even physiological inclinations. The complexity of the religious existence of Africans as ex-slaves in the New World seriously increased the importance of this unique issue and raised in a basic way the question of the relationship between religious and cultural orientations.[54]

Looking around the platform, Arnett went on to note, "I am also, by the Chairman, announced to give color to this vast Parliament of Religions. [Laughter] Now, I think it is very well colored itself. I think the color is in the majority this time." Just before ending by thanking the Parliament president for inviting him, Arnett noted, "There is not a slave among us to-day, and we are glad that you did not come while we were in chains, because, in that case, we could not have got here ourselves." The next day the *Daily Inter-Ocean*, which covered the Parliament more extensively than the other Chicago papers, ran synopses of a number of the opening addresses but did not mention Arnett's.⁵⁵

On the thirteenth day of the Parliament—dedicated to the "Love of Humanity as an Outgrowth of Religion"—the paper delivered by Fannie Barrier Williams was titled, "What Can Religion Do to Further the Condition of the American Negro?" The Christian Mrs. Williams was not in a mood to mince words in her talk, perhaps partly as a result of her having been run around by the bureaucracy of the fair as an on-again, off-again employee. Speaking in defense of a true Christianity, Williams claimed that as slaves African Americans were afforded only a negligible amount of the full gospel. This was to keep them in ignorance of the saving power of the Christian religion, Williams claimed, and to render them more docile than they would have been. Williams found this ludicrous because of the fact that during the Civil War, blacks had to be trusted in order to be employed as soldiers desperately needed in the fight against slavery, and they showed that they indeed could be.

Williams then contributed to the recurrent theme of criticizing Christian missionary work initiated by the Asians by posing a painfully ironic question: "When [African] mothers saw their babes sold on the auction block in order to raise money to send missionaries to foreign lands . . .is it not remarkable if such people have any sense of the purities of Christianity?" Still, Williams refused to disparage her Christian faith, noting that countless individual Christians had been the friends of blacks both before and after slavery. She concluded, as would the other black speakers at the Parliament, by conjoining religious sentiments with cultural realities: "The hope of the negro and other dark-skinned races in America depends upon how far the White Christians can assimilate their own religion." The following day, the *Daily Inter-Ocean* ran a brief summary of Mrs. Williams's comments, touching only lightly on her criticisms and concluding on a positive note.⁵⁶

The main event for African Americans at the World's Parliament of Religions took place, appropriately, on September 22, the twelfth day of the Parliament and the thirty-first anniversary of the Emancipation Proclamation. The day was dedicated to "The History of Religion and Civil Society." It was the third of three days focused ostensibly on social issues. At a special night session, the presiding officer, Bishop Daniel Alexander Payne of the AME Church, was introduced by Bishop Arnett as the oldest Methodist bishop in the world at eighty-four years of age. The evening was to be a special celebration of the new status of blacks and the role played by religion in helping their plight. Nonetheless, the social climate of the times dictated that any new status for African Americans would be won only slowly and with great difficulty. In his introductory comments for the evening, Charles Bonney took what now appears as an odd tack in hinting at the necessity of slavery so that the blacks of the world could find their way into civilization. "Man at last takes place in the world as man," Bonney began. "Africa in America is the hope of Africa throughout the world. Every sorrow which your race has suffered in this country . . . shall yet be repaid to your race in the Dark Continent a myriad-fold in the blessings which shall follow your experience in the New World. No more touching a chapter can be found in the history of your race than that which will record the religious experiences of that race in America." The clash between Bonney's triumphalist Swedenborgianism, representative of the Protestant stance at the Parliament as a whole, and the historical circumstances of African Americans is revealing. How the African experience in America could be characterized as "touching" is difficult to comprehend. The propensity for the transcendent rhetoric of the Parliament to flow easily over the most difficult of social realities was seemingly limitless.[57]

The events of the evening were to provide starker contrasts still between religious ideals and cultural realities. While Bishop Arnett sat on the stage poised to speak, a Professor O'Gorman of the Catholic University of Washington, D.C., read a paper written by J. R. Slattery of St. Joseph's seminary in Baltimore called "The Catholic Church and the Negro Race." Slattery began by recounting how famous Catholics dating back to Augustine had fought against slavery in every era. If Africans did not deserve to be slaves, however, they were in need of Catholic aid in their quest to emerge as legitimate religious beings. Slattery asserted that Africans are

> a people one-half of whom have no religion and the other half are professing only a shade of sentimental belief. In their childish way they desire to love God; they long for and relish the supernatural. Michelangelo sees an angel in an uncarved block of marble. A similar block of marble is the negro; far harder to work upon than the Carrara lump of Michelangelo, because the chisel is to be applied to the human heart. And has the negro a human heart? Is he a man? Yes, thank God. It is his manhood that is our first ground of hope.[58]

While a crowd of African Americans and officers from the AME Church looked on, Slattery made an appeal—a reversion, if you will—to morality: "In the formation of his character, which is his weak spot, chief stress should be laid on moral training and education. Neither by nature nor by training can the colored people, taken as a body, stand as yet on the same footing of moral independence as their white brethren. The careful, patient, and Christian intervention of the whites . . . is their right as well as their need in the present hour. In all this Catholics will lead the way." Slattery then listed fifteen positive Catholic traits only to conclude, "In regard to the negro race, however, these hardly exist."[59]

Thus, it was up to Bishop Arnett to follow this speech, with his task being to put into hopeful perspective the religious position of nine million African Americans. Arnett began his paper "Christianity and the Negro" by emphasizing the need for a humanistic interpretation of the gospel and by calling for a movement away from metaphysics and toward a greater concern for more immediate issues like social justice. "All we ask is the right of an American citizen," Arnett asserted, that "belong[s] to every citizen of a Christian commonwealth. It is not pity we ask for, but justice. We do not shun justice, but we ask to be judged justly." Arnett continued by recounting the history of the relationship between African American culture and Christianity:

> The negro is older than Christianity, as old as man, for he is one of the legitimate sons of his father and grandfather. We know what has been done in the name of Christianity, in the name of religion, in the name of God. We were stolen from our native land in the name of religion, chained as captives and brought to this continent in the name of the liberty of the gospel; they bound our limbs in fetters in the name of the Nazarene in order to save our souls. When the price of flesh went down the interest in our souls became small. When the slave trade was abolished by the strong hand of true Christianity then false Christianity had no interest in our souls at all.[60]

Arnett placed the accent on the positive in his conclusion, however, by noting that "Christianity has always had some strong friends for the negro in the South and in the North, men who stood by him under all circumstances." The next day, the *Daily Inter-Ocean* emphasized what a powerful evening it had been, though it was a bit overzealous in claiming, "the union of the race is likely to result from the gathering." Nevertheless, the paper tried to help the cause along by running a greatly edited version of Arnett's challenging speech. Arnett's earlier, more positive comments about organ music issuing from the

CHICAGO'S COLUMBIAN EXPOSITION                                    165

homes of blacks playing "Home, Sweet Home" were substituted as a conclusion in place of Arnett's comments on the deeply ironic relationship historically between black slavery and Christianity.[61]

The theme of emphasizing religion as social reality rather than theology was echoed again by the irrepressible Frederick Douglass, who was in the audience and was asked to make some impromptu comments on the occasion of the great Emancipation. Douglass stood up and basically questioned the efficacy of the World's Parliament of Religions itself: "If I had not been studying man all my life rather than theology, I should be able to make a speech to you to-day, but I have been studying the great question of human rights instead of human religions. People are asking me about the race problem—the negro problem. I know of no race problem. The great problem that confronts the American people to-day is a national problem—whether this great nation of ours is great enough to live up to its own convictions, carry out its declaration of independence, and execute the provisions of its constitution."[62]

In his comments at the closing ceremony, Bishop Arnett would echo the emphasis on the social particularities of religion voiced above by Douglass yet again: "The unity of the spirituality of God is the one thing we all have agreed upon. We have differed as to how to approach him and how to receive his favor and blessing."[63]

The goal of religious unity was indeed the main topic about which none could agree at the World's Parliament of Religions. To recall the sentiments of H. W. Burrows at the end of chapter 2, it must remain an open question whether cross-cultural discussion based on religion leads more readily to a satisfactory unification, or conversely, to an insurmountable impasse. On the one hand, "religion" does appear as an obvious point of departure for discussion between peoples greatly removed from one another, since it has most commonly been employed to reflect the essence of a given cultural orientation. On the other hand, it is just this comparing of essences that causes comparison in general its greatest difficulty. When the surface is reduced to that which is believed to lie beneath it, something is inevitably lost and a distortion occurs. In the long run, parties on both sides of the act of comparison experience this distortion negatively.

Even more central to the discussion of religious comparison in particular, however, is the question of whether religion can ever be finally separated from culture. Is it really possible to imagine acts of religious comparison apart from the inevitable economic power differential that defines them? If Swami Vivekananda and D. T. Suzuki used the Parliament setting to imagine and advance the notion of the ultimacy of their own religious sects, they nonetheless did so from a disadvantaged economic cultural perspective, and this was primarily what distinguished their vision of unity from that of the Protestants. This was the essential difference that marked how each approached the question of, in Bishop Arnett's words, "the unity of the spirituality of God."

The setting of the Columbian Exposition made it appear clear to Protestants that their deity was shining on them a little more brightly than were those of their religious compatriots. Conversely, for the Asians and Bishop Arnett, the Chicago exposition indicated that Protestant countries had abused their privileges, appeared willing to continue to do so, and would use their religious vision as justification for such activity. Still, the very fact that this message emerged at the Parliament, along with the implausible success of the Asian delegates—a success that continues clearly to this day—calls for a fundamental reassessment of what exactly constitutes "power" in all of its potential appearances. The subject of religion is, at the very least, as good a point as any through which this particular and peculiar question might be addressed.

In the end, the World's Parliament of Religions demonstrated that if religion had become a separable aspect of culture in the past half-century, it could never ultimately be extracted from its cultural setting and engaged in nonpolitical acts of comparison and quests for religious unity. By taking the initial step of directly engaging religious representatives from beyond the West, the Parliament charted a course for the future development of a field of religion where peoples outside the West would not merely be represented by Western theorists but actively engaged in a complex and ongoing discussion about both religion and culture. This willingness to engage peoples from major civilizational centers in philosophical and religious discussion, regardless of the initial motivations, is one of the positive legacies left by the World's Parliament of Religions to the field of religion. Such ambitious forms of comparison have provided the field of religion with a powerful excitement, but also with the sternest of challenges.

# CONCLUSION
## A PARLIAMENT FOR THE WORLD'S RELIGIONS?

FROM THE perspective of the history of religions, the postevent commentary on the World's Parliament of Religions was written by a relatively small and enclosed circle of persons. John Henry Barrows gave a series of Christian victory speeches that attempted to set the Parliament in world-historical perspective. Barrows's lecture tour across Asia in 1896 forged some connection between the Parliament and the academic study of religion in that it was endowed by a grant made through the University of Chicago. There were other Christian apologetics as well, generally exploring one or another angle of Christian supremacy. Paul Carus, editor of the philosophical quarterly the *Monist*, who initially found the idea of a World's Parliament of Religions dubious, used the event as a launching pad for asserting a new convergence of science. He then used this vision to claim a grand unity between East and West. Carus went on to write fifteen books on Oriental thought, while his Open Court Press published thirty-eight such books from 1893 to 1915.[1]

Asian visibility in the United States was pronounced immediately following the Parliament, but as Kenten Druyvestyn has pointed out, the significant press accorded such figureheads as Swami Vivekananda distorted the real extent of Asian influence. The essence of the Vedanta movement was formed by Vivekananda giving classes on yoga in New York City in 1896, but after receiving much early fanfare the movement grew slowly. Parliament participant Shaku Soyen's student D. T. Suzuki would eventually be employed by Paul Carus at the Open Court Press and would become the person primarily responsible for popularizing Zen in America. In a quantitative sense, however, both of these movements must be viewed retrospectively as having a negligible social impact until much later. The unfolding fate of Native

American and African American groups, which largely reflected their status at the Parliament, became a much larger issue.[2]

One unfortunate legacy of the Columbian Exposition and World's Parliament of Religions took a favorable turn when African Americans were represented at the opening ceremony of Atlanta's Cotton States and International Exposition in 1895 and managed to have their own separate building at the event. In delivering his famous "Atlanta Compromise" speech at the Atlanta exposition, Booker T. Washington claimed that blacks were best suited to agricultural and industrial labor, should be eager and proud to work, and would be best off keeping their culture separate from white culture. Nonetheless, black participation at the fair was controversial. Many blacks felt that the government appropriation for a separate black exhibit was only a token gesture aimed at securing cheap black labor for an industrial market ready to expand overseas. Audiences were segregated at the fair's events, and blacks could only purchase refreshments in the Negro Building. The expanded black participation at Atlanta's exposition thus needs to be strongly qualified, and a similar pattern developed at other Southern expositions. Still, visibility and participation has to be seen as preferable to the nearly complete refusal to acknowledge blacks at the Northern expositions.[3]

Native Americans were not as fortunate as blacks at ensuing international expositions—much as had been the case at the World's Parliament of Religions. Ethnic villages increasingly became a studied practice at later fairs that represented Native American peoples only as reminders of the American past. At the 1904 Louisiana Purchase Exposition in St. Louis, some of the same Kwakiutl recruited from British Columbia by F. W. Putnam for the Columbian Exposition took part in the event, which indicates that particular groups did choose to participate more than once. It is hard to know if the recurring participation on the part of native peoples was because it offered some level of enjoyment, reflected a desire for social visibility in even less than ideal circumstances, or simply represented acts of economic desperation.[4]

A more scholarly congress of religions was held at the Paris exposition of 1900, and while the connection of this event to the Chicago Parliament of Religions is historically obscure, it is probably fair to claim some relationship between the two. The Paris meetings provided a more credible foundation for, and reflection of, the surfacing of a full-scale academic study of religion. These congresses gave rise to an intellectual tradition that in 1950 officially became the International Association of the History of Religions (IAHR). Originally

# CONCLUSION

formed in Amsterdam, the group still meets every five years. A second strand resulting ostensibly from the 1893 Parliament was a series of interfaith meetings that occurred regularly from Japan to India to the United States during the first half of the twentieth century. A third Parliament lineage is marked by a Christian ecumenical movement that resulted in the establishment of the World Council of Churches in 1948, also in Amsterdam.[5]

Considering the disparate religious voices that emerged from the Columbian Exposition and World's Parliament of Religions, the centenary of the events represented interesting challenges for the various religious strands they spawned. The *quin*centenary world's fair commemorating the arrival of Columbus in the New World was solicited by and awarded to the city of Chicago, but the event proved to be too controversial for the ethnically diverse city. The arrival of Columbus could no longer be considered cause for unabashed celebration in the political climate of a multicultural urban center in the America of 1992, and the event had to be moved to the alternate location of Barcelona amid ongoing protests.[6]

Despite the fate of the more secular-minded centenary of the Chicago fair, plans for a similar reprise of the World's Parliament of Religions went forward, finally reaching fruition at Chicago's plush Palmer House hotel in late August and early September of 1993. The bureaucratic structure of the event, along with its location, made it appear very similar to one of the American Academy of Religion's annual meetings. If it were one of the Academy's meetings, however, it would have appeared that a special costume party had been called for the year in question. Delegates from across the world, and especially from neo-pagan groups from within the United States, attended in traditional attire, lending an aura of religious authenticity and existentiality to the proceedings. Unlike the 1893 Parliament, which excluded Native Americans and allowed blacks only token representation, Native American groups were prominent at the 1993 Parliament, and the African-American Leadership Partnership of Chicago was one of many cosponsors at the event. In fact, the 1993 Parliament was dominated by all of the groups who were, or who would have been, mostly excluded from the 1893 event. Then again, it was all of the most liberal religious groups from across the world who attended the 1893 event as well. In the preceding century, the definition of religious liberalism had changed dramatically, as the center drifted continually to the left.[7]

Planning for the 1993 Parliament began in the late 1980s. There was increased sensitivity to issues of religious diversity, as was to be expected, beginning with the title of the event. A definite article, "the," had become an indefinite "a," and "parliament" came to precede "world" as the focus of the title. The idea that any one group in particular could host *The World's* Parliament of Religions, thus defining "world" on its own terms, was at some point perceived as politically incorrect. To help further, the value-neutral "of" had been replaced by the affirmative "for." Thus, the event was redefined as *A Parliament for* the World's Religions, indicating that it was just that: *a* parliament, defined by, and belonging to no one in particular, but which was a proponent of its subject matter.

The literary theory was solid and the political sensitivity refined, but the cultural reality of the 1993 Parliament was largely the same as it had been a hundred years prior. Religious representatives of the most liberal religious persuasions from across the world, though mostly from the West and America, met to discuss difficulties and identify commonalities in and between the world's religions. In 1893, the American participants were mostly liberal-leaning Protestants, Catholics, and Jews. In 1993, the participants included predominantly middle- to upper-class religious liberals who could first afford to travel to Chicago and then to stay there for a week at a posh hotel. Some Protestant groups were present, but there was negligible participation by the more mainline liberal denominations who found excessive the manner in which religious liberalism had come to be defined at such an event. So prevalent were such nontraditional religious groups that the Greek Orthodox Diocese of Chicago pulled out of the event due to "certain quasi-religious groups with which Orthodox Christians share no common ground," groups that "possess no belief in God or a supreme being." Alan Neely has observed that Christians like Erwin Lutzer of the Moody Church in Chicago, who complained that "Jesus did not get a fair representation" at the 1993 event, had only themselves to blame for the predominance of less traditional religious groups at the Parliament. Evangelicals simply refused to show up in any significant numbers and for the most part remained passive observers when they did. A prime example of how the 1993 Parliament was not conducive to more traditional religion is the fact that 142 years after the Great Exhibition and a full century after the first Parliament, the Archbishop of Canterbury was *still* sending regrets—now in even greater earnest, we might presume—about being unable to justify his presence at the more invitingly titled "A Parliament for the World's Religions."[8]

The minimal presence of Jews and Catholics at the 1993 event indicated the extent to which radical religious liberalism in the United

States had come to be defined by the kind of amorphous boundaries that only the most liberal edge of Protestantism is able to tolerate extensively. Jews and Catholics have found niches in contemporary American culture that have generally left them less motivated to engage in interreligious dialogue in an attempt to promote their social legitimacy than are many other religious groups. Further, in no way did they desire to be defined as fringe groups, a status they had worked so hard to overcome in the preceding century. The marginal American religious groups who were present in great numbers at the 1993 Parliament—"neo-pagans" remains the best one-word definition of such people—were generally seeking to do what groups like the Catholics and Jews sought to do at the 1893 event. They sought to promote their legitimacy as widely acceptable forms of religion in America.

The split between science and religion, which was in its embryonic stages at the 1893 event, was pronounced and definitive at the 1993 Parliament. On the first full night of presentations, Dr. Gerald Barney of the Millennium Institute was given a prestigious slot at eight o'clock in the Palmer House's largest meeting hall. The context of the meeting was religion, but a scientist had been asked to deliver some sobering facts about the plausible future of the exponentially growing human race. An unprecedented global threat in the form of food shortages was announced in a dramatic manner. The numbers looked bad. On charts that made Malthusian economics look prophetic, population growth was placed next to the world's available farmland to show that by current projections, the mass of humankind had no more than a half-century to live. In an attempt at theater, Barney pulled up a slide of a famous, award-winning photograph taken by photographer Kevin Carter in which a vulture sat perched near a prone African child who appeared ready to starve to death. The situation was irremediably grim.

While science was able to diagnose the problem, however, the proposed solution produced a kind of hermeneutic circle beyond which science was not able to see clearly. At the close of his talk, Barney thus called on religionists for help: "Now, I have a request, to you, our spiritual leaders—a request I make on behalf of not just all humans, but on behalf of the whole community of life. Would you devote the next 7 years of your lives to helping all 6 billion of us humans to learn from each other and from Earth how to live sustainably, justly, and humanely on the Earth in the next millennium?" Focused on the event of the millennium as a potentially eschatological moment in history, Barney went on to extol the world's religious leaders: "*If you will,* the original source of creative energy will show us all a new future. *Then,* with hope in our hearts, we can die in peace—*all 6 billion of us*—to our old, immature, 20th-century ways of being and thinking." Here, after a seamless presentation, Barney's voiced trembled as he concluded: "We can cross the waters together. And we can *celebrate earth's arrival in a new era* in a way that will be remembered forever." The goal, then, was not Darwinian survival; the goal was the collective creation of a new historical era that would go down in history for all of time. The goal was Spencerian evolution—a progressive triumph led again by the West. How much things changed and how much they stayed the same from one Parliament to the next.⁹

At least one of the religious leaders upon whom Barney called was having none of it. On Wednesday of Parliament week, the most prominent Orthodox Christian present at the Parliament, Paulos Mar Gregorious, Metropolitan of Delhi and the North Syrian Orthodox Church of India and a past president of the World Council of Churches, had given a memorable talk about the role of religion in modern society. Gregorious challenged the notion that religion could be employed to change the existing cultural order. With the title "Towards a New Enlightenment—This Time Global, Spiritual and Comprehensive," he began his talk by saying, "We need to do something more than just put some religion into the existing civilization. The civilization itself needs to have a new enlightenment in which it will see reality in a new perspective."¹⁰

Sounding a hopeful note, Gregorious worked the notion of enlightenment from a cultural perspective by observing that in Europe the Enlightenment had been hindered by conservative elements that are not present in the United States. He noted, however, that the new civilization brought about by the eighteenth-century Enlightenment "pays deference and lip service to religion but pushes it to the margins." As an example of the cultural impotence of religion, Gregorious cited the peripheral, marginalized status of the 1893 Parliament in its relation to the Columbian Exposition. He then directly challenged the notion of the important role of religionists set forth by Gerald Barney:

> When they [the society] say to us, "You religious people have a big role," it is not true, nobody believes it. They see us as some kind of global people, kind of interesting to watch. Sometimes we might get a little notice in the newspaper or on the television, but they do not think religion is the decisive factor in human life. So let us not have

any thoughts that somebody is going to ask us religious people to shape the world. We have to be a little more wise. See, only the scientists have the center. And the scientists and the technologists who are at the center are now saying we do not have the answers. We need to sit down with you and talk to you. But we have not developed the capacity to talk to them. We are afraid. We are afraid these scientists know so much, but it is not true.[11]

Gregorious concluded by focusing on the economic circumstances behind the search for human solutions. He noted that all the money is in the hands of the scientists, who in turn are bound by those giving out the money. The problem has to be traced to the source, Gregorious lectured the audience, because most of the money is in the hands of those focused on defense and profit rather than humanistic concerns. Barring some change in this economic circle, the upshot of Gregorious's comments was that it would be both ludicrous and hypocritical to solicit the help of religionists in such a circumstance in order to solve global problems. For the most part, Gregorious's observations about the potency of the 1993 Parliament of Religions were borne out in press reports of the event. In the *National Review,* John R. Coyne Jr. wrote a bemused article about the event and dubbed the proceedings "Ultimate Reality in Chicago." *Christianity Today* called the Parliament "The Supermarket of the Gods."[12]

By the end of the 1993 Parliament, the sophisticated attempts to find an encompassing language in which everyone could find something to like broke down completely. Father Hans Küng, the Swiss Roman Catholic, spent more than two years drafting "A Global Ethic," a statement designed to identify and promote commonalities between the world's religions at the level of ethics. In its construction, "more than one hundred and fifty experts from diverse religious traditions and perspectives had been consulted by July of 1993." The document was a "minimal ethic" decrying all of the worst aspects of human culture—the condemnation of oppression is the best simple summary. It pointed to commonalities in the moral teachings of the ancient religious traditions through which contemporary social problems might be approached. The language of "A Global Ethic" was definitive and forceful; many would characterize it as Germanic in the context of Western scholarship. The word "God" had been eliminated; in its place was "ultimate reality." In the end, The Assembly of Spiritual and Religious Leaders of the Parliament found the statement lacking—if not in principle, then at least in tone: "What happened at the meeting of the Assembly on September 4 was a confusing and frustrating descent into chaos. There was no possibility of editing the statement on ethics at the moment, and there was little debate on the document itself. Because some representatives feared the tone of the statement was too Western and Christian, it was proposed to endorse the text as an initial statement *toward* a global ethic."[13]

The 1993 Parliament closed with Kung and the Dalai Lama sharing the same platform. The former read his "declaration," searching for the right language to incorporate all religious beings into a single global ethic. The latter, exiled from his homeland because of the same oppressive forces the global ethic sought to undermine, talked about the need for many religions among the world's many peoples. In essence, the Dalai Lama called for *real* pluralism, *cultural* pluralism, not theoretical religious pluralism with an underlying theme of unity. An edict promoting the ethical commonalities between religions drawn up by scholars in state-of-the-art language seemed unable to touch the Dalai Lama's particular situation and the very real threat with which his people's own set of ethics was faced.

It is easy to disparage religious gatherings such as the 1993 Parliament of Religions. The collectivity who is willing to actually congress around the occasion of comparative religion rather than to merely imagine it as an academic construction often presents a disconcerting image. Another way to consider the value of such meetings is to ask not what they do for the world and its problems, but rather to consider what the world might be like if such events never occurred at all. One observer, Peter Gardella, chair of religion at Manhattanville College in New York, found the whimsy of the 1993 Parliament, with its profusion of neo-pagans, to be the perfect antidote to the "solemn optimism" of the event of a century before. While other writers noted the negligible representation of "established religion" and a triumph of "religious pluralism," Gardella came away from the later Parliament "feeling much better" about the revamped version of the religious global village. Despite the chaotic light in which globally based interfaith meetings cast the congressing religious world when it actually meets itself face-to-face, such actual encounters may bring some necessary humility to each separate religious conception arising in privacy from all the others. Such gatherings may also serve as a reminder to the academic study of religion that when concepts are put into practice, it is quite common to gain unforeseen results.[14]

THIS STUDY has attempted to demonstrate the extent to which the appearance of a "field" of religion was dependent on a wider variety of factors than has generally been acknowledged, originating both within the West itself and also from beyond it. In an internal sense, the ability of evolutionists to convince Westerners—both the elite and laypersons alike—that evolutionism had a positive contribution to make to their societies was crucial in allowing for traditional religious authority to be countered by an alternative mode of cultural, and finally religious, orientation. The international exposition tradition was instrumental in demonstrating, in a visceral way that could be understood at all levels of society, how evolutionary theory could be applied to the interpretation of cultural and religious differences so as to be advantageous to Western peoples. Evolutionism gained ascendancy within the West itself, in fact, when it became attractive to enough members of the intelligentsia and populace that churches were pressed to incorporate it into their dogma. When this happened, an evolution-based interpretation of religious differences began to appear as a plausible addition to—and in some cases replacement for—traditional biblical religion.

Equally, and in an external sense, the cumulative effects of colonial interactions transformed much of Western religious thought into being comparative rather than theologically based. However, this new field of comparative religion was greatly informed by the political and economic intercultural reality out of which it emerged. For this reason, it becomes critical to identify some of the ways the new field of comparative-based religious thought functioned in particular historical contexts. The problem with the manner in which early comparative thinking about religion manifested for the contemporary United States in particular, with its distinct division between "primitive" and "civilized" peoples, is that the "primitives" and the "civilized" of 1893 have come to inhabit a truly interdependent social world at the end of the twentieth century. What was significant about the first World's Parliament of Religions to most contemporary observers before, during, and after the event was the degree to which it incorporated into a single gathering what were perceived as the ten great world religions. But given the extent to which certain cultural groups were excluded by this seemingly inclusive rubric of the Parliament, it seems all the more important to assess the event's significance for the world of the new millennium by carefully considering the religions that appeared simply too opaque to be incorporated into it.

The decisions about denying religious representation to certain cultural groups at the Parliament were not really religious decisions per se. Rather, those judgments were largely obligatory given the hierarchy of world cultures that predominated within the international exposition tradition during the latter half of the nineteenth century. This taxonomy was based on industrial, economic, and sociopolitical considerations rather than specifically religious ones, but it nonetheless defined the Parliament's religious categories, leading them to be inadequately representative and hence ineffective as a model for serious religious study. Clearly, the inclusion of Native American groups at the event would have been a real leap for Parliament organizers in light of the cultural context in which it occurred. It would have necessitated a direct acknowledgment of an element of American culture that was being either systematically excluded elsewhere at the Columbian Exposition or reconfigured within Euro-American historical conceptions. On the other hand, the relatively recent emancipation of so many African Americans made it more likely that they would be included in some way at an American congress of religion in 1893 built around the theme of human progress. This much granted, it was still just one member of the AME Church and one local African American woman who represented the nine million African Americans of the period. The notion that actual *African* religions would find a place at the Parliament was never seriously entertained. The Parliament was constructed out of colonial categories rather than anything representing a plausible methodology for a field of religion. It merits our attention for just this reason, demanding that we ask the question of whether adequate progress has been made in overcoming this particular early legacy within the field of religion of today.

With no exotic representatives from distant lands symbolizing the subordinate domestic groups of the United States at the World's Parliament of Religions, their religious legacy was marked by their limited presence at the Columbian Exposition and on the basis of the commercialized ethnographic images by which they became defined along the midway. This carnivalesque section of the fair made whatever genuine expressions of religion of which these peoples may have been capable appear as caricatures that could be easily dismissed as childish, freakish, and finally unevolved. A history of ideas could point to Benjamin W. Arnett's fine speeches or Alice Fletcher's detailed academic description of Indian religion as examples of minority representation at the World's Parliament of Religions. As a matter of cultural history, however, it was the midway, with its images of violence, rumors of cannibalism, and theories of fetishism that ultimately informed the culture of the time about the religions of those American peoples who fell into the fair's cultural category of the "primitive."

## CONCLUSION

What of the phenomenon of the "primitive," then? Has the "primitive" been adequately incorporated into Western religious thought and its potential messages been heard, given the considerable suffering it incurred by its hand? If it has not, what is to be learned from this fact? While much scholarship related to the "primitive" has been written off as "nostalgic"—a hopeless reversion to a past that is not recoverable—its dismissal is not quite that simple. The way that primitiveness became defined as such, for instance, was on the basis of a lack of industry. If we recall the angle of Gerald Barney's critique of modernity at the 1993 Parliament, however, we find too much "industry" being blamed for creating a set of conditions that make it appear that the future of human life on the planet is rapidly becoming mathematically impossible. If the many peoples discovered across the world in the past few centuries who have been deemed "primitive" did not "industrialize" to any significant degree, this may have been due to choice rather than inability. Considering Barney's figures, if this was a choice, it has now become quite possible to see it as a potentially wise one. Similarly, while the "primitive" has provided the repository for the projection of the violent inclinations in Western society, whether the "primitive" or the "civilized" is more inherently violent is both quantitatively and qualitatively debatable in view of the events of the twentieth century.

The message of the "primitive," whatever it may have been, was repressed at the World's Parliament of Religions. Whether it has been adequately brought into consciousness in the field of religion today is yet another very open question. While Mircea Eliade's conceptions of the "archaic" or "primitive" have been dismissed as a degeneration into romanticism in many quarters, his work can also be viewed as a cognizance that there was something vital in the particular inquiry into the nature of the "primitive" that had not been adequately incorporated into the developing field of religion. The serious consideration of little-industrialized societies and their importance for the field of religion in today's world still presents a difficult challenge for religious studies. The inherently theological background of the field of religion today, which was very much in evidence at the World's Parliament of Religions, has not lent itself readily to this mode of analysis, nor to conducting it effectively when it has undertaken it. Nonetheless, the field of the "primitive" still marks a viable arena in which conceptions of religion specifically might be distinguished from the broader cultural biases to which they stand in relation.

If religion is to be defined as a vital force that is clearly separable from its specific cultural settings, it needs to contribute something that cannot be otherwise found in the politicized reality of daily, secular life. The example of the first World's Parliament of Religions shows how little a field of religion can be capable of contributing to either cultural or intercultural discussion. The Parliament also demonstrated that the concept of religion can be employed by a field bearing its name—much as other comparable rubrics such as "culture" can be employed in the guise of "anthropology"—to reinforce the more negative aspects of intercultural relations. Using the World's Parliament of Religions as a guide, one of the critical tasks for the field of religion in the future is to develop a means by which the religious categories that are used to explore interreligious relationships can avoid becoming defined excessively by the cultural and political climate out of which they emerge. When this is accomplished, the unique voice of "religion" might be heard.

# NOTES

## Preface

1. Flood, *Beyond Phenomenology*, 42–64. King, *Orientalism and Religion*, 35–41.
2. Chidester, *Savage Systems*, 5. Maurice, *The Religions of the World and Their Relationship to Christianity*. Maurice's lectures include observations of foreign religions based strictly on how they might be viewed as subordinate to Christianity, rather than how they all relate to a purportedly scientific conception of nature as in evolutionary theory.
3. See Eagleton, *Idea of Culture*, 1–31; Young, *Colonial Desire*, 29–54.
4. Novick, *That Noble Dream*. 1–86.
5. I am thinking here of studies like Eric Sharp's *Comparative Religion*, Walter Capps's *Religious Studies*, or J. Samuel Press's *Explaining Religion*, each eminently useful as theoretical guides to the field of religion but with little attention given to the deep historical contexts that informed the theories recounted. There have been a number of recent studies concerned with contextualizing the history of the study of religion, but they have done so in a more immediate and narrow sense than what is being attempted here. I would point specifically to Ivan Strenski's *Four Theories of Myth in the Twentieth Century* and *Religion in Relation*, Russell McCutcheon's *Manufacturing Religion*, or Donald Wiebe's *The Politics of Religious Studies*. An example of a much broader approach to the history of the field can be found in Chidester, *Savage Systems*.
6. At different points in the text, I have had recourse to employ the potentially vague term "traditional biblical religion." By this phrase, I simply mean pre-evolutionary biblical religion, which consisted of literal interpretations of scripture that varied depending on societal contexts. The term is inadequate as a descriptive term but must be used as a way of demarcating post-evolutionary religion, with the profound changes it brought about, from what existed before it. I use it only in opposition to post-evolutionary conceptions of religions and the concept "religion."

## 1. International Expositions in Historical Context

1. Braudel, *The Mediterranean*. See also his *Civilization and Capitalism* series.

2. Representatives from African countries participated in the Columbiad's Congress on Africa as well, and this meeting did contain some discussion about religious issues, even if that was not its central focus. About the Congress on Africa, see Reid, *All the World Is Here!* 179–91.

3. Thomas Richards's *The Commodity Culture of Victorian England* effectively clarifies certain confusions prevalent in neo-Marxist thought; specifically, the inclination to forget the extent to which Marx emphasized (following Hegel) that largely disembodied discourse can affect material exchange every bit as much as, if not more than, material exchange shapes the structure of any given discourse. See his "Introduction," 1–16.

4. Paul Greenhalgh has argued that international expositions differ from trade fairs in their "specific aim of promoting the *principle* of display [emphasis mine]." See his *Ephemeral Vistas*, 3, which is the best thematic study of the international exposition tradition. In a similar vein, Kenneth Luckhurst has traced the etymological history of the various terms for fairs and noted that while trade fairs involve an actual exchange of goods, at "exhibitions" (as in the example of an art exhibition) one would not expect any actual sales. The word "exposition" represents a bridging of the gap between the original meanings of the words "fair" and "exhibition." See his *The Story of Exhibitions*, 1–10. The expositions did represent a clear point of departure from the trade fairs, but the principle of display was always a critical element of the success of early trade fairs, with their inclusion in various times and places of noncommercial, aesthetically minded exhibits, entertainments, and educational displays. Further, international expositions and the earlier trade fairs can both be viewed as involving concerted attempts to define and influence exchange values across unfamiliar borders. The importance of this common central focus of both kinds of fairs makes less significant whether actual commodities were exchanged at one kind of fair and not the other.

5. Braudel, *The Wheels of Commerce*, 91.

6. Ibid.

7. The phrase "imagined communities" is from Benedict Anderson, *Imagined Communities*.

8. See Richard Altick, *Shows of London*, 5. Geary, *Furta Sacra*.

9. Altick, *Shows of London*, 5.

10. Ibid., 5–7.

11. Ibid., 26.

12. For a history of the display of human beings for profit, see Robert Bogdan, *Freak Show*, especially 176–99. Altick, *Shows of London*, 46.

13. McGrane, *Beyond Anthropology*, 19–20.

14. Benedict, *The Anthropology of World's Fairs*, 7–10.

15. Anderson, *Imagined Communities*, 5.

16. See Braudel's evocative opening chapter to *The Structures of Everyday Life*, 31–103; see also Hobsbawm, *The Age of Capital*, 146–61. Hobsbawm notes,

however, that "an ethnic-linguistic definition of nations . . . was, essentially, invented in the nineteenth century" (146).

17. See Chidester, *Savage Systems*, 59; Hobsbawm, *The Age of Revolution*, 22–23.

18. Anderson, *Imagined Communities*, 194.

19. See F. M. Barnard, *Herder's Social and Political Thought;* Robert S. May, *Herder and the Beginnings of Comparative Literature*. See also Eagleton, *Idea of Culture*, 1–31.

20. On the French national expositions and *expositions universelles*, see Greenhalgh, *Ephemeral Vistas*, especially 3–7.

21. Ibid., 5.

22. Ibid, 7–8.

23. Ibid., 9.

## 2. Britain's Great Exhibition

1. The most useful survey of world's fair literature can be found in Robert Rydell's bibliographic essay in *The Books of the Fairs*.

2. Paul Greenhalgh has argued that the show of industrial might by the British government at the Great Exhibition was designed in part to intimidate revolutionary-minded individuals such as the Chartists into conformity through the careful staging of the most impressive industrial exhibits. See his *Ephemeral Vistas*, 29–30. To a certain extent, it was the case that the British government advanced specific political agendas. It remains important to remember, however, that in 1851, hegemonic inclinations were infinitely more simplistic and naïve than they were at the end of the nineteenth century, and especially through the first half of the twentieth century. All of the most recent interpretations of the Great Exhibition, Thomas Richards's *Commodity Culture of Victorian England*, Greenhalgh's *Ephemeral Vistas*, and Larry Lutchmansing's "Commodity Exhibitionism at the London Great Exhibition of 1851" can be accused of having fallen into this problem of anachronism in interpreting the Great Exhibition at various points.

3. I have given both of these themes—design and architecture—very little attention. For more on the debates about the nature of the exhibition displays, see Yvonne Ffrench, *The Great Exhibition: 1851*, which is the best general history of the Great Exhibition; Christopher Hobhouse, *1851 and the Crystal Palace;* and Nikolaus Pevsner, *High Victorian Design: A Study of the Exhibits of 1851*. The best work on the architecture of the "Crystal Palace," as the Great Exhibition building came to be called, can be found in Antony Bird, *Paxton's Palace*.

4. Chidester, *Savage Systems*, 1; McGrane, *Beyond Anthropology*, 19–20.

5. I am indebted to David Chidester for clarifying the distinction between the terms "savage" and "primitive" in his unpublished paper "Classify and Conquer." For more insight into how little-industrialized societies have participated in and contributed to this process of cultural exchange with the West, see Chidester, *Savage Systems*, and Thomas, *Entangled Objects*. McGrane, *Beyond Anthropology*, 113–14. See the Introduction for a longer explanation of the history of the usages of the term "culture."

6. Matthew Digby Wyatt, "A Report on the Eleventh French 'Exposition of the Products of Industry,'" 22. Royal Society Archives.

7. In the years following the Great Exhibition, when the historical significance of the event became more fully apparent, the matter of who had what part in making the idea of the first international exhibition a reality became a matter of in-fighting within the Royal Society. The precise story may never be finally known. For more on Henry Cole's role, see Bonython, "The Planning of the Great Exhibition of 1851," and Burris, "Religion and Anthropology at Nineteenth-Century International Expositions," 51–52. Henry Cole, *Fifty Years of Public Work*, 124–25.

8. Commissioners Records, 4.

9. I have referred to the event primarily as the Great Exhibition because I am emphasizing its nature as a dynamic event initiating a sequence of other events, rather than as an isolated historical phenomenon within British history that is affiliated with the particular building in which it was displayed.

10. Commissioners Records, 19.

11. *Morning Chronicle* (London), 18 November 1850.

12. *Punch*, vol. 20 (1851), 189; *London Times*, 2 May 1851; "Religious Aspects of the Great Exhibition," 626; *Illustrated London News*, 3 May 1851.

13. Reverend W. Pashley, *The Morning Stars*.

14. *Illustrated London News*, 3 May 1851.

15. Paul Greenhalgh has argued, however, that while the price of admission was reduced significantly for the working classes, it was lowered to a point that guaranteed that the lowest reaches of the working class would be absent. See *Ephemeral Vistas*, 30.

16. *Illustrated London News*, 31 May 1851.

17. *Punch*, vol. 20 (1851), 42.

18. *London Times*, 1 May 1851.

19. Walton explores this theme in *France at the Crystal Palace* by conducting a feminist reading of the interplay at the level of industrial philosophy between France and Britain at the Great Exhibition.

20. *London Times*, 15 May 1851; Ibid., 24 May 1851; *Illustrated London News*, 10 May 1851.

21. Meinig, *Continental America*, 46–50, 114–19. For an analysis of transatlantic relations between the United States and Britain at the time of the Great Exhibition, see Cunliffe, "America at the Great Exhibition of 1851."

22. This occurred through the signing of the Treaty of Guadalupe Hidalgo with Mexico on February 2, 1848. See Meinig, *Continental America*, 146.

23. *London Times*, 28 December 1850.

24. *Illustrated London News*, 17 May 1851.

25. *London Times*, 2 May 1851.

26. *London Times*, 15 May 1851.

27. *Punch*, vol. 20, 209. In all fairness, the abolition of the slave trade in Britain had to do with the economic circumstances of the declining sugar trade in the Caribbean as well as humanitarian concerns. This fact partly explains the

earlier abolishment of slavery in that country than in the United States. See, for instance, David Brion Davis, *The Problem of Slavery in Western Culture*.

28. *Morning Chronicle*, 5 May 1851.
29. *Morning Chronicle*, 28 October 1851.
30. *Journal of the Royal Society of Arts*, vol. 1, 475.
31. Quoted by Robert Dalzell, *American Participation in the Great Exhibition of 1851*, 54.
32. Anderson, *Imagined Communities*, 180n.
33. *Illustrated London News*, 24 May 1851.
34. Ibid.
35. *Morning Chronicle*, 16 May 1851.
36. *London Times*, 24 May 1851; *Morning Chronicle*, 16 May 1851.
37. Ibid.
38. *London Times*, 10 April 1851.
39. *London Times*, 25 January 1851. On Mormon participation, see T. Edgar Lyon Jr., "In Praise of Babylon," 49–61.
40. Aveling, *Great Sights*, 16.
41. *London Times*, 2 May 1851.
42. Commissioners Reports, vol. 1, 125–26.
43. Ibid.
44. Commissioners Records, 374–75.
45. Anonymous, *A Walk through the Crystal Palace*, n.p.; Aveling, *Great Sights*, 5.
46. John Cumming, *The Great Exhibition: Suggestive and Anticipative*, 55–56; Reverend J. W. Milner, *The Design of God in the Great Exhibition*, 13.
47. William Paley, *Natural Theology*; Anonymous, "Religious Aspects of the Great Exhibition," 635–36.
48. Binney, *The Royal Exchange and the Palace of Industry*, 95–98.
49. Higginson, *A World Embracing Faith*, n.p.
50. Ibid.
51. *London Times*, 5 March 1850.
52. Anonymous, *The Great Assembly*, (London: J. P. Snow, [1853?]), 6–10.
53. Ibid.
54. Henry Cole, *Lectures on International Results*, vol. 1, 422–29.
55. This observation is made by Reid Badger, *The Great American Fair*, 6.
56. "The Exhibition Jury Reports," 492; *Illustrated London News*, 8 November 1851.
57. H. W. Burrows, *The Great Exhibition: A Sermon*, (London: Skeffington and Southwell, 1851), 12.

## 3. Social Evolutionism and International Expositions

1. Writing in a more nuanced way about the theory of evolution in the context of the history of anthropology, George Stocking has opted for the term "sociocultural evolutionism" to describe more fully the complete range of the concept in

his study *Victorian Anthropology*. I have chosen the simpler and more common term "social evolutionism" to avoid becoming jargonistic in a study that is less specific in a disciplinary sense. I have included the "ism" to signify that social evolution was not a single unified theory, but rather a conglomerate of several competing theories that were applied across a wide range of contexts in a variety of ways.

2. The following argument about evolutionism has been gleaned from a variety of texts. The best survey of the field is provided by Peter Bowler in *Evolution: The History of an Idea*. See also Himmelfarb, *Darwin and the Darwinian Revolution*, for a concise discussion of the theoretical issues and Stocking, *Victorian Anthropology*, 9–45, for a historical contextualization of the phenomenon.

3. Stocking, *Victorian Anthropology*, 5.

4. For an analysis of the progress of archaeology in the nineteenth century, see Daniel and Renfrew, *The Idea of Prehistory*.

5. An account of the internalist perspective on the phenomenon of the Darwinian revolution can be found in Ruse, *Taking Darwinism Seriously*.

6. Accounts of the externalist perspective can be found in Bowler, *The Non-Darwinian Revolution*, and Young, *Darwin's Metaphor*.

7. Ellegard, *Darwin and the General Reader*, 17.

8. *Essays and Reviews* was published in London in 1860 by six prominent liberal clergymen. Ellegard cites another book, *The Pentateuch and the Book of Joshua Critically Examined*, seven parts, 1862–1879, by Bishop J. W. Colenso, as causing nearly as much controversy. Both became involved in court cases. See Ellegard, *Darwin and the General Reader*, 105–6.

9. Ellegard, *Darwin and the General Reader*, 33.

10. Darwin, *The Origin of Species*, 373.

11. Ibid., 919–20.

12. Nandy, *The Intimate Enemy*, 69.

13. Quoted in Chidester, "Classify and Conquer," 2.

14. Benedict, *Anthropology of World's Fairs*, 30.

15. Sweet, "The Face of Australia."

16. Greenhalgh, *Ephemeral Vistas*, 86–87.

17. Benedict, *Anthropology of World's Fairs*, 46.

18. Sweet, "Face of Australia," 65; Benedict, *Anthropology of World's Fairs*, 42.

19. Greenhalgh, *Ephemeral Vistas*, 87–89.

## 4. Exhibitionism, American Style

1. Adams, *The Education of Henry Adams*, 343.

2. Hilton, *Here Today, Gone Tomorrow*, 11–12.

3. Davis, *Parades and Power*, 1–22.

4. Steen, "New York 1853–1854," 12, in Findling and Pelle, *Historical Dictionary*.

5. Hilton, *Here Today, Gone Tomorrow*, 20.

6. Ibid.

## NOTES TO CHAPTER FOUR

7. Badger, *Great American Fair*, 16.
8. Hilton, *Here Today, Gone Tomorrow*, 24–29.
9. Ibid., 21–32.
10. Ibid., 23–27.
11. Ibid., 21.
12. Badger, *Great American Fair*, 16; Allwood, *The Great Exhibitions*, 31–33.
13. Steen, in Findling and Pelle, *Historical Dictionary*, 13–14.
14. On the Civil War fairs, see Hilton, *Here Today, Gone Tomorrow*, 12. On the genesis of the Philadelphia Centennial, see Rydell, *All the World's a Fair*, 17; Heller, "Philadelphia, 1876," in Findling and Pelle, *Historical Dictionary*, 55. Rydell's works are the best guide to the American international expositions. All world's fair researchers owe a debt of gratitude to his pioneering studies and state-of-the-art historiographical work. The concluding quote is from Heller, "Philadelphia Centennial," in Findling and Pelle, *Historical Dictionary*, 63.
15. Quoted by Rydell, *All the World's a Fair*, 14. Heller, "Philadelphia Centennial," in Findling and Pelle, *Historical Dictionary*, 61.
16. Rydell, *All the World's a Fair*, 16.
17. Ibid., 21. Wagner quote is from Hilton, *Here Today, Gone Tomorrow*, 38. Heller, "Philadelphia Centennial," in Findling and Pelle, *Historical Dictionary*, 58–61.
18. For more on women at international expositions, see Paul Greenhalgh, *Ephemeral Vistas*, 174–97.
19. Tenkotte, "Kaleidoscopes of the World," 5–29.
20. Hoxie, *A Final Promise*, 87. Richard Slotkin has explored this theme thoroughly and used the Centennial Exhibition as a leitmotif in *The Fatal Environment*.
21. Rydell, *All the World's a Fair*, 26. There is considerable confusion about whether living Indians were displayed, or in what manner, at the Philadelphia Centennial. I have found nothing to confirm actual displays of live Indians in any manner commensurable with the later institution of "ethnic villages" at the Paris and Chicago expositions
22. Rydell, *All the World's a Fair*, 22–23.
23. Ibid., 27–29.
24. Vile, *Encyclopedia of Constitutional Amendments*, 50; Roberts, *Darwinism and the Divine*, 32.
25. McCabe, *Illustrated History of the Centennial Exhibition*, 274–75.
26. For the participation of the American Bible Society at international expositions, see Cordato, "The Bible on Display." On the Centennial congresses, see McCabe, *Illustrated History*, 274–75.
27. Regarding the origination of the Columbian Exposition, see Lederer, "The Genesis of the World's Columbian Exposition."
28. Johnson, ed., *A History of the World's Columbian Exposition*, vol. 4, 4–10.
29. Dexter, "Putnam's Problems," 316. Putnam had to argue for this particular name of the building at a time when it was not certain that the new science of culture would be called "anthropology."

30. Ibid.
31. Frederick Starr Papers.
32. Hinsley, in *Exhibiting Cultures*, 348; Dexter, "Putnam's Problems," 318.
33. For this insight, which is borne out in the official literature, I am indebted to an eminently useful Ph.D. dissertation by Gertrude Scott called "Village Performance: Villages at the Chicago World's Columbian Exposition, 1893," New York University, 1991, 97. Scott conducts an impressive archaeology of the villages at the fair, and her work serves as a useful index to the newspaper articles about the Columbiad that are not indexed.
34. For more on the East Indian presence at early international expositions and the manner in which India was represented and perceived, see Breckenridge, "The Aesthetics and Politics of Colonial Collecting," 195–216.
35. Allwood, *Great Exhibitions*, 6. For an analysis of Japanese participation at early American world's fairs, see Harris, "All the World a Melting Pot?" 29–55.
36. An account of Japan's careful planning for the fair, stated intentions, and studied approach toward the United States was written up by the Japanese foreign minister to the United States, Gozo Tateno, in "Foreign Nations at the World's Fair," 34–43.
37. See, for example, "An Esquimaux Revolt," *Daily Inter-Ocean*, 31 March 1893, 7, and "Exodus of Eskimos," *Daily Inter-Ocean*, 21 April 1893, 1, as well as Scott, "Village Performance."
38. "Weird Funeral Rite," *Daily Inter-Ocean*, 22 August 1893, 7.
39. Rudwick and Meier, "Black Man in the White City," 358.
40. Wilson, "Black Involvement." See also Reid, *All the World Is Here!*
41. Rudwick and Meier, "Black Man in the White City," 361.
42. Wilson, "Black Involvement," 13.
43. *Daily Inter-Ocean*, 2 May 1893, 5; *Chicago Tribune*, 2 May 1893, 1–2.
44. Headlines were regularly given such captions as "Two Redskins on the Rampage," *Daily Inter-Ocean*, 2 September 1893, 5. On the Apache chief, see "White City Chips," *Daily Inter-Ocean*, 15 September 1893, 7.
45. This complex problem of the reenactment of Native American rituals in the context of expositions has been explored in Jacknis, "Northwest Coast Indian Culture," 91–118. For a discussion of differences in the way particular Native American groups were represented at American world's fairs, see Trennert, "Fairs, Expositions, and the Changing Face of Southwestern Indians," 127–50.
46. Johnson, *History of the Exposition*, 341.
47. For an example of how seriously Hindu magic was beginning to be taken in this period, see Hensholdt, "The Wonders of Hindoo Magic," 46–60.
48. On the "No" drama, see Scott, "Village Performance," 133.
49. On the participation and representation of predominantly Islamic countries at international expositions, see Mitchell, "The World as Exhibition," 217–36, and Celik, *Displaying the Orient*. Bloom contracted for the Algerian act while in Paris at the 1889 exposition before taking over the Chicago midway. For the record, Bloom insisted that the legendary belly dancer "Little Egypt" never performed at the Chicago fair. See his *Autobiography*, 134–35.

50. See Reid, *All the World Is Here!* passim.

51. For an analysis of the extent to which reports of cannibalism have been grossly exaggerated and misrepresented in many regions within anthropological writings, see Arens, *The Man-Eating Myth.*

52. "From Away Up North," *Daily Inter-Ocean,* 22 May 1893, 2.

53. Scott, "Village Performance," 212.

54. For more on Peneé and the display of Africans at international expositions, see Rydell, "Darkest Africa."

55. Wilson has claimed that the music played in the Dahomean village was the first instance of ragtime being played in the United States, which developed by slowing down existing African rhythms ("Black Involvement in Chicago's Previous Fairs"). Various sources have proposed more significant degrees of influence issuing from the Dahomean music, claiming that the drumming in particular may have left a mark on Chicago jazz. See "Black Involvement."

56. An excellent account of Douglass's activities at the fair can be found in McFeely, *Frederick Douglass,* and Reid, *All the World Is Here!*

57. Scott, "Village Performance."

58. Benedict, "Rituals of Representation," passim.

59. Howard Eilberg Schwartz has conducted an illuminating investigation into the way in which the analysis of "primitive" religion has been carefully demarcated from analyses of comparable religious phenomena within the history of classically Western religions such as that of ancient Judaism. See his *The Savage in Judaism.*

## 5. Exhibiting Religion at Chicago's Columbian Exposition

1. The participation of women at the World's Parliament of Religions and at international expositions in general is a topic that sorely needs current reflection. Unfortunately, the potential immensity of such a project—especially as a matter of cultural history, which is the focus here—has caused it to fall almost completely outside of the present inquiry. Paul Greenhalgh's *Ephemeral Vistas* is the best introduction to the activities of women at international expositions. See also Robert Rydell's important essay "A Cultural Frankenstein?" In an analysis of oppressed factions at the fair, Rydell makes the important observation that the women at the fair, as distinct from the ethnic minorities, were middle- and upper-class persons of considerable means within the society in which they sought change. Richard Seager has also explored the role of women at the Columbiad and Parliament in some depth in *The World's Parliament of Religions.*

In general, the status of women at the Chicago fair and Parliament of Religions was ambiguous. On the one hand, they had their own distinguished building; on the other hand, they were taking part in displays like the "World's Congress of Beauties" along the midway, where "forty ladies from forty nations" sat in booths, occupied themselves with idle tasks, and were thoroughly objectified like the ethnic villagers alongside them. The central problem with writing a relatively simple, separate analysis of the religious presence of women at nineteenth-century international expositions and at the intellectual congresses is that with the forbidding complexity of contemporary feminist hermeneutics, such attempts can all too easily appear patronizing and as token concessions. I have elected to generally avoid any analysis of the early feminist movement at international expositions primarily because the subject does not fit well into my governing heuristic device of social evolutionism. A very different structure would be needed for the feminist project. World's fair scholarship has generally been too broad in scope, reflective of its data; it is important that firmer boundaries be drawn around the topic. The rising status of women at early international expositions—especially those in America, where their presence was especially noteworthy—was nonetheless an important aspect of the total phenomenon, and it is unfortunate that I must generally omit treatment of it here.

2. Paul Carter ends his survey of the cultural and religious history of the period with the Chicago fair and parliament in *The Spiritual Crisis of the Gilded Age*, while Martin Marty begins his projected four-volume study, *Modern American Religion*, with these events. There are innumerable other examples. One of the problems with previous attempts to analyze the influence of social evolutionism in particular on American religious thought in the nineteenth century has been an emphasis on a "history of ideas" approach, reflective perhaps of a latent theological tendency within the writing of American religious history. Paul Boller Jr.'s *American Thought in Transition* is useful in showing the many manifestations of social evolutionism in American thought, but it lacks full cultural contextualization. James Turner's *Without God, without Creed* seeks to contextualize evolutionism within the history of Western thought extending back to the post-Reformation period, but in its attempts to do so, it sacrifices full cultural contextualization of the lengthy period it treats. Jon Roberts has conducted an exhaustive survey of the impact of evolutionary thought on religion in America in the later nineteenth century in *Darwinism and the Divine in America*. Roberts's stated methodological bias, however, is toward "the public posture of Protestants who assessed the theological implications of the theory of organic evolution," and concentrates on "the views of members of the more 'main-line' Protestant denominations" (xiii). This approach addresses the impact of evolutionism on a relatively narrow cross section of American society as a whole, and it makes difficult the attempt to address the impact of social evolutionism on those who bore the brunt of it, as it were—the non-Protestant peoples who were most adversely affected by it, which is the focus here.

3. Szasz, *The Divided Mind of Protestant America*.

4. One recent study observes, in fact, that opinion is almost evenly divided in the contemporary United States as to whether or not a deity specially and separately created human beings within the last ten thousand years. See Eve and Harrold, *The Creationist Movement in Modern America*. Szasz places the transition to the predominance of evolution-based religion after the turn of the century—later than most American evolution scholars—due in part to his emphasis on the contributions of the higher criticism. George Marsden concurs with the later dating of the evolutionary transition in *Fundamentalism and American Culture*,

where he emphasizes the distinct dichotomization of the debate after the turn of the century, leading up to its culmination in the 1920s as symbolized by the Scopes Trial. Whenever the transition to the predominance of evolutionism is marked, the seeds for the change were clearly being sewn much earlier, and its ubiquitous presence at the Columbian Exposition provides strong evidence of this.

5. Herve Varenne, "Creating America," 15–33.

6. The numbers are from *The Statistical History of the United States*.

7. A good source for identifying the many uses to which social evolutionism was put in the period can be found in Boller, *Evolutionary Naturalism*.

8. See, for instance, the second chapter of Marty's *Modern American Religion: The Irony of It All*, titled "A Cosmopolitan Habit in Theology," 17–24, where the recurrent interaction between religious groups is viewed as making inevitable an ecumenically based American theology that never would have arisen earlier. See Cross, *The Emergence of Liberal Catholicism in America*; Sorin, *A Time for Building*.

9. Catherine L. Albanese, for instance, has shown that the theme of "nature" has permeated the religious understanding of the most diverse groups from across the Americas, and there are certainly other themes that could be advanced as unifying rather than separating forces. See her *Nature Religion in America*.

10. In his article "Pluralism and the American Mainstream," Richard Seager has extended the work of R. Laurence Moore in tracing the history of a bias in the writing of American religious history that places excessive emphasis on mainline Protestant denominations in defining the field. Non-Judeo-Christian groups have been even more inadequately represented than marginal Judeo-Christian groups in this academic context.

11. *The World's Columbian Exposition, 1893, Official Catalogue*, Liberal Arts Department. For more on Adler and the exhibiting and presence of Jews at international expositions, see Barbara Kirshenblatt-Gimblett, *Destination Culture*, 77–106.

12. *Illustrations of the Different Languages and Dialects in Which the Holy Bible Has Been Circulated by the American Bible Society*, n.p.

13. On the placement of the Native American encampments, see Johnson, *History of the Exposition*, 424–25. Religion was certainly a central focus, and quite plausibly *the* central focus, of anthropology early on, as evidenced by the much greater and more enduring popularity of the second volume of E. B. Tylor's founding, two-volume study *Primitive Culture* entitled *Religion in Primitive Culture*. If it was not "religion" that early anthropology focused on in the classically Western sense, then at the very least it was religion as expression of ultimate societal concerns. For more on the native perspective on ritual performance at international exposition, see Jacknis, "Northwest Coast Indian Culture."

14. Johnson, *History of the World's Columbian Exposition*, 424.

15. Dean, *White City Chips*, 232.

16. John C. Eastman, "Japan and the Japanese."

17. Denton J. Snider, *World's Fair Studies*, 262.

18. Ibid., 237.

19. Ibid., 255, 258, 334.

20. Cameron, *History of the Exposition*, 313–14.

21. The complex discourse about the fetish has been one of the more compelling theoretical results of the modern Western encounter with cultures it has deemed "primitive." About the idea of the fetish, see especially the three illuminating articles by William Pietz, "The Problem of the Fetish," I, II, and IIIa, especially the second, where Pietz effectively contextualizes the long history of ambivalence toward matter inhering within Christian theology. Marx employed the notion of the fetish to show how the profound preoccupation with the many commodities of modern society—a phenomenon seemingly infused with religious fervor—had diverted energy away from concern about the proper adjudication of and dissemination of those commodities. See "The Fetishism of Commodities and the Secret Thereof," in *Capital*, vol. 1, 82–96. Walter Benjamin forged a link between fetishism and the practice of international expositions, with their unprecedented displays of commodification, when he wrote, "Fetishism, which is subject to the sex appeal of the inorganic, is its [commodification's] vital nerve. The cult of commodities places it [the sex appeal of fetishism] in its service," (*Reflections* 153). Benjamin's observation echoes the notion advanced here: that international expositions were themselves the greatest displays of fetishism in history. McClure, ed., *World's Fair Sermons*, 106.

22. Anonymous, *A Sentence of Holy Writ in 100 Languages*, n.p.

23. Chandler, "Paris 1867, Exposition Universelle," 42.

24. The precise connection between the 1867 congress on weights and measures and the founding of the International Bureau in 1875 is not clear. Chandler has written that the International Bureau occurred "Partly as a result of this exhibit [of weights and measures]," (Ibid., 42). Burton Benedict links the formation of the bureau to the exposition's international congress on weights and measures more directly, claiming it "led to the signing" of the treaty (*Anthropology of World's Fairs*, 42).

25. Benedict, *Anthropology of World's Fairs*, 46.

26. The original papers pertaining to the organization of the World's Parliament of Religions of both Charles Carroll Bonney and Parliament president John Henry Barrows apparently have been lost to posterity. See Druyvestyn, "The World's Parliament of Religions," 28. Bonney, "The Genesis of the World's Religious Congresses of 1893," 79. For more on the mechanics of the planning of the Parliament, see Burris, "Religion and Anthropology." Richard Seager has speculated on the possibility of doing a Foucauldian archaeological analysis of the period by examining the papers from throughout the Congress Auxiliary. Though a casual aside, this notion is untenable for a number of reasons that nonetheless are revealing about the nature of the Congress Auxiliary. First, many of the congresses did not publish their proceedings. Seager's point of departure for this notion apparently is a statement made by Charles Bonney, who estimated that the auxiliary's papers would fill fifty volumes at six hundred pages apiece *(World's Parliament of Religions*, xx). Unfortunately, the records of most of those other congresses do not exist. The Parliament collection forms a signifi-

cant percentage of the remaining papers from congresses related to the humanities. Second, papers from exposition congresses tend to be overly general and melodramatic, in keeping with the context in which they occur. In this, they parallel Nickolaus Pevsner's critique of the aesthetic success of the Great Exhibition's displays mentioned in chapter 1. See his *High Victorian Design*. I have examined all of the papers pertaining to religion from the nonreligion congresses, for instance, and it is almost uniformly the case that the papers are too broad and general to be groundbreaking. There are always exceptions, of course, such as Frederick Jackson Turner's little-known frontier thesis (discussed below), or the unexpected results of the interaction with the Asians at the Parliament, which nevertheless was more significant as a historical encounter between peoples than for any brilliant doctrines that were advanced. Third, Foucault's odd style of history, as evidenced in *The Order of Things*, involves scanning a broad historical epoch and then organizing the data around novel themes. On the contrary, the papers from the Columbian Exposition's Congress Auxiliary are eminently bound by their historical context and redundant as such.

27. Because of my emphasis on the intercultural aspect of the World's Parliament of Religions, which I have attempted to contextualize throughout this book, I have deemphasized the other religious congresses besides the Parliament. These meetings were not generally focused on international issues and were not comprised of many non-Euro-Americans. They were also not unprecedented, unlike the international Parliament of Religions, with similar meetings having occurred among at least a few groups at the Philadelphia Centennial Exposition of 1876 as mentioned earlier. What is important to remember in terms of how the many Protestant religious groups participated, and especially in determining how liberal and conservative, or evangelical, groups participated, is that the sharp division between liberal and conservative was just beginning to sort itself out in this period. Donald W. Dayton has argued that use of the term "evangelical" is anachronistic for 1893 and not an effective gauge for assessing the extent to which such conservative groups were represented at the Parliament. Regarding the negligible evangelical presence at the Parliament, Dayton argues that if the activities of the evangelist Dwight L. Moody outside the fair are included, those who would later become definitive evangelicals were actually at the fair in force. See his paper "Voices Not Heard." Moody set up his crusade outside the fair during its run and drew in hundreds of thousands of people. For more on Moody's activities at the fair, see James Gilbert, *Perfect Cities*. Regarding the nonreligion congresses, see Johnson, *History of the Exposition*, 173–75.

28. One place where the objectified study of religion did not reach was into the Congress on Philosophy. None of the twenty-four philosophy papers by notables such as Josiah Royce and John Dewey had anything to do with religion. Philosophy, with its ancient Western roots, was a discipline that reached very little toward intercultural comparative projects that often challenged some of its longstanding epistemological assumptions.

29. Adler, "Museum Collections," 322–26. Jastrow, "The Scope and Method of the Historical Study of Religions," 291.

30. Johnson, *History of the Exposition*, 412–13.

31. "The General Program of the World's Congress Auxiliary of the World's Columbian Exposition of 1892," n.p. "Genesis of the Congress on Africa," n.p.

32. Quoted in Reid, *All the World Is Here!* 183.

33. Quoted in "Genesis of the Congress on Africa," n.p.

34. Turner, *The Significance of the Frontier in American History*, 28–37.

35. Barrows, *The World's Parliament of Religions*, 2:1570.

36. Bonney, "The Genesis of the World's Religious Congresses of 1893," 79.

37. Swedenborg, *Divine Providence* XVII: 326–29, quoted in Druyvestyn, "World's Parliament of Religions," 19.

38. Ibid., 87

39. Barrows, *World's Parliament of Religions*, 1:22.

40. Seager has emphasized the role of the Asians at the Parliament in *The World's Parliament of Religions*, though his work on the ecumenical aspect of the event is significant. Eric Ziolkowski's collection of contemporary comment on the Parliament, *A Museum of Faiths*, also shows a predominant focus on the Asians. Ziolkowski has also drawn attention to the notion that religion was exhibited as well as discussed at the Parliament. His study is the best guide to the particularities of the Parliament and its legacies.

41. Kirshenblatt-Gimblett, *Destination Culture*, 99–106.

42. Seager, *World's Parliament of Religions*, 45.

43. McCann, "Catholics at the Parliament." Seager, *World's Parliament of Religions*, 44.

44. Barrows, "Results of the Parliament of Religions," 11. Joseph M. Kitagawa, *The 1893 World's Parliament of Religions and Its Legacy*.

45. One letter was read from J. Sanna Abou Naddara, a Muslim from Paris. The main Muslim presentations were made by Alexander Russel Webb, an American who converted to Islam in 1888, and missionary George Washburn. Some of the women were in fact criticized by the Christian men for becoming a little too enamored with the exotic and charismatic Asian representatives. There is considerable confusion on the question of Asian participation depending on how one views the category of "Asia" and how one counts Parliament participants. Representatives can be counted either by country or by religion, and also by whether or not they participated in person or just sent a paper to be read. Seager identifies thirty Asian delegates by defining Asia as it would have been defined in 1893 and counting by religion rather than by religion and nationality combined *(World's Parliament of Religions*, 50). However, Homer Jack identifies just sixteen participants from Asian religions. He names six Buddhists, three Hindus, one Confucian, one Jain, and one Shintoist. The final four of the sixteen are marginal choices: three Muslims—two from India who did not speak and a recent American convert—and an American theosophist. From the "Asia" of today, then, there was one Chinese, three Indians, one Ceylonese, and five Japanese, making my total of twelve. On top of this, several of these twelve never actually addressed the audience. The number of Asians who actually addressed the Parliament in English was perhaps as few as a half-dozen out of the 183 participants. I consider this a small number

by comparison, for instance, to the fact that there were eighteen Catholics participants alone. The Asians who could address the audience in English were understandably given several presentations apiece, making it inevitable that they would become highly visible and significant figureheads for the whole of the event. See Jack, "The World's Parliament of Religions." Carl T. Jackson has also emphasized the negligible presentations on Asian religions by Asians. Jackson further notes that two of the most significant participants from Asia, H. Dharmapala of Ceylon and Hirai Kinzō of Japan, were actually Theosophists rather than adherents of traditional Asian religions. See his *The Oriental Religions and American Thought*.

46. Jack, "The World's Parliament of Religions," 4.

47. Barrows, "Results of the Parliament," 2.

48. The best account of the activities of the Asian representatives at the Parliament and the cultural contexts that informed them can be found in Seager, *World's Parliament of Religions*.

49. Houghton, ed., *Neely's History of the Parliament of Religions*, 585–87

50. Ibid., 587.

51. For more on the AME Church and the life of Richard Allen, see George, *Segregated Sabbaths*; Allen, *Life Experience and Gospel Labors*; and Richardson, *Dark Salvation*.

52. See Dickerson, "Perspectives on African-American Christianity." This question of the "locus" of religion has been explored at length by Albert J. Raboteau in *Slave Religion*. On the planning of the Parliament, see Druyvestyn, "World's Parliament of Religions," 48.

53. I have excluded here the impromptu comments made by Frederick Douglass included below.

54. Barrows, *The First World's Parliament of Religions*, 1:107-8.

55. Ibid., 1:107.

56. Houghton, ed., *Neely's History of the Parliament of Religions*, 631. *Daily Inter-Ocean*, 24 September 1893, 1.

57. Bonney, *World's Congress Addresses*, 41.

58. Houghton, *Neely's History of the Parliament*, 603–4.

59. Ibid., 603–4.

60. Houghton, *Neely's History of the Parliament*, 606–7. For more on the manner in which Arnett and the AME Church contributed to the Parliament, see Naylor, "The Black Presence at the World's Parliament of Religions."

61. Ibid. "Wealth Has Duties," *Daily Inter-Ocean*, 23 September 1893, 1. Barrows's collection of parliament papers includes a thoroughly edited version of Arnett's speech, without a title and under the heading "Addresses of Bishop B. W. Arnett and the Hon. J. M. Ashley." Ashley was a key congressional figure in the passing of the Emancipation Proclamation. His speeches of the period had been gathered together and published and were being presented to him as a token of black gratitude on the evening of the addresses. Barrows thus went so far as to edit out all of Arnett's negative comments about the role of Christianity in slavery and grouped Arnett's address with Slattery's, who was identified as a prominent white who had aided blacks.

62. Ibid., 702.
63. Barrows, *World's Parliament of Religions,* 1:180

## Conclusion

1. See, for instance, Barrows's *The Christian Conquest of Asia.* For a counterpoint to Barrows's particular triumphalism, see Jenkin Lloyd Jones, "The Parliament's Challenge to the Unitarians," 306–7. On Barrows' activities following the Parliament, see Seager, *World's Parliament of Religions,* 140. For the Catholic version of this vision, see Hewitt, "Christian Unity in the Parliament of Religions," and "The Lessons of the White City." For a Jewish analysis of the Parliament, see Hirsch, "After the Parliament, What?" Carus, "The Dawn of a New Religious Era," 1–20; and "The World's Religious Parliament Extension," 345–53. See also Henderson, "Catalysts: Paul Carus and the Parliament."

2. On Vivekananda, see Druyvestyn, "World's Parliament of Religions," 258–62; Seager, *World's Parliament of Religions,* 155. Henderson, "Catalysts: Paul Carus and the Parliament."

3. Ibid.

4. See Jacknis, "Northwest Coast Indian Culture," 109.

5. Ziolkowski, *A Museum of Faiths,* 23–27.

6. Records of the political issues pertaining to the 1992 world's fair can be found at the Chicago Historical Society.

7. I attended the 1993 Parliament for the World's Religions. Whatever is not footnoted below is based on observation.

8. Virginia Baron has noted the glaring difference between the 1893 Parliament at the modest Art Institute and the 1993 event at the opulent Palmer House hotel. Despite the expense, a thousand potential attendees had to be turned away when the seven-thousand-person capacity was reached. See Baron, "The 1993 Parliament of the World's Religions." On the Orthodox withdrawal, see Zipperer, "The Elusive Quest for Religious Harmony." On "pagan" participation, see Lefebure, "Global Encounter." On evangelical participation, see Neely, "The 1993 Parliament of the World's Religions," 122. David Toolan has bemoaned that the 1993 parliament lacked "any clear sense on the part of the organizers" of what progress had been made in interreligious dialogue since the 1893 parliament. See his "Chicago's Parliament of the World's Religions," 3.

9. Barney, "Global 2000 Revisited," 38–39.

10. Metropolitan Paulos Mar Gregorious, "Towards a New Enlightenment," tape recording.

11. Ibid.

12. John R. Coyne Jr., "Ultimate Reality in Chicago," 26–27; David Neff, "The Supermarket of the Gods," 20–21.

13. Regarding the development of the global ethic, see O'Connor, "Does a Global Village Warrant a Global Ethic?" *Christian Century* (22–29 September 1993), 888.

# BIBLIOGRAPHY

## Sources of Archival Materials

British Museum Library
Chicago Historical Society, Department of Special Collections
DePaul University, Department of Special Collections
Guildhall Library, London
Harold Washington Library, Department of Special Collections, Chicago
National Arts Library, Victoria and Albert Museum, London
Newberry Library, Department of Special Collections, Chicago
Royal Society of Arts Library, Royal Society of Arts, London
University of Chicago, Regenstein Library, Department of Special Collections

## Primary Sources

Adams, Henry. *The Education of Henry Adams.* Boston: Houghton Mifflin, 1961.
Adler, Cyrus. "Museum Collections to Illustrate Religious History and Ceremonials," in *Memoirs of the International Congress of Anthropology,* C. Stainland Wake, ed. Chicago: Schulte Publishing, 1894, 322–26.
Allen, Rt. Rev. Richard, *The Life Experience and Gospel Labors of the Rt. Reverend Richard Allen.* New York: Abingdon, 1960.
Anonymous. *A Sentence of Holy Writ in 100 Languages.* London: Partridge and Oakley, 1851.
Anonymous. *The Great Assembly.* London: J. P. Snow, [1853?].
Aveling, Thomas. *Great Sights.* London: Snow, Gurney, and Turner, 1851.
Barney, Gerald. "Global 2000 Revisited: What Shall We Do?" Unpublished paper. Council for a Parliament of the World's Religions Collection, DePaul University, Department of Special Collections. Lincoln Park Library.
Baron, Virginia. "The 1993 Parliament of the World's Religions." *Parabola* 18, no. 4 (winter 1993): 122–24.
Barrows, John Henry. "Results of the Parliament of Religions." Reprint. *Forum* (September 1894): 1–14.
Barrows, John Henry, ed. *The World's Parliament of Religions: An Illustrated and Popular Story of the World's First Parliament of Religions, Held in Chicago in Connection with the Columbian Exposition of 1893.* Two volumes. Chicago: Parliament Publishing, 1893.

*Beautiful Scenes of the White City.* Chicago: Laird and Lee, 1894.
Binney, Rev. Thomas. *The Royal Exchange and the Palace of Industry or, The Possible Futures of Europe and the World.* London: The Religious Tract Society, 1851.
Bloom, Sol. *The Autobiography of Sol Bloom.* New York: Putnam and Sons, 1948.
Boas, Franz. "Ethnography at the Columbian Exposition." *Cosmopolitan* 15 (1893): 607–9.
Bonney, Charles Carroll. "The Genesis of the World's Religious Congresses of 1893." *New-Church Review* I (January 1894): 73–100.
———. *World's Congress Addresses.* Chicago: Open Court, 1900.
———. "The World's Parliament of Religions." *Monist* 5 (April 1895): 321–43.
Buel, J. W. *The Magic City: A Massive Portfolio of Original Photographic Views of the Great World's Fairs.* St. Louis: Historical Publishing, 1894.
Burrows, H. W. *The Great Exhibition: A Sermon.* London: Skeffington and Southwell, 1851.
Cameron, William E. *History of the World's Columbian Exposition.* Chicago: Columbian History, 1893.
Carus, Paul. "Charles Carroll Bonney." *Open Court* 17 (September 1903): 516–19.
———. "The Dawn of a New Religious Era." Appendix, *Monist* 4 (April 1894): 1–20.
———. "The World's Religious Parliament Extension." *Monist* 5 (April 1895): 345–53.
Chambers, Robert. *Vestiges of the Natural History of Creation.* Leicester: Leicester University Press, fourth ed., 1845.
*Chicago Times Portfolio of Midway Types.* Chicago: Chicago Times, 1893.
Cole, Henry. *Fifty Years of Public Work.* Two volumes. London: George Bell and Sons, [1884?].
Cole, Henry, ed. *Lectures on the International Results of the Great Exhibition of 1851.* London: David Bogue, [1853?].
"Commissioners Records of the Great Exhibition of Industry of All Nations." National Arts Library Archives.
"Commissioners Reports of the Great Exhibition of the Industry of All Nations." Vols. I–II. National Arts Library Archives.
Coyne, John R., Jr. "Ultimate Reality in Chicago." *National Review* (4 October 1993): 26–27.
Culin, Stewart. "Retrospect of the Folklore of the Columbian Exposition." *Journal of American Folklore* 7 (January-March, 1894): 51–59.
Cumming, John. *The Great Exhibition: Suggestive and Anticipative.* London: John Farquar Shaw, 1851.
Dall, William H. "Anthropology." *The Nation* 57 (28 September 1893): 224–26
Darwin, Charles. *The Origin of Species.* New York: Modern Library, [1960?].
———. *The Descent of Man.* New York: Modern Library, [1960?].
Dean, Teresa. *White City Chips.* Chicago: Warner Publishing, 1895.
Douglass, Frederick, and Ida B. Wells. *The Reason Why the Colored American is Not in the Columbian Exposition.* No imprint. Chicago Historical Society.

Eastman, John C. "Japan and the Japanese." *The Graphic* (25 February 1893).
———. "Eccentric Features of the World's Fair." *The Chautaquan* 17 (April 1893): 12–14.
"The Exhibition Jury Reports," *Fraser's Magazine* No. 245 (November 1852): 491–92.
Fleming, Rev. Fletcher. *The Parable of the Pearl of Great Price Explained and Applied with Reference to the Great Exhibition.* London: Whitaker and Company, 1851.
Fuller, Francis. "Diary of Francis Fuller." John Scott Russell Papers. Royal Society of Arts Archives.
Gardella, Peter. "Two Parliaments, One Century." *Cross Currents* (spring 1994): 97–104.
"General Program of the World's Congress Auxiliary of the World's Columbian Exposition of 1892." May 1 ed., Department of Science and Philosophy, African Ethnology Section, preliminary publication.
"Genesis of the Congress on Africa." *The World's Congress Auxiliary of the World's Columbian Exposition*, Department of Science and Philosophy, General Division of African Ethnology. Newberry Library.
Hawthorne, Julian. "A Description of the Inexpressible." *Lippincott's Monthly Magazine* 51 (April 1893): 496–503.
———. "The Lady of the Lake." *Lippincott's Monthly Magazine* 52 (August 1893): 240–42.
Henrotin, Ellen M. "The Great Congresses at the World's Fair." *Cosmopolitan* 14 (March 1893): 626–32.
Hensholdt, Heinrich. "The Wonders of Hindoo Magic." *Arena* 9 (December 1893): 46–60.
Hewitt, Augustine. "Christian Unity in the Parliament of Religions," *Catholic World* 59 (May 1894): 152–63.
———. "The Lessons of the 'White City'." *Catholic World* 59 (September 1894): 770–79.
———. "The Lessons of the 'White City'." *Catholic World* 60 (October 1895): 73–82.
Higginson, Edward. *A World Embracing Faith or Religious Whispers from the Exhibition of Industry.* London: E. T. Whitfield, 1851.
Hirsch, Emil. "After the Parliament, What?" *Reform Advocate* 3 (February 1894): 398–400.
Houghton, Walter R., ed. *Neely's History of the Parliament of Religions and Religion Congresses at the World's Columbian Exposition.* Chicago: F. T. Neely, 1983.
*Illustrations of the Different Languages and Dialects in Which the Holy Bible Has Been Circulated by the American Bible Society.* Souvenir edition. No imprint [1893?].
Jastrow, Morris, Jr. "The Scope and Method of the Historical Study of Religions," in Wake, *Memoirs of Anthropology Congress*, 291.
———. *The Study of Religion.* New York: Scribner's, 1902.

Johnson, Rossiter, ed. *A History of the World's Columbian Exposition Held in Chicago in 1893*. Four volumes. New York: D. Appleton, 1897.

Jones, Jenkin Lloyd. "The Parliament's Challenge to the Unitarians," *Unity* 32 (January 1894): 306–7.

*The Juvenile and Missionary Record and Sabbath Scholars Magazine* XII (September 1851), National Arts Library Archives.

Lefebure, Leo D. "Global Encounter: At the Parliament of the World's Religions." *Christian Century* 110 n. 26, (22 September 1993): 886–89.

Maurice, F. D. *The Religions of the World and Their Relations to Christianity*. London: Boston, Gould, and Lincoln, 1854.

McClure, J. B., ed. *World's Fair Sermons by Eminent Divines at Home and Abroad*, vol. I. Chicago: Rhodes and McClure, 1893.

Milner, Rev. J. W. *The Design of God in the Great Exhibition: Our Duty as Christians in Reference to It*. London: Thomas Hatchard, [1851?].

Neff, David. "The Supermarket of the Gods." *Christianity Today* (13 September 1993): 20–21

*Official Descriptive and Illustrated Catalogue*. London: Spicer Brothers, Wholesale Stationers; W. Clowes and Sons, Printers, 1851.

Paley, William. *Natural Theology; or, Evidences of the Existence and Attributes of the Deity, Collected from the Appearances of Nature*. Charlottesville: Lincoln-Rembrandt, twelfth ed., 1997. Originally published, London: printed for J. Faulder, 1809.

Pashley, Rev. W. *The Morning Stars*. London: T. Hatchard, 1851.

Pipe, William. "The Parliament of Religions." *Outlook* 48 (August 1893): 385–87.

"Religious Aspects of the Great Exhibition." *The Eclectic Review*, vol. II (November 1851): 624–38.

"Reports by the Juries on the Thirty Classes Into Which the Great Exhibition was Divided." Royal Commission. National Arts Library.

"Results of American Participation in the Great Exhibition." *Journal of the Royal Society of Arts*, vol. I (1852): 474–76.

Rodgers, Charles T. *American Superiority at the World's Fair*. Philadelphia: John J. Hawkins, 1852.

Smith, Harlan I. "The Anthropology Building at the World's Columbian Exposition." *American Antiquarian* 15 (January-November, 1893): 115–17.

Snider, Denton J. *World's Fair Studies*. Chicago: Sigma Publishing, 1895.

Starr, Frederick. "Anthropology at the World's Fair." *The Popular Science Monthly* 43 (1893): 610–21.

———. Frederick Starr Papers. University of Chicago Press, Regenstein Library, Department of Special Collections.

Tateno, Gazo. "Foreign Nations at the World's Fair." *North American Review* 156 (January 1893): 34–43.

Toolan, David. "Chicago's Parliament of the World's Religions." *America* 169, no. 8 (25 September 1993): 3–4.

Turner, Frederick Jackson. *The Significance of the Frontier in American History*. New York: Frederick Ungar Publishing, 1963.

Wake, C. Stainland, ed. *Memoirs of the International Congress of Anthropology.* Chicago: Schulte Publishing, 1894.
Whewell, William. "The General Bearing of the Great Exhibition on the Progress of Art and Science." *Lectures on the International Results of the Great Exhibition.* Henry Cole, ed. (London: David Bogue, [1853?]).
Wyatt, Matthew Digby. "A Report on the Eleventh French 'Exposition of the Products of Industry'." Royal Society of Arts Archives.
Zipperer, John. "The Elusive Quest for Religious Harmony." *Christianity Today* 37, no. 11 (4 October 1993): 42–44.

## Secondary Sources

Albanese, Catherine L. *Nature Religion in America.* Chicago: University of Chicago Press, 1991.
Allwood, John. *The Great Exhibitions.* London: Studio Vista, 1977.
Arens, W. *The Man-Eating Myth: Anthropology and Anthropophagy.* Oxford: Oxford University Press, 1979.
Altick, Richard D. *The Shows of London.* Cambridge: Harvard University Press, 1978.
Anderson, Benedict. *Imagined Communities.* London: Verso, 1991.
*Annotated Bibliography: The World's Columbian Exposition of 1893, with Illustrations and Price Guide.* Albuquerque, N.M.: Cooper, 1992.
Badger, Reid. *The Great American Fair: The World's Columbian Exposition and American Culture.* Chicago: Nelson Hall, 1979.
Barnard, F. M. *Herder's Social and Political Thought: From Enlightenment to Nationalism.* Oxford: Clarendon, 1965.
Benedict, Burton. *The Anthropology of World's Fairs.* Berkeley, Calif.: Scolar Press, 1983.
———. "Rituals of Representation: Ethnic Stereotypes and Colonized Peoples at World's Fairs." In *Fair Representations: World's Fairs and the Modern World.* Robert W. Rydell and Nancy Gwinn, eds. (Amsterdam: V.U. University Press, 1994).
Benjamin, Walter. *Reflections.* Translated by Edmund Jephcott. New York: Harcourt, Brace, Jovanovich, 1978.
Bogdan, Robert. *Freak Show: Presenting Human Oddities for Amusement and Profit.* Chicago: University of Chicago Press, 1988.
Boller, Paul, Jr. *American Thought in Transition: The Impact of Evolutionary Naturalism, 1865–1900.* Boston: University of Massachusetts, 1969.
Bonython, Elizabeth. "The Planning of the Great Exhibition of 1851." *Journal of the Royal Society of Arts.* (May 1995): 1–4.
*The Books of the Fairs: Materials about World's Fairs, 1834–1916, in the Smithsonian Institution Libraries.* Introductory essay by Robert W. Rydell. Chicago: American Library Association, 1992.
Bowler, Peter. *Evolution: The History of an Idea.* Rev. ed. Berkeley: University of California Press, 1989.

———. *The Non-Darwinian Revolution.* Baltimore: Johns Hopkins University Press, 1989.

Braudel, Fernand. *Civilization and Capitalism, Fifteenth through Eighteenth Century,* vol. 1: *The Structures of Everyday Life: The Limits of the Possible.* Translated by Sian Reynolds. New York: Harper and Row, 1979.

———. *Civilization and Capitalism, Fifteenth through Eighteenth Century,* vol. 2: *The Wheels of Commerce.* Translated by Sian Reynolds. New York: Harper and Row, 1979.

———. *Civilization and Capitalism, Fifteenth through Eighteenth Century,* vol. 3: *The Perspective of the World.* New York: Harper and Row, 1979.

———. *The Mediterranean and the Mediterranean World in the Time of Phillip II.* Two volumes. Translated by Sian Reynolds. New York: Harper and Row, 1966.

Breckenridge, Carol A. "The Aesthetics and Politics of Colonial Collecting: India at World's Fairs." *Comparative Studies in Society and History* 31 (April 1989): 195–216.

Brown, Julie K. *Contesting Images: Photography and the World's Columbian Exposition.* Tucson: University of Arizona Press, 1994.

Burg, David. *Chicago's White City of 1893.* Lexington: University Press of Kentucky.

Burris, John P. "Religion and Anthropology at International Expositions: From the Great Exhibition to the World's Parliament of Religions, 1851–1893." Ph.D. dissertation, University of California, Santa Barbara, 1997.

Capps, Walter. *Religious Studies: The Making of a Discipline.* Minneapolis: Fortress, 1995.

Carter, Paul. *The Spiritual Crisis of the Gilded Age.* Dekalb: Illinois University Press, 1971.

Caudill, Edward. *Darwinism in the Press: The Evolution of an Idea.* Hillsdale, N.J.: Lawrence Erlbaum Associates, 1989.

Celik, Zeynep. *Displaying the Orient: Architecture of Islam at Nineteenth-Century World's Fairs.* Berkeley: University of California Press, 1992.

Chandler, Arthur. "Paris 1867, Exposition Universelle," in *Historical Dictionary of World's Fairs,* John E. Findling and Kimberly F. Pelle, eds., New York: Greenwood, 1990.

Chidester, David. *Savage Systems: Colonialism and Comparative Religion in Southern Africa.* Charlottesville: University Press of Virginia, 1996.

———. "Classify and Conquer: Imperial Classifications and Colonial Constructions of Religions." Unpublished paper.

Cooper, John W. "The Christ-Logos and Beyond: A Christian Perspective on Unity Among the Monotheistic Religions." Unpublished paper. Council for a World's Parliament of Religions Collection, DePaul University, Department of Special Collections.

Cordato, Mary Frances. "The Bible on Display: The American Bible Society's Participation at World's Fairs, 1867–1982." ABS Working Historical Paper Series, Working Paper 1990–1994. American Bible Society, Department of Archives/Library Services, New York, N.Y.

———. "Representing the Expansion of Woman's Sphere: Women's Work and Culture at the World's Fairs on 1876, 1893, and 1904," Ph.D. dissertation, New York University, 1989.
Cross, Robert. *The Emergence of Liberal Catholicism in America.* Cambridge: Harvard University Press.
Cunliffe, Marcus. *In Search of America.* Contributions in American Studies, Number 98. (New York: Greenwood, 1991).
Dalzell, Robert F., Jr. *American Participation in the Great Exhibition of 1851.* Amherst, Mass.: Amherst College, 1960.
Daniel, Glyn, and Colin Renfrew. *The Idea of Prehistory.* Edinburgh: Edinburgh University Press, 1988.
Darney, Virginia Grant. "Women and World's Fairs: American International Expositions, 1876–1904." Ph.D. dissertation, Emory University, 1982.
Davis, David Brion. *The Problem of Slavery in Western Culture.* New York: Oxford University Press, 1966.
Davis, Susan G. *Parades and Power: Street Theater in Nineteenth-Century Philadelphia.* Philadelphia: Temple University Press, 1986.
Dayton, Donald W. "Voices Not Heard: Evangelicals." Unpublished paper. Council for a World's Parliament of Religions Collection, DePaul University, Department of Special Collections.
Dexter, Ralph W. "Putnam's Problems Popularizing Anthropology." *American Scientist* 54 (1966): 315–32.
Dickerson, Dennis C. "Perspectives on African-American Christianity: Arnett, Douglass, and Early at the World's Parliament of Religions." Unpublished paper. Council for a Parliament of the World's Religions Collection, DePaul University, Department of Special Collections.
Doenecke, Justus D. "Myths, Machines and Markets: The Columbian Exposition of 1893." *Journal of Popular Culture* 6 (spring 1973): 535–49.
Druyvestyn, Kenten. "The World's Parliament of Religions." Ph.D. dissertation, University of Chicago Press, 1976.
Du Bois, W. E. B. *The Souls of Black Folk.* New York: Vintage, 1990.
Eagleton, Terry. *The Idea of Culture.* Oxford: Blackwell Publishers, 2000.
Eilberg-Schwarz, Howard. *The Savage in Judaism: An Anthropology of the Israelite Religions in Ancient Judaism.* Bloomington: Indiana University Press, 1987.
Ellegard, Alvar. *Darwin and the General Reader: The Reception of Darwin's Theory of Evolution in the British Periodical Press, 1859–1872.* Goteborg: University of Goteborg, 1958.
Eve, Raymond A., and Harrold, Francis B. *The Creationist Movement in Modern America.* Boston: Twayne, 1991.
Findling, John E., and Kimberly F. Pelle, eds. *Historical Directory of World's Fairs.* New York: Greenwood, 1990.
Flood, Gavin. *Beyond Phenomenology: Rethinking the Study of Religion.* London: Cassell, 1999.
Fogelson, Raymond D. "The Red Man in the White City." In *Columbian Conse-*

*quences*. David Hurst Thomas, ed. (Washington, D.C.: Smithsonian, 1991): 73–90.

Foreman, Carolyn Thomas. *Indians Abroad: 1493–1938*. Norman: University of Oklahoma Press, 1943.

Foucault, Michel. *The Order of Things: An Archaeology of the Human Sciences*. New York: Vintage, 1973.

George, Carol V. R. *Segregated Sabbaths: Richard Allen and The Emergence of Independent Black Churches 1760–1840*. New York: Oxford University Press, 1973.

Greenhalgh, Paul. *Ephemeral Vistas: The Expositions Universelles, Great Exhibitions and World's Fairs, 1851–1939*. Manchester, U.K.: Manchester University Press, 1988.

Gilbert, James. *Perfect Cities: Chicago's Utopias of 1893*. Chicago: University of Chicago Press, 1991.

———. "World's Fairs as Historical Events." In *Fair Representations: World's Fairs and the Modern World*. Robert W. Rydell and Nancy Gwinn, eds. Amsterdam: V.U. University Press, 1994.

Harris, Neil. *Cultural Excursions: Marketing Appetites and Cultural Tastes in Modern America*. Chicago: University of Chicago Press, 1990.

Harrison, Peter. *"Religion" and the Religions in the English Enlightenment*. Cambridge: Cambridge University Press, 1990.

Heller, Arthur. "Philadelphia Centennial, 1876." In John E. Findling and Kimberly F. Pelle, eds. *Historical Dictionary of World's Fairs*. New York: Greenwood, 1990.

Henderson, Harold. "Catalysts: Paul Carus and the Parliament." Unpublished paper. Council for a Parliament of the World's Religions Collection, DePaul University, Department of Special Collections.

Hilton, Suzanne. *Here Today, Gone Tomorrow: The Story of World's Fairs and Expositions*. Philadelphia: Westminster, 1978.

Himmelfarb, Gertrude. *Darwin and the Darwinian Revolution*. New York: Norton, 1959.

Hinsley, Curtis M. "The World as Marketplace: Commodification of the Exotic at the World's Columbian Exposition, 1893." In *Exhibiting Cultures: The Poetics and Politics of Museum Display*. Ivan Karp and Steven D. Lavine, eds. Washington, D.C.: Smithsonian Institution, 1991, 344–65.

Hobhouse, Hermoine. "The Legacy of the Great Exhibition." *Royal Society of Arts Journal* (May 1995): 49–53.

Hobsbawm, Eric J. *The Age of Capital, 1848–1875*. New York: Scribner's, 1975.

———. *The Age of Empire, 1875–1914*. New York: Vintage, 1987.

———. *The Age of Revolution, 1789–1848*. New York: New American Library, 1962.

Hodgen, Margaret. *Early Anthropology in the Sixteenth and Seventeenth Century*. Philadelphia: University of Pennsylvania Press, 1964.

Hoxie, Frederick E. *A Final Promise: The Campaign to Assimilate the Indians, 1880–1920*. Lincoln: University of Nebraska Press, 1984.

Jack, Homer. "The World's Parliament of Religions." *World's Fair* 9 (October–December, 1989): 4.

———. "The World's Parliament of Religions: How Some Religions Participated." Unpublished paper. Council for a Parliament of the World's Religions Collection, DePaul University, Department of Special Collections.

Jacknis, Ira. "Northwest Coast Indian Culture." In *Columbian Consequences*. David Hurst Thomas, ed. (Washington, D.C.: Smithsonian, 1991): 91–118.

———. "Franz Boas and Exhibits: On the Limitations of the Museum Method of Anthropology." In *Objects and Others: Essays on Museums and Material Culture*. George P. Stocking Jr., ed. Madison: University of Wisconsin Press, 1985, 75–111.

Jackson, Carl T. *The Oriental Religions and American Thought: Nineteenth-Century Explorations*. Westport, Conn.: Greenwood, 1981.

Karp, Ivan, and Steven D. Levine, eds. *Exhibiting Cultures: The Poetics and Politics of Museum Display*. Washington, D.C.: Smithsonian, 1991.

King, Richard. *Orientalism and Religion: Postcolonial theory, India and "the Mystic East."* London: Routledge, 1999.

Kirshenblatt-Gimblett, Barbara. *Destination Culture: Tourism, Museums, and Heritage*. Berkeley: University of California Press, 1998.

Kitagawa, Joseph M. *The 1893 World's Parliament of Religions and Its Legacy*. Eleventh John Nuveen Lecture, 1983. Chicago: University of Chicago Divinity School; Baptist Theological Union, 1983.

Leakey, Richard, and Roger Lewin. *Origins Reconsidered: In Search of What Makes Us Human*. New York: Doubleday, 1992.

Lederer, Francis II. "The Genesis of the World's Columbian Exposition." M.A. Thesis, University of Chicago Press, 1967.

Lewis, Russell. "Everything Under One Roof: World's Fairs and Department Stores in Paris and Chicago." *Chicago History* 12 (fall 1983): 28–47.

Lindfors, Bernth. *Africans on Stage: Studies in Ethnological Show Business*. Bloomington: Indiana University Press, 1999.

Long, Charles H. *Significations*. Philadelphia: Fortress, 1986.

———. "Fair: No Fair." Unpublished paper.

Luckhurst, Kenneth W. *The Story of Exhibitions*. London: Studio Publications, 1951.

Lutchmansing, Larry. "Commodity Exhibitionism at the London Great Exhibition of 1851," *Annals of Scholarship* VII (1990): 203–16.

Lyon, T. Edgar, Jr. "In Praise of Babylon: Church Leadership at the 1851 Great Exhibition in London." *Journal of Mormon History* 14 (1988): 49–61.

Marsden, George. *Fundamentalism and American Culture: The Shaping of Twentieth-Century Evangelicalism, 1880–1925*. New York: Oxford University Press, 1980.

Marty, Martin E. *Modern American Religion*, vol. I: *The Irony of It All*. Chicago: University of Chicago Press, 1986.

Marx, Karl. *Capital: A Critique of Political Economy*. Frederick Engels, ed. New York: Charles H. Kerr, 1906.

Mauss, Marcel. *The Gift: Forms and Functions of Exchange in Archaic Societies.* Translated by Ian Cunnison. New York: Norton, 1967.

May, Robert S. *Herder and the Beginnings of Comparative Literature.* Chapel Hill: University of North Carolina Press, 1969.

McCabe, James D. *The Illustrated History of the Centennial Exhibition.* Philadelphia: National Publishing, 1975.

McCann, Dennis P. "Catholics at the Parliament: An Americanist Breakthrough" Unpublished paper. Council for a Parliament of the World's Religions Collection, DePaul University, Department of Special Collections.

McCutcheon, Russell T. *Manufacturing Religion: The Discourse on Sui Generis Religion and the Politics of Nostalgia.* New York: Oxford University Press, 1997.

MeFeely, William S. *Frederick Douglass.* New York: Norton, 1991.

McGrane, Bernard. *Beyond Anthropology: Society and the Other.* New York: Columbia University Press, 1989.

Meinig, Donald. *The Shaping of America,* vol. 1: *Atlantic America, 1492–1800.* New Haven, Conn.: Yale University Press, 1986.

———. *The Shaping of America,* vol. 2: *Continental America, 1800–1867.* New Haven, Conn.: Yale University Press, 1993.

Mitchell, Timothy. "The World as Exhibition." *Comparative Studies in Society and History* 31, no. 2 (April 1989): 217–36.

Moses, L. G. "Indians on the Midway: Wild West Shows and the Indian Bureau at World's Fairs, 1893–1904." *South Dakota History* 21 (fall 1991): 206–29.

Nandy, Ashis. *The Intimate Enemy: Loss and Recovery of Self under Colonialism.* New York: Oxford University Press, 1989.

Naylor, D. Keith. "The Black Presence at the World's Parliament of Religions, 1893." *Religion* 26, no. 3 (July 1996): 249–59.

Novick, Peter. *That Noble Dream: The "Objectivity Question" and the American Historical Profession.* Cambridge: Cambridge University Press, 1988.

O'Connor, June. "Does a Global Village Warrant a Global Ethic?" *Religion* 24, no. 2 (April 1994): 155–64.

Pietz, William. "The Problem of the Fetish, I." *Res: Anthropology and Aesthetics* 13 (spring 1985): 5–17.

———. "The Problem of the Fetish, II." *Res: Anthropology and Aesthetics* 13 (spring 1987), 23–45.

———. "The Problem of the Fetish, IIIa." *Res: Anthropology and Aesthetics* 16 (autumn 1988): 105–23

Preuss, J. Samuel. *Explaining Religion: Criticism and Theory from Bodin to Freud.* New Haven, Conn.: Yale University Press: 1987.

Raboteau, Albert J. *Slave Religion: The "Invisible Institution" in the Antebellum South.* New York: Oxford University Press, 1978.

Reid, Christopher Robert. *All the World Is Here!: The Black Presence at White City.* Bloomington: Indiana University Press, 2000.

Richards, Thomas. *The Commodity Culture of Victorian England.* Stanford, Calif.: Stanford University Press, 1990.

Richardson, Harry V. *Dark Salvation.* New York: Anchor, 1976.

Roberts, Jon. *Darwinism and the Divine in America: Protestant Intellectuals and Organic Evolution, 1859–1900*. Madison: University of Wisconsin, 1988.
Rudwick, Elliot M., and August Meier. "Black Man in the "White City": Negroes and the Columbian Exposition, 1893." *Phylon* 26 (1965).
Ruegamer, Lana. "The Paradise of Exceptional Women: Chicago Women Reformers, 1863–1893." Ph.D. dissertation, Indiana University, 1982.
Ruse, Michael. *Taking Darwinism Seriously*. Chicago: University of Chicago Press, 1979.
Rydell, Robert. *All the World's a Fair: Visions of Empire at American International Expositions, 1876–1915*. Chicago: University of Chicago Press, 1984.
———. "'Darkest Africa': African Shows at American World's Fairs, 1893–1940." From *Africans on Stage: Studies in Ethnological Show Business*. Bernth Lindfors, ed. Bloomington: Indiana University Press, 1999.
———, and Nancy Gwinn, eds. *Fair Representations: World's Fairs and the Modern World*. Amsterdam: V.U. University Press, 1994.
———. *World of Fairs: The Century of Progress Expositions*. Chicago: University of Chicago Press, 1993.
Scott, Gertrude. "Village Performance: Villages at the Chicago World's Columbian Exposition, 1893." Ph.D. dissertation, New York University, 1991.
Seager, Richard Hughes, ed. *The Dawn of Religious Pluralism: Voices from the World's Parliament of Religions, 1893*. La Salle, Ill.: Open Court, 1993.
———. "Pluralism and the American Mainstream: The View from the World's Parliament of Religions." *Harvard Theological Review* 82:3 (1989): 301–24.
———. "The World's Parliament of Religions." Ph.D. dissertation, Harvard University, 1986.
———. *The World's Parliament of Religions: The East/West Encounter, Chicago, 1893*. Bloomington: Indiana University Press, 1995.
Slotkin, Richard. *The Fatal Environment: The Myth of the Frontier in the Age of Industrialism*. New York: Atheneum, 1985.
Sorin, Gerald. *A Time for Building: The Jewish People in America*. The Jewish People in America series. Baltimore: Johns Hopkins University Press, 1982.
*Statistical History of the United States from Colonial Times to the Present*. Stamford, Conn.: Fairfield, 1965.
Steen, Ivan D. "New York, 1853–1854." In John E. Findling and Kimberly F. Pelle, eds. *Historical Dictionary of World's Fairs*. New York: Greenwood, 1990.
Stocking, George P., Jr., ed. *Objects and Others: Essays on Museums and Material Culture*. Madison: University of Wisconsin Press, 1985.
———. *Victorian Anthropology*. New York: Free Press, 1987.
Strenski, Ivan. *Four Theories of Myth in Twentieth-Century History*. Iowa City: Iowa University Press, 1987.
———. *Religion in Relation: Method, Application, and Moral Location*. Columbia: University of South Carolina Press, 1993.
Susman, Warren. "Ritual Fairs." *Chicago History* 12 (fall 1983): 4–9.
Sweet, Jonathan. "The Face of Australia: International Exhibitions, 1851–1888."

Unpublished M.A. thesis, Royal School of Arts, 1991. National Arts Library Archives.

Szasz, Ferenc. *The Divided Mind of Protestant America, 1880–1930.* Tuscaloosa: University of Alabama Press, 1982.

Tenkotte, Paul A., Jr. "Kaliedoscopes of the World: International Exhibitions and the Concept of Culture Place." *American Studies* 28, no. 1 (spring 1987): 5–29.

Thomas, David Hurst, ed. *Columbian Consequences,* vol. 3. Washington, D.C.: Smithsonian, 1991.

Thomas, Nicholas. *Entangled Objects: Exchange, Material Culture, and Colonialism in the Pacific.* Cambridge: Harvard University Press, 1991.

Trennert, Robert A. "Fairs, Expositions, and the Changing Face of Southwestern Indians, 1876–1904." *New Mexico Historical Review* 62 (April 1987): 127–50.

———. "Selling Indian Education at World's Fairs and Exhibitions, 1893–1904." *American Indian Quarterly* 11, no. 3 (1987): 203–20.

Turner, James. *Without God, without Creed.* Baltimore: Johns Hopkins University Press, 1985.

Varenne, Herve, ed. *Symbolizing America.* Lincoln: University of Nebraska Press, 1986.

Vile, John R. *Encyclopedia of Constitutional Amendments, Proposed Amendments, and Amending Issues, 1785–1995.* Santa Barbara, Calif.: ABC-CLIO, Inc., 1996.

Walton, Whitney. *France at the Crystal Palace: Bourgeois Taste and Artisan Manufacture in the Nineteenth Century.* Berkeley: University of California Press, 1994.

Webb, George. *The Evolution Controversy in America.* Lexington: University Press of Kentucky, 1994.

Weiman, Jane Madeline. *The Fair Women.* Chicago: Academy Chicago, 1981.

Wilson, Dreck Spurlock. "Black Involvement in Chicago's Previous World's Fairs." Unpublished paper, Chicago Historical Society, n.d.

Wim, De Wit. *Grand Illusions: The Chicago World's Fair of 1893,* Chicago: Chicago Historical Society, 1993.

Young, Robert. *Darwin's Metaphor.* Cambridge: Cambridge University Press, 1985.

Young, Robert J. C. *Colonial Desire: Hybridity in Theory, Culture, and Race.* London: Routledge, 1995.

Ziolkowski, Eric J., ed. *A Museum of Faiths: Histories and Legacies of the 1893 World's Parliament of Religions.* American Academy of Religion Classics in Religious Studies, No. 9. Atlanta: Scholars Press, 1993.

———. "Heavenly Visions and Worldly Intentions: Chicago's Columbian Exposition and World's Parliament of Religions." *Journal of American Culture* 13, no. 4 (winter 1990): 9–15.

———. "Waking Up from Akbar's Dream: The Literary Prefiguration of Chicago's 1893 World's Parliament of Religions." *Journal of Religion* 73, no. 4 (January 1993): 42–60.

# INDEX

Adams, Henry, 87
Adler, Cyrus, 132–33, 142–43, 152
Africa: at Columbian Exposition, 144–45; at Congress on Africa, 144–45; Dahomeans at Columbian Exposition, 117, 119–20; at Philadelphia Centennial, 96; at World's Parliament of Religions, 160, 163, 176
African Americans: at Columbian Exposition, 107–9, 117, 119–20; during Gilded Age, 130–31; at 1993 Parliament of Religions, 169; at Philadelphia Centennial, 96–97; at World's Parliament of Religions, 125–26, 151, 160–62, 176; after World's Parliament of Religions, 168
Albert, Prince, xiii, 35, 59; planning Great Exhibition, 26–27, 30
Allen, Richard, 160
Anderson, Benedict, 15
anthropology: in America, 101, 126, 158–60; origin of academic study of, 19, 189 n. 13
Archbishop of Canterbury, 51–52, 54, 151
Aristotle, 17
Arnett, Bishop Benjamin W., 145, 161–62, 163–66
Austria, 37, 38

Barney, Gerald, 171
Barnum, P. T., 90, 92
Barrows, John Henry, 147, 153, 155, 167, 193 n. 61
Bartholdi, Frédéric, 94
Benedict, Burton, 14, 121, 156
Bible: authority of, 127, 129; at Columbian Exposition, 133; at Great Exhibition, 52–53; higher criticism of, 68, 74–75, 127

Bloom, Sol, 103, 111, 116, 136, 186 n. 49
Boas, Franz, 111, 134
Bonaparte, Napoleon, 33
Bonney, Charles C., 99, 143–44, 147–48, 163
Braudel, Fernand, 1, 15; on early trade fairs, 5
Britain, 125; Church of England at World's Parliament of Religions, 151; competition with France, 37–38, 140; 1862 international exhibition, 82, 140; as world leader, 39
British Museum, 11
Burnham, Daniel H., 102
Burrows, H. W., 62
Burton, Sir Richard, 120

Carter, Kevin, 171
Carus, Paul, 167
Catholicism: American, during Gilded Age, 130–31; at 1993 Parliament of Religions, 170; and southern Europe, 26; at World's Parliament of Religions, 126, 150, 157, 163–64, 193 n. 45
Chambers, Robert, 68
Chandler, Arthur, 141
China: absence at Great Exhibition, 25, 39; at Columbian Exposition, 113–14, 136; at World's Parliament of Religions, 154–55
Christy, Henry, 69
civilization: concept of, xiii; definition of, xv–xvi; influence of concept on religion, 58–59
Clarke, James Freeman, 97
Cleveland, President Grover, 110
Cody, Buffalo Bill, 110
Cole, Henry, 37, 59; as founder of Great Exhibition, 26–27, 182 n. 7
Colt, Samuel, 43, 90
Columbus, Christopher, 6, 98, 99–101

comparative religion: in America, 97–98; at Columbian Exposition, 132; at Great Exhibition, 25–26, 55–59, 62; origins of, xvi; pre–evolutionary, 179 n. 6; and social evolutionism, 80–81, 123–28
Cook, Captain James, 18
Corliss, George, 94
Cromwell, Thomas, 10
Crystal Palace, xiii; coining of name, 30; novelty of, 33; reconstructed at Sydenham, 63–64
culture: versus civilization, xvi–xvii; defined, xv–xvi; as subject of anthropology, xvii
Custer, General George, 95

Daguerre, Louis, 82
Dalai Lama, 174
Darwin, Charles: and religion, 68–69; split with Lyell, 67
De Perthes, Boucher, 26
Dewey, Melville, 94
Dickens, Charles, 35
Dickerson, Dennis C., 160
Douglass, Frederick, 108–9, 120, 145, 165

Eagleton, Terry, xv
East India Company (British), 25, 46
Egypt, 39
Eliade, Mircea, 177
Eliot, George, 68
Elizabeth I, Queen, 10
Ellegard, Alvar, 73–75
evolution, theory of: in America, 97; Darwin's ethnocentrism, 78; effect on traditional religion, 175; influence on human sciences, 81; internalist versus externalist explanations, 72–74; after Mendelian genetics, 73; neo–Lamarckism versus Darwinism, 65, 73, 75–80, 143–44; role of *The Origin of Species*, 74
exhibitions (*see also specific exhibitions*): defined, 180 n. 4; history of, 21–22, 180 n. 4; as movable museums, 11–12; national, in Britain, 21; —, in France, 20–21, 26–27

Ferris, George, 99
fetishism, 137–38, 190 n. 21
Fillmore, President Millard, 41
Flood, Gavin, xiv
France, 125; competition with Britain, 37–38; at the Great Exhibition, 41

Gardella, Peter, 174
Geary, Patrick, 10
Germany, 37; American Germans during Gilded Age, 131; at Columbian Exposition, 113; as the Zollverein, 37–38, 41
Gibbons, James Cardinal, 153
Gilded Age, 126–30
Goodyear, Henry, 43
Grant, Ulysses S., 93
Great Exhibition of the Industry of All Nations (*see also* Crystal Palace): awards at, 31–32; classification of exhibits, 30; closing of, 59–62; criticism of, 36, 60–62; cultural hierarchies at, 37, 39, 47, 49; display of Bibles at, 52–53; as distinct from Crystal Palace, 182 n. 7; as educational tool, 52–53; feminist reading of, 182 n. 19; funding of, 28; historical uniqueness of, 22; influence on field of religion, 24; initial planning of, xiii; juried meetings at, 16–17, 31, 59–60; materiality at, 54–55, 139–40; as museum, 9; opening of, 32; origin of, 26–28; percentage of British attending, xiv, 69; politics behind, 23–24, 181 n. 2, 182 n. 7; press coverage of, 36; profit from, 59; purpose of, 27–28; religion at, 39, 49–59; utilitarianism at, 37–38
Greely, Horace, 44, 89, 91
Greenhalgh, Paul, 180 n. 4, 181 n. 2, 182 n. 15
Gregorious, Paulos Mar, 172–73

Herder, Johann Gottfried, 19–20, 139
Higginson, Rev. Edward, 55–56
Hinduism, 134
Hirsch, Emil, 153
history, academic study of, 19
Hobsbawm, Eric, 15; on globalism, 17
Hoxie, Frederick E., 95

India, 25, 39; at Columbian Exposition, 104–5, 114–15, 134; at World's Parliament of Religions, 151, 155–56
international expositions (*see also specific exhibitions*): American, before Chicago, 86–98; colonial displays at, 104; as commercial enterprises, 2; compared to potlatch ceremony, 14; compared to trade fairs, 2, 6–7; early precursors of ethnic

villages at, 11–13, 83; educational aspect of, 9; element of spectacle within, 3; European, 82–85; exchange within, 141; historical context of, 4–8, 180 n. 4; intellectual congresses at, 3, 98, 125, 139–42; as museums, 2; nationalism at, 3; religion at, 49; tradition of, xiv; women at, 91, 94–95, 187 n. 1
Islam: at Columbian Exposition, 115, 120, 135–36; at Great Exhibition, 39, 56, 61; at World's Parliament of Religions, 154, 192 n. 45
Italy, 37, 38

Jacknis, Ira, 111
Japan: absence at Great Exhibition, 25, 39; at Columbian Exposition, 105–7, 114–15, 134–35; at Vienna exposition (1873), 105; at World's Parliament of Religions, 155
Jastrow, Morris, Jr., 143
Jones, Owen, 46
Judaism: American, during Gilded Age, 130–31; at Columbian Exposition, 133, 152; within Congress Auxiliary, 143; at Great Exhibition, 49, 56; at 1993 Parliament of Religions, 170–71; at World's Parliament of Religions, 126, 150, 152–53, 157

King, Richard, xiv
Kipling, Rudyard, 78
Kirschenblatt-Gimblett, Barbara, 152
Kitagawa, Joseph, 154
*Kultur*, xvi
Küng, Father Hans, 173

LePlay, Frederic, 82
Linnaeus (Carl Linné), 17
London: 1886 Colonial and Indian Exhibition, 83; photography at 1862 international exposition, 82
Lyell, Charles, 67–68, 70

Marty, Martin, 130
Marx, Karl: and dialectical materialism, 3–4, 180 n. 3; on the fetish, 190 n. 21
Maurice, F. D., xiv
Mauss, Marcel, 14
McCann, Dennis P., 153
McCormick, Cyrus, 43, 90
McGrane, Bernard, 12, 45
Midway Plaisance: described, 99
Mivart, St. George, 75

Morse, Samuel, F. B., 90
Müller, F. Max, 68, 80–81, 83

Nandy, Ashis, 78
nationalism, 14–15
Native Americans: at Columbian Exposition, 101–2, 107, 109–12, 119, 121, 133–34; displayed at Philadelphia Centennial, 95–96; during Gilded Age, 130–31; Kwakiutl, 111–12, 134; at 1993 Parliament of Religions, 169; at World's Parliament of Religions, 125–26, 151–52, 157–60, 176; after World's Parliament of Religions, 168
Neely, Alan, 170
New York Crystal Palace (1853), 14, 45, 88–92; class consciousness of, 91–92
Novick, Peter, xvi

Paley, William, 54
Paris Expositions Universelles: of 1855, 140; of 1878, 141; of 1889, 83–84, 102, 141; of 1967, 72, 82–83, 141
Parliament for the World's Religions (1993), 169–74
Paxton, Sir Joseph, 29–30, 89
Payne, Bishop Daniel Alexander, 162
Peneé, Captain Xavier, 120
Philadelphia Centennial Exhibition (1876), 45, 85, 88, 92–98, 108, 141; Bible at, 98; race at, 96–97; women at, 94–95
Pierce, President Franklin, 90–91
Pitt-Rivers, Gen. Augustus, 69
Pomare, Queen, 46
potlatch ceremony, 14, 156
Powers, Hiram, 42
Prichard, James C., 68
"primitive," the (*see also* "savage," the): at Columbian Exposition, 117–22, 133–34, 137, 146, 175–76; defined, 24; distinguished from "savage," 24–25; as mode of display, 8; studies of Western exchange with, 181 n. 5
Protestantism: ambivalence toward materiality, 10, 81, 138, 190 n. 21; American, during Gilded Age, 127, 130; at Great Exhibition, 49–51; host of World's Parliament of Religions, 132, 149–50; and northern Europe, 26; at Philadelphia Centennial, 98
Putnam, Frederic Ward, 101–2, 111

Raboteau, Albert, 160
Reid, Christopher Robert, 144–45

religion (*see also* comparative religion): academic study of, 69, 124–25, 168–69, 174, 179 n. 5; American, during Gilded Age, 126–32; concept of, 85, 123–24, 132, 134; distinguished from culture, xvii, 24, 97–98, 123–24, 126–27, 130, 132, 134, 138–39, 145, 160–61, 164–66; versus ethnicity, 126; at Great Exhibition, 49–59; material exhibiting of, 128, 132–34, 138; within national traditions, xx; origin of concept, xiii–xvi; at Philadelphia Centennial, 97–98; principal influences on field of, xviii; and social evolutionism, 127–28, 135–36, 175; traditional biblical, defined, xviii, 179 n. 6

*Religionswissenschaft*, xvi
Royal Commission, 23
Royal Society, xiii
Royal Society of Arts, 26
Rydell, Robert, 112

"savage," the (*see also* "primitive," the): at Columbian Exposition, 121; defined, 24; distinguished from "primitive," 25; at Great Exhibition, 8–9, 45–49; as mode of display, 11; noble, 11, 47–49
Schwarz, Howard Eilberg, 187
Scott, Gertrude, 121, 186 n. 33
Sibthorpe, Col., 28
Sloane, Sir Hans, 11
Smithsonian Institution, 91, 93, 95, 132–34
Snider, Denton J., 136–38
social evolutionism, 63–81: advanced by Great Exhibition, 66–67, 70–71; choice of term explained, 183–84 n. 1; and colonialism, 78–81; at Columbian Exposition, 121–22, 135–37; defined, xviii, 64; and European international expositions, 82–85; and evolutionary theory proper, 71; history of, 67–70; influence on field of religion, 64–65, 127–28; relation to biblical religion, 66; and religion, 127–32, 135–36; role of neo-Lamarckism in, 78–80; in United States, 127–30, 188 n. 4
Sousa, John Philip, 109
Spain, 37, 39
Spencer, Herbert, 69, 78–80, 129, 144
Starr, Frederick, 101, 111
Stocking, George, 183–84 n. 1
Strauss, David, 68

Suzuki, D. T., 155–56, 165, 167
Swedenborg, Emanuel, 148
Szasz, Ferenc, 127

Tenkotte, Paul A., 95
Thackeray, William Makepeace, 32
Tiele, C. P., 81
Tilden, Samuel J., 94
trade fairs: connection to international expositions, 180 n. 4; defined, 4; as systems of exchange, 4–5
Tunisia, 39
Turkey, 39
Turner, Frederick Jackson, 146–47
Turner, Henry McNeal, 145
Tylor, E. B., xvi, 69; on the "primitive," 25

United States: competition with Britain, 40–41; as forum for World's Parliament of Religions, 124–25; Gilded Age religion, 126–32; at Great Exhibition, 25, 40–45; international relations of, 41

Varenne, Herve, 128
*Vedas*, 68
Victoria, Queen, xiii, 28, 83
Vienna international exposition (1873), 105, 141
Vivekananda, Swami, 155–56, 165
Von Humboldt, Alexander, 17
Von Ranke, Leopold, xvi

Wagner, Richard, 94
Walton, Whitney, 37
War of 1812, 40
Washington, Booker T., 168
Wells, Ida B., 108
Whitman, Walt, 94
Williams, Fannie Barrier, 108, 161–62
World's Columbian Exposition: attendance at, xiv; awards juries at, 104; Department of Ethnology and Archaeology at, 100–103; as forum for education, 100–102, 122, 138, 149; Midway Plaisance at, 112–22; nature of, 2; planning of, 98–100; "primitive" at, 104, 107–8, 117–22; religion at, 45, 121–22; White City within, 99, 102, 103–12; Woman's Building at, 133; women at, 187–88 n. 1
World's Columbian Exposition Congress Auxiliary, 99–100, 142–47, 190 n. 26; Congress of Anthropology, 142–43;

Congress of Folklore, 142; Congress of Women, 142; Congress on Africa, 125, 144–46, 151; Congress on Evolution, 142, 144; Jewish Religious Congress, 153; Jewish Women's Congress, 153; "primitive" within, 142, 144–47; religion congresses within, 191 n. 27; World's Congress of Representative Women, 142

World's Parliament of Religions, 147–66; as American phenomenon, 124–26, 150–53; Asian participation at, 153–57, 192–93 n. 45; Christian agenda of, 143; compared to Great Exhibition, 139; criticism of missionary activity at, 149, 162; as expression of colonialism, 85, 123–26, 148, 150, 157–58, 175; as forum for world religions, xix, 125; influence of Columbian Exposition on, 104, 112–22, 126, 154, 166; limitations of format, 125–26; location of, 99–100; planning of, 147–48; politics of, 148–49, 175–76; purpose of, 149–50; significance of, 125–26; unity of religions within, 150–51, 156

Wyatt, Matthew Digby, 27

Young, Robert J. C., xvi

# STUDIES IN RELIGION AND CULTURE

| | |
|---:|:---|
| Edmund N. Santurri | *Perplexity in the Moral Life: Philosophical and Theological Considerations* |
| Robert P. Scharlemann | *Inscriptions and Reflections: Essays in Philosophical Theology* |
| James DiCenso | *Hermeneutics and the Disclosure of Truth: A Study in the Work of Heidegger, Gadamer, and Ricoeur* |
| David Lawton | *Faith, Text, and History: The Bible in English* |
| Robert P. Scharlemann, editor | *Theology at the End of the Century: A Dialogue on the Postmodern* |
| Robert P. Scharlemann, editor | *Negation and Theology* |
| Lynda Sexson | *Ordinarily Sacred* |
| David E. Klemm and William Schweiker, editors | *Meanings in Texts and Actions: Questioning Paul Ricoeur* |
| Guyton B. Hammond | *Conscience and Its Recovery: From the Frankfurt School to Feminism* |
| Roger Poole | *Kierkegaard: The Indirect Communication* |
| John D. Barbour | *Versions of Deconversion: Autobiography and the Loss of Faith* |
| Gary L. Ebersole | *Captured by Texts: Puritan to Postmodern Images of Indian Captivity* |
| David Chidester | *Savage Systems: Colonialism and Comparative Religion in Southern Africa* |
| Laurie L. Patton and Wendy Doniger, editors | *Myth and Method* |
| Orrin F. Summerell, editor | *The Otherness of God* |
| Langdon Gilkey | *Creationism on Trial: Evolution and God at Little Rock* |
| Michael L. Raposa | *Boredom and the Religious Imagination* |
| Peter Homans, editor | *Symbolic Loss: The Ambiguity of Mourning and Memory at Century's End* |
| Winston Davis, editor | *Taking Responsibility: Comparative Perspectives* |
| John P. Burris | *Exhibiting Religion: Colonialism and Spectacle at International Expositions, 1851–1893* |